T0137252

The Information Retrieval Series

Volume 46

Information Retrieval (IR) deals with access to and search in mostly unstructured information, in text, audio, and/or video, either from one large file or spread over separate and diverse sources, in static storage devices as well as on streaming data. It is part of both computer and information science, and uses techniques from e.g. mathematics, statistics, machine learning, database management, or computational linguistics. Information Retrieval is often at the core of networked applications, web-based data management, or large-scale data analysis.

The Information Retrieval Series presents monographs, edited collections, and advanced text books on topics of interest for researchers in academia and industry alike. Its focus is on the timely publication of state-of-the-art results at the forefront of research and on theoretical foundations necessary to develop a deeper understanding of methods and approaches.

This series is abstracted/indexed in Scopus.

More information about this series at http://www.springer.com/series/6128

Yi Chang • Hongbo Deng

Editors

Query Understanding for Search Engines

 Springer

Editors
Yi Chang
Jilin University
Jilin, China

Hongbo Deng
Alibaba Group
Zhejiang, China

ISSN 1871-7500   ISSN 2730-6836   (electronic)
The Information Retrieval Series
ISBN 978-3-030-58336-1   ISBN 978-3-030-58334-7   (eBook)
https://doi.org/10.1007/978-3-030-58334-7

This Springer imprint is published by the registered company Springer Nature Switzerland AG.
The registered company address is: Gewerbestrasse 11, 6330 Cham, Switzerland

Foreword

Web search engines have made such incredible advances in the past three decades that interacting with them has become part of all connected people's daily routines. With such success, come high expectations, and searchers do not tolerate search engines not perfectly understanding and satisfying their needs. Regular Web searchers rarely realize however that understanding their queries is a really hard technical challenge, which is yet to be completely solved.

One of the sources that is of challenge is that queries are just an approximate projection of users' needs: they are not necessarily well, and almost never fully expressed. I like to use Plato's cave allegory to explain this point. In Plato's allegory, chained prisoners facing the back of the cave can only see the shadows of objects passing behind them. They mistake them for the actual objects, as they are not exposed to any other reality. In the same spirit, I see queries as shadows of our needs. Unless search engines develop full telepathic capabilities (hey, a SciFi fan like me can always dream), they can only work with queries as a proxy to users' needs and as such, may never be able to fully comprehend them. Nevertheless, search engines need to do their best at understanding queries, as hard as it may be, if they want to have a shot at satisfying users.

On the positive side however, query understanding has made a clear progress in the past two decades, together with the evolution of search engines, and this even without telepathic capabilities:-). The increasing availability of personal/contextual signals about searchers (as long as privacy is enforced), especially with new mediums, such as voice search in mobile or digital assistants, makes me hopeful for the future.

I am delighted to see that two prominent researchers in the field such as Yi Chang and Hongbo Deng have taken upon themselves to rally search experts from leading academia and industrial research institutions in order to dive deep into this important topic. The book contributors examine the different elements of query understanding and most notably:

1. core understanding, where the search engine tries to associate deeper semantic meaning with the issued query; this covers, for instance, query classification, query tagging, or inferring the intent behind queries,
2. query rewrite, which consists of augmenting or transforming queries in such a way that the search engine can manipulate them and produce better results, and finally,
3. query suggestion, one of my favorite topics (as I had the privilege to lead the team that launched Google Suggest more than a decade ago), which consists in assisting the searcher in expressing their needs. Following the Plato allegory, this mechanism helps the "shadow" to be closer to the real user's need, via dynamic query autocompletion, related query suggestions, etc.

I am sure that researchers and practitioners in the field, from students to experts, will greatly benefit from reading this book, which provides a framework to "understand understanding" (pun intended), as well as a comprehensive overview of the state of the art. I sincerely hope that it will inspire developers to improve their solutions and researchers to continue innovating in that area, which remains as fascinating as ever.

Haifa, Israel   Yoelle Maarek

Contents

Editors and Contributors

About the Editors

Dr. Yi Chang is the Dean of School of Artificial Intelligence, Jilin University, China. He was a Technical Vice President at Huawei Research America and a research director at Yahoo Research before that. His research interests include information retrieval, data mining, machine learning, natural language processing, and artificial intelligence. He has published more than 100 papers on premium conferences or journals, and he has served as the conference general chair for ACM WSDM'2018 and ACM SIGIR'2020. He was elected as an ACM Distinguished Scientist in 2018, for his contributions to intelligent algorithms for search engines.

Dr. Hongbo Deng is a senior staff engineer and director in the Search and Recommendation Business Unit at Alibaba Group. Before that, he was a senior software engineer at Google and a senior research scientist at Yahoo! Labs. His research interests include information retrieval, Web search, data mining, recommendation system, and natural language processing. He obtained his Ph.D. from the Department of Computer Science and Engineering at The Chinese University of Hong Kong. He has published more than 40 papers on top conferences and journals and won several best paper awards, including the Best Paper Award in SIGKDD 2016 and the Vannevar Bush Best Paper Award in JCDL 2012. In addition, he has been actively serving as a program committee member in KDD, WWW, SIGIR, WSDM, and CIKM as well as co-organizing several workshops. Dr. Hongbo Deng is a senior member of ACM.

Contributors

David Carmel Amazon Research, Haifa, Israel

Yi Chang Jilin University, Jilin, China

Hongbo Deng Alibaba Group, Zhejiang, China

Zhicheng Dou Renmin University of China, Beijing, China

Jiafeng Guo Chinese Academy of Sciences, Beijing, China

Yanyan Lan Chinese Academy of Sciences, Beijing, China

Yanen Li LinkedIn Inc., Mountain View, CA, USA

Liangda Li Yahoo Research, Sunnyvale, CA, USA

Zhen Liao Facebook Inc., Menlo Park, CA, USA

Hui Liu Michigan State University, East Lansing, MI, USA

Jian-Yun Nie University of Montreal, Montreal, QC, Canada

Yang Song Google Research, Mountain View, CA, USA

Jiliang Tang Michigan State University, East Lansing, MI, USA

Xuanhui Wang Google Research, Mountain View, CA, USA

Dawei Yin Baidu Inc., Beijing, China

Dengyong Zhou Google Research, Mountain View, CA, USA

Chapter 1
An Introduction to Query Understanding

Hongbo Deng and Yi Chang

Abstract This book aims to present a systematic study of practices and theories for query understanding of search engines. The studies in this book can be categorized into three major classes. One class is to figure out what the searcher wants by extracting semantic meaning from the searcher's keywords, such as query classification, query tagging, and query intent understanding. Another class is to analyze search queries and then translate them into an enhanced query that can produce better search results, such as query spelling correction, query rewriting. The third class is to assist users to refine or suggest queries so as to reduce users' search effort and satisfy their information needs, such as query auto-completion and query suggestion. This chapter discusses organization, audience, and further reading for this book.

1.1 Introduction

Query understanding is a fundamental part of search engine. It is responsible to precisely infer the intent of the query formulated by search user, to correct spelling errors in the query, to reformulate the query to capture its intent more accurately, and to guide search user in the formulation of query with precise intent. Query understanding methods generally take place before the search engine retrieves and ranks search results. If we can understand the information needs of search queries in the best way, we can better serve users. Therefore, query understanding has been recognized as the key technology for search engines.

Before we dive into the details of query understanding, let us briefly review how do search engines work. In general, search engines need to understand exactly what

H. Deng (✉)
Alibaba Group, Zhejiang, China
e-mail: hbdeng@acm.org

Y. Chang
Jilin University, Jilin, China
e-mail: yichang@jlu.edu.cn

© Springer Nature Switzerland AG 2020
Y. Chang, H. Deng (eds.), *Query Understanding for Search Engines*,
The Information Retrieval Series 46, https://doi.org/10.1007/978-3-030-58334-7_1

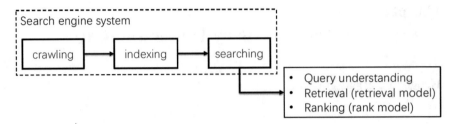

Fig. 1.1 Fundamental actions of a search engine system

kind of information is available and then present it to users logically according to their query. The way they accomplish this is through three fundamental actions: crawling, indexing, and searching, as shown in Fig. 1.1. Web search engines get their information by crawling from site to site, while some e-commerce search engines collect their information according to their own providers without crawling. The indexing process is to store and organize their collected information on their servers, as well as prepare some positive and negative signals for the following search process. Searching is a process that accepts a text query as input and returns a list of results, ranked by their relevance to the query. The search process can be further divided into three steps, which include query understanding, retrieval, and ranking.

Because query understanding is the first step in the search process, it is the core part of the process that the user interacts with search engines. The basic search interface features include query auto-completion and query refinement suggestions. More specifically, query auto-completion is becoming the primary surface for the search experience, which suggests relevant completed queries as the user types. Suppose a user wants to query "britney spears," Fig. 1.2 shows the most relevant completions for prefixes from "b" to "brit." Once a query is submitted, the primary objective is to conduct semantic analysis, so as to understand the intention behind the query, such as query classification (classifying the query according to the categories) and query tagging (extracting the entities and concepts mentioned in the query). Given the query "britney spears pretty girls" as shown in Fig. 1.2 (step 2), it can be classified to the category [music] with probability 0.5, and then "britney spears" and "pretty girls" are tagged as [singer] and [song], respectively. Before retrieving search results, another important type of query understanding is to alter a given query to alternative queries through query expansion, spelling correction, and query rewriting, which can improve relevance performance by bridging the vocabulary gap between a query and relevant documents. Much of query understanding takes place before retrieving a single result; however, some query suggestions are returned to users along with the search results, which is also called post-ranking query suggestions. It can assist users to refine queries in order to satisfy their information needs. An overview diagram of searching process is shown in Fig. 1.2.

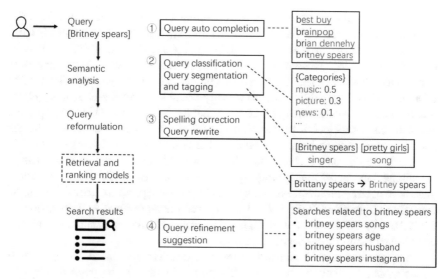

Fig. 1.2 An overview diagram of searching process

What is not covered in this book? We do not cover crawling, indexing, retrieval, and ranking problems. Some basic query processing stacks, such as stemming and lemmatization, are not covered. For more details in these areas, please refer to [12, 41].

What is covered in this book? In this book, we aim to present a systematic study of practices and theories for query understanding of search engines. This chapter will discuss how the organization of the book is related to the different areas of query understanding and will briefly discuss each of these issues in the following sections.

1.2 Query Classification

Query classification, which is to assign a search query into a given target taxonomy, has been recognized as one important technique that can bring improvements in both efficiency and effectiveness of general Web search. Various classification of taxonomies have been proposed in order to understand users' search query from different viewpoints, including intent taxonomy, topic taxonomy, performance taxonomy, and so on. Basically, these tasks of query classification include, but are not limited to, identifying the type of search goals and demanded resources required by a user, identifying the topical categories a query belongs to, determining query performance of a query for a given retrieval system, and selecting vertical services a query might be relevant to.

Query topic classification aims to determine the topical category of queries according to some predefined topic taxonomy. Typical topic taxonomies used in literature include that proposed in the KDD Cup 2005 [37] and a manually collected one from AOL [6]. Researchers may also use some specific topic taxonomy constructed in some target domains for commercial search engine. The task of KDD Cup 2005 competition was to classify 800,000 internet user search queries into 67 predefined categories. It is obvious that the KDD Cup 2005 is an important event in this area, since it provides an opportunity for researchers from different countries to develop techniques to enhance the task of query topic classification. In this competition, many methods have been proposed to tackle the main challenges of training data sparsity and feature sparsity problems. Even after the competition, there have been continuous research work to improve the performance of query topic classification. In Chap. 2, Sect. 2.3, we reviewed the representative work proposed for KDD Cup 2005 and AOL taxonomy, as well as some representative work on other topic taxonomy or specific domains.

Query performance classification aims to categorize queries according to their *difficulty*, i.e., the likely quality of results returned by the search system for a query, in the absence of relevance judgments and without user feedback. In practice, query difficulty could be further specified in two ways, namely *system query difficulty* and *collection query difficulty* [2]. System query difficulty captures the difficulty of a query for a given retrieval system run over a given collection. In other words, the query is difficult for a *particular* system. System query difficulty is typically measured by the average precision of the ranked list of documents returned by the retrieval system when run over the collection using the query in question. Collection query difficulty captures the difficulty of a query with respect to a given collection. In this way, the difficulty of a query is meant to be largely *independent* of any specific retrieval system. For more details in this direction, please refer to Chap. 2, Sect. 2.4.

In Chap. 2, we discuss several different query classification tasks, from some major interests, such as intent classification, topic classification, performance classification, to classification tasks on other "dimensions" such as geographic location and time requirement. For each classification task, there have been multiple classification taxonomies proposed in the past due to finer analysis of users' needs or specific application requests. Although different types of features have been proposed for different tasks, they are mainly from the resources such as query logs, click logs, retrieved documents, search corpus, and queries themselves. Supervised, unsupervised, and semi-supervised models have been employed in these tasks.

1.3 Query Segmentation and Tagging

Query segmentation is one of the first steps towards query understanding. Its goal is to split a query string into a few segments. The basic bag-of-words (BOW) model can be thought of as segmenting queries based on individual words. Such an approach is simple but can be less meaningful. For Chinese language, most of the individual words have little meaning by themselves and the meaning of a sentence is carried by a sequence of words. However, there are no natural boundaries such as spaces in Chinese language, and query segmentation is a necessary step for Chinese queries [44, 52] as well as for many other languages. For English language, spaces are presented inside sentences and individual words obtained in the BOW model are more meaningful compared with Chinese language. However, the BOW model can still be less effective because the meaning of a phrase can be totally different from its individual words. For example, knowing that "new york" is a city name and treating them as a whole is better than treating them as two individual words "new" and "york." Moreover, it is also beneficial to know whether some words comprise an entity like an organization's name, which makes it possible to enforce word proximity and ordering constraints on document matching. Therefore, it is necessary to go beyond the BOW model. A search engine that can automatically split a query into meaningful segments is highly likely to improve its overall user satisfaction.

In Chap. 3, Sect. 3.1, we formulate the problem of query segmentation as finding boundaries to segment queries into a list of semantic blocks. Various approaches have been proposed for query segmentation, which can be categorized into three different approaches, including heuristic-based approaches, supervised learning approaches, and unsupervised learning approaches. Heuristic-based approaches are based on some statistics obtained from external resources, such as pointwise mutual information (PMI) [8], connexity [46], and naive segmentation [22]. In the supervised learning setting, query segmentation is formulated as a classification problem that takes a query as input and outputs a vector with $n - 1$ binary values, where y_i means that there is a break between word x_i and x_{i+1}. Recently, a query segmentation method based on conditional random fields (CRF) is proposed by Yu et al. [58]. Supervised learning approaches rely on human annotated training data, while unsupervised learning approaches have unique advantage that no labeled data is needed. Existing approaches mainly use EM as their main algorithms. For more details about query segmentation, please refer to Chap. 3, Sect. 3.1.

The problem of query tagging is to assign labels from a set of predefined ones at word level, and it can be classified into query semantic tagging and query syntactic tagging according to different labels. One important type of semantic labels is defined along with named entity, including "Game," "Movie," "Book," "Music," etc. Given a query, the tasks of name entity recognition (NER) are to identify which words in the query represent named entities and classify them into different classes. For Web search queries, Guo et al. [21] found that only 1% of the named entity queries contain more than 1 entity and the majority of named entity queries contain exactly a single one. For e-commerce search, the semantic labels can be different properties and their values, such as brand, color, model, style, and so on. An example from [42] of query semantic tagging in the *product* domain is shown in the following where the labels are in parentheses.

cheap (SortOrder) **garmin** (Brand) **steetpilot** (Model) **c340** (Model) **gps** (Type)

Semantic labels can be used to provide users with more relevant search results. For example, based on the structured information or labels generated by query tagging, many specialized search engines conduct structured matching with documents where structured information are available, such as in e-commerce search.

Another type of query tagging is related to traditional syntactic analysis, which is usually conducted over complete sentences in NLP. Its goal is to understand a sentence's grammatical constituents, POS of words, and their syntactic relations. The task of query syntactic tagging is to apply NLP techniques to search for queries. However, search queries are short and their word order is family free, which make it very challenging to directly apply syntactic parsing NLP techniques on search queries. The majority of existing approaches [5, 7, 53] transfer information from sentences in search results or snippets to search queries.

In Chap. 3, we reviewed a few representative methods for both query semantic tagging and syntactic tagging, including template-based approach, weakly supervised learning approach, transfer learning based approaches, etc.

1.4 Query Intent Understanding

Query intent itself is an ambiguous word and it is still a challenge to have a scientific definition of query intent. Intent itself means the perceived need for information that leads to a search, but how to describe or classify the need is still in an exploratory stage. Till now, different kinds of query intent understanding tasks have been explored towards discovering the implicit factors related to real user information needs according to some predefined intent taxonomy.

As a starting point, a Web search intent taxonomy with broad consensus was proposed by Broder [11], which aims to classify user goals into navigational, informational, and transactional. For instance, when a user issues the query "amazon," she could be trying to navigate the specific website http://www.amazon.com, while a user submitting "Olympic history" is most likely to be interested in finding information on that topic but not concerned about the particular website. Since the proposal of Broder's taxonomy, several other taxonomies have been proposed along the development of this area, including Rose and Levinson's taxonomy [47], Baeza-Yates's taxonomy [3], and so on.

Another well-known query intent is defined with the emergence of numerous vertical search services (e.g., job search, product search, image search, map search, news search, weather search, or academic search). Identifying the vertical intent of a given search query is becoming important in search engines to present aggregated results from multiple verticals through the standard general web search interface. This is the so-called aggregated search or universal search. For example, given the query "beijing weather," it is good to directly show the latest weather forecast information of Beijing city in the search result, while for query "tom cruise," it would be better to show the images or videos of "tom cruise" in the search result. At the same time, irrelevant vertical results within the search engine result page (SERP) may disturb users. Therefore, it is critical to have query vertical intent classifiers in a general or aggregated search engine that can predict whether a query should trigger respective vertical search services.

In Chap. 4, Sect. 4.3, we introduce the detailed query intent classification. Different classification methods have been leveraged for this task, from manual classification [30, 47] to automatic ones [3, 26, 28] such as decision tree and support vector machine. A majority of work in this area focuses on proposing effective features for query intent identification. Different kinds of features have been extracted mainly from three data resources, including search corpus, query strings, and user logs. Although the research community has consensus on the intent taxonomy, there is no standard benchmark dataset constructed for this particular task. Most researchers conducted experiments on their own labeled datasets, with query size ranging from tens to thousands.

1.5 Query Spelling Correction

Queries issued by users usually contain errors and misused words/phrases. Recent studies show that about 10 to 12% of all query terms entered into Web search engines are misspelled [16, 17]. The ability to automatically correct misspelled queries has become an indispensable component of modern search engines. Automatic spelling correction for queries helps the search engine to better understand the users' intents and can therefore improve the quality of search experience. However, query spelling is not an easy task, especially under the strict efficiency constraint. More importantly, people not only make typos on single words (insertion, deletion, and substitution), but can also easily mess up with word boundaries (concatenation and splitting). Moreover, different types of misspelling could be committed in the same query, making it even harder to correct.

Query spelling correction has long been an important research topic [29]. Traditional spellers focused on dealing with non-word errors caused by misspelling a known word as an invalid word form. Early works on query spelling correction were based on edit distance and the Trie data structure. A common strategy at that time was to utilize a trusted lexicon and certain distance measures, such as Levenshtein distance [31]. Later, noisy-channel model was introduced for spelling correction, in which the error model and n-gram language model were identified as two critical components. Brill and Moore demonstrated that a better statistical error model is crucial for improving a speller's accuracy [10]. In addition, there are many more types of spelling errors in search queries, such as misspelling, concatenation/splitting of query words, and misuse of legitimate yet inappropriate words. Research in this direction includes utilizing large web corpora and query log [1, 14, 16], training phrase-based error model from clickthrough data [54] and developing additional features [19]. More recently, [35] addressed multi-types of spelling errors using a generalized Hidden Markov Model. In Chap. 5, we will cover the detailed topics and other components for supporting a modern query spelling correction system.

1.6 Query Rewriting

It is well-known that there exists a "lexical chasm" [45] between web documents and user queries. The major reason is that web documents and user queries are created by different sets of users and they may use different vocabularies and distinct language styles. Consequently, even when the queries can perfectly match user's information needs, the search engines may be still unable to locate relevant web documents.

Query rewriting (QRW) enables the search engine to alter or expand a given query to alternative queries that can improve relevance performance by returning additional relevant results. It is a critical task in modern search engines and has attracted increasing attention in the last decade [20, 27, 45]. At the early stage, methods have been developed to find terms related to these in a given query and then substitute terms in the original queries with these related ones (or substitution-based methods) [27]. Then if we treat queries as the source language and web documents as the target language, the query rewriting problem can be naturally considered as a machine translation problem; thus, machine translation techniques have been applied for QRW (or translation-based methods) [45]. Recently, deep learning techniques have been widely applied in information retrieval [32] and natural language processing [57]. There are very recent works applying deep learning in query rewriting that achieve the state-of-the-art performance [24]. In Chap. 6, we will review the representative query rewriting methods with traditional shallow models including substitution-based methods and translation-based methods, as well as the advanced algorithms based on deep learning techniques such as word embedding, seq2seq models, learning to rewrite frameworks, and deep reinforcement learning.

1.7   Query Auto-Completion

Query auto-completion (QAC) has been widely used in all major search engines, and has become one of the most important and visible features in modern search engines. The main objective of QAC is to predict users' intended queries and assist them to formulate a query while typing. The QAC engine generally offers a list of suggested queries that start with a user's input as a prefix, and the list of suggestions is changed to match the updated input after the user types each character. The interaction with the QAC engine ends until the user clicks one of the suggestions from the list or presses return.

The most popular QAC algorithm is to suggest completions according to their past popularity. Generally, a popularity score is assigned to each query based on the frequency of the query in the query log from where the query database was built. This simple QAC algorithm is called most popular completion (MPC), which can be regarded as an approximate maximum likelihood estimator [4]. The main drawback of MPC is that it assumed user's interest is stable within the range of the collected historical query logs. However, user's interest changes from time to time and can be influenced by various types of information, including temporal information, contextual information, personal information, user's interaction in QAC, and user's interaction besides QAC. In Chap. 7, we will introduce existing metrics utilized in measuring the QAC performance and the most prominent QAC approaches in the literature, including context-sensitive QAC [4], time-sensitive QAC [49, 56], personalized QAC [48], interaction-based QAC [33, 34, 36], and so on.

1.8   Query Suggestion

Query suggestion is one of the few fundamental problems in Web search. It assists users to refine queries in order to satisfy their information needs. Most commercial search engines provide query suggestions on their search result pages to help user formulating queries. Search engine logs contain information on how users refine their queries as well as how users click on suggested queries. As a result, most query suggestion techniques leverage search logs as a useful source of information. From the perspective of modeling and organizing search logs, query suggestion techniques can be categorized into four classes: (1) query co-occurrence; (2) query-URL bipartite graph; (3) query transition graph; and (4) short-term search context methods.

In general, co-occurrence methods [18, 25, 27, 39] use co-occurrence of query pairs in sessions or tasks. This type of method is usually straight-forward to understand and compute. Query-URL bipartite graph methods [15, 43, 50] use clicked URLs of a query to find similar queries. This type of method usually conducts random walk on the click graph to propagate the similarities. Query transition graph methods [9, 51, 55] use the query refinement information in search logs to find next possible queries in the search process. This type of method usually constructs a query transition graph and performs random walk on the graph starting from testing queries. Short-term search context methods [13, 23, 25, 38, 40] use search sequence information (e.g., queries within current session) to improve the relevance of suggestions. Sequence mining approaches [13, 23, 38] are usually applied to predict next possible queries given current search sequence. In Chap. 8, we introduce the aforementioned techniques in detail and summarize other related suggestion techniques as well as future directions.

1.9   Discussion and Future Directions

The problem of query understanding has been widely studied in the Web search and data mining literature. Query understanding is not about determining the relevance of each result to the query, while it is the communication channel between the searcher and the search engine. The query understanding problem has numerous variations that allow the use of either additional domain knowledge or cross-language in order to improve the underlying results. Moreover, a wide variety of methods are available for query understanding beyond keyword query, such as natural language question understanding and dialog query conversational query understanding. With the success of deep learning in many research areas, it has started to explore deep learning based techniques to various query understanding problems, including but not limited to query classification, query tagging, query rewrite, query suggestions. In Chap. 9, we will further discuss a few other interesting cases, including personalized query understanding, temporal dynamics of queries, and semantic understanding for search queries. In many cases, these advanced techniques and algorithms may be used to significantly improve the quality of the underlying results.

References

1. Farooq Ahmad and Grzegorz Kondrak. Learning a spelling error model from search query logs. In *Proceedings of the Human Language Technology Conference and Conference on Empirical Methods in Natural Language Processing*, pages 955–962, 2005.
2. Javed A. Aslam and Virgiliu Pavlu. Query hardness estimation using Jensen-Shannon divergence among multiple scoring functions. In *Proceedings of the 29th European Conference on IR Research*, volume 4425, pages 198–209, 2007.
3. Ricardo A. Baeza-Yates, Liliana Calderón-Benavides, and Cristina N. González-Caro. The intention behind web queries. In *Proceedings of the 13th International Conference on String Processing and Information Retrieval*, volume 4209, pages 98–109, 2006.
4. Ziv Bar-Yossef and Naama Kraus. Context-sensitive query auto-completion. In *Proceedings of the 20th International Conference on World Wide Web*, pages 107–116, 2011.
5. Cory Barr, Rosie Jones, and Moira Regelson. The linguistic structure of English web-search queries. In *Proceedings of the 2008 Conference on Empirical Methods in Natural Language Processing*, pages 1021–1030, 2008.

6. Steven M. Beitzel, Eric C. Jensen, Ophir Frieder, David D. Lewis, Abdur Chowdhury, and Aleksander Kolcz. Improving automatic query classification via semi-supervised learning. In *Proceedings of the 5th IEEE International Conference on Data Mining*, pages 42–49, 2005.
7. Michael Bendersky, W. Bruce Croft, and David A. Smith. Structural annotation of search queries using pseudo-relevance feedback. In *Proceedings of the 19th ACM Conference on Information and Knowledge Management*, pages 1537–1540, 2010.
8. Shane Bergsma and Qin Iris Wang. Learning noun phrase query segmentation. In *Proceedings of the 2007 Joint Conference on Empirical Methods in Natural Language Processing and Computational Natural Language Learning*, pages 819–826, 2007.
9. Paolo Boldi, Francesco Bonchi, Carlos Castillo, Debora Donato, Aristides Gionis, and Sebastiano Vigna. The query-flow graph: model and applications. In *Proceedings of the 17th ACM Conference on Information and Knowledge Management*, pages 609–618, 2008.
10. Eric Brill and Robert C. Moore. An improved error model for noisy channel spelling correction. In *38th Annual Meeting of the Association for Computational Linguistics*, pages 286–293, 2000.
11. Andrei Z. Broder. A taxonomy of web search. *SIGIR Forum*, 36 (2): 3–10, 2002.
12. Stefan Büttcher, Charles L. A. Clarke, and Gordon V. Cormack. *Information Retrieval - Implementing and Evaluating Search Engines*. MIT Press, 2010.
13. Huanhuan Cao, Daxin Jiang, Jian Pei, Qi He, Zhen Liao, Enhong Chen, and Hang Li. Context-aware query suggestion by mining click-through and session data. In *Proceedings of the 14th ACM SIGKDD International Conference on Knowledge Discovery and Data Mining*, pages 875–883, 2008.
14. Qing Chen, Mu Li, and Ming Zhou. Improving query spelling correction using web search results. In *Proceedings of the 2007 Joint Conference on Empirical Methods in Natural Language Processing and Computational Natural Language Learning*, pages 181–189, 2007.
15. Nick Craswell and Martin Szummer. Random walks on the click graph. In *Proceedings of the 30th Annual International ACM SIGIR Conference on Research and Development in Information Retrieval*, pages 239–246, 2007.
16. Silviu Cucerzan and Eric Brill. Spelling correction as an iterative process that exploits the collective knowledge of web users. In *Proceedings of the 2004 Conference on Empirical Methods in Natural Language Processing*, pages 293–300, 2004.
17. Hercules Dalianis. Evaluating a spelling support in a search engine. In *Proceedings of the 6th International Conference on Applications of Natural Language to Information Systems*, volume 2553, pages 183–190, 2002.
18. Bruno M. Fonseca, Paulo Braz Golgher, Bruno Pôssas, Berthier A. Ribeiro-Neto, and Nivio Ziviani. Concept-based interactive query expansion. In *Proceedings of the 2005 ACM CIKM International Conference on Information and Knowledge Management*, pages 696–703, 2005.
19. Jianfeng Gao, Xiaolong Li, Daniel Micol, Chris Quirk, and Xu Sun. A large scale ranker-based system for search query spelling correction. In *Proceedings of the 23rd International Conference on Computational Linguistics*, pages 358–366, 2010.
20. Jianfeng Gao, Shasha Xie, Xiaodong He, and Alnur Ali. Learning lexicon models from search logs for query expansion. In *Proceedings of the 2012 Joint Conference on Empirical Methods in Natural Language Processing and Computational Natural Language Learning*, pages 666–676, 2012.
21. Jiafeng Guo, Gu Xu, Xueqi Cheng, and Hang Li. Named entity recognition in query. In *Proceedings of the 32nd Annual International ACM SIGIR Conference on Research and Development in Information Retrieval*, pages 267–274, 2009.
22. Matthias Hagen, Martin Potthast, Benno Stein, and Christof Bräutigam. Query segmentation revisited. In Sadagopan Srinivasan, Krithi Ramamritham, Arun Kumar, M. P. Ravindra, Elisa Bertino, and Ravi Kumar, editors, *Proceedings of the 20th International Conference on World Wide Web*, pages 97–106, 2011.
23. Qi He, Daxin Jiang, Zhen Liao, Steven C. H. Hoi, Kuiyu Chang, Ee-Peng Lim, and Hang Li. Web query recommendation via sequential query prediction. In *Proceedings of the 25th International Conference on Data Engineering*, pages 1443–1454, 2009.

24. Yunlong He, Jiliang Tang, Hua Ouyang, Changsung Kang, Dawei Yin, and Yi Chang. Learning to rewrite queries. In *Proceedings of the 25th ACM International Conference on Information and Knowledge Management*, pages 1443–1452, 2016.
25. Chien-Kang Huang, Lee-Feng Chien, and Yen-Jen Oyang. Relevant term suggestion in interactive web search based on contextual information in query session logs. *J. Assoc. Inf. Sci. Technol.*, 54 (7): 638–649, 2003.
26. Bernard J. Jansen, Danielle L. Booth, and Amanda Spink. Determining the informational, navigational, and transactional intent of web queries. *Inf. Process. Manag.*, 44 (3): 1251–1266, 2008.
27. Rosie Jones, Benjamin Rey, Omid Madani, and Wiley Greiner. Generating query substitutions. In *Proceedings of the 15th international conference on World Wide Web*, pages 387–396, 2006.
28. In-Ho Kang and Gil-Chang Kim. Proceedings of the 26th annual international ACM SIGIR conference on research and development in information retrieval. pages 64–71, 2003.
29. Karen Kukich. Techniques for automatically correcting words in text. *ACM Computing Surveys*, 24 (4): 377–439, 1992.
30. Uichin Lee, Zhenyu Liu, and Junghoo Cho. Automatic identification of user goals in web search. In *Proceedings of the 14th international conference on World Wide Web*, pages 391–400, 2005.
31. V. I. Levenshtein. Binary codes capable of correcting deletions, insertions and reversals. *Soviet Physics Doklady*, 10 (8): 707–710, February 1966.
32. Hang Li and Zhengdong Lu. Deep learning for information retrieval. In *Proceedings of the 39th International ACM SIGIR conference on Research and Development in Information Retrieval*, pages 1203–1206, 2016.
33. Liangda Li, Hongbo Deng, Anlei Dong, Yi Chang, Hongyuan Zha, and Ricardo Baeza-Yates. Analyzing user's sequential behavior in query auto-completion via Markov processes. In *Proceedings of the 38th International ACM SIGIR Conference on Research and Development in Information Retrieval*, pages 123–132, 2015.
34. Liangda Li, Hongbo Deng, Anlei Dong, Yi Chang, Ricardo Baeza-Yates, and Hongyuan Zha. Exploring query auto-completion and click logs for contextual-aware web search and query suggestion. In *Proceedings of the 26th International Conference on World Wide Web*, pages 539–548, 2017.
35. Yanen Li, Huizhong Duan, and ChengXiang Zhai. A generalized hidden Markov model with discriminative training for query spelling correction. In *The 35th International ACM SIGIR conference on research and development in Information Retrieval*, pages 611–620, 2012.
36. Yanen Li, Anlei Dong, Hongning Wang, Hongbo Deng, Yi Chang, and ChengXiang Zhai. A two-dimensional click model for query auto-completion. In *The 37th International ACM SIGIR Conference on Research and Development in Information Retrieval*, pages 455–464, 2014.
37. Ying Li, Zijian Zheng, and Honghua (Kathy) Dai. KDD CUP-2005 report: facing a great challenge. *SIGKDD Explorations*, 7 (2): 91–99, 2005.
38. Zhen Liao, Daxin Jiang, Enhong Chen, Jian Pei, Huanhuan Cao, and Hang Li. Mining concept sequences from large-scale search logs for context-aware query suggestion. *ACM Trans. Intell. Syst. Technol.*, 3 (1): 17:1–17:40, 2011.
39. Zhen Liao, Yang Song, Li-wei He, and Yalou Huang. Evaluating the effectiveness of search task trails. In *Proceedings of the 21st Conference on World Wide Web*, pages 489–498, 2012.
40. Zhen Liao, Daxin Jiang, Jian Pei, Yalou Huang, Enhong Chen, Huanhuan Cao, and Hang Li. A vlHMM approach to context-aware search. *ACM Trans. Web*, 7 (4): 22:1–22:38, 2013.
41. Christopher D. Manning, Prabhakar Raghavan, and Hinrich Schütze. *Introduction to information retrieval*. Cambridge University Press, 2008.
42. Mehdi Manshadi and Xiao Li. Semantic tagging of web search queries. In *Proceedings of the 47th Annual Meeting of the Association for Computational Linguistics and the 4th International Joint Conference on Natural Language Processing of the AFNLP*, pages 861–869, 2009.

43. Qiaozhu Mei, Dengyong Zhou, and Kenneth Ward Church. Query suggestion using hitting time. In *Proceedings of the 17th ACM Conference on Information and Knowledge Management*, pages 469–478, 2008.
44. Fuchun Peng, Fangfang Feng, and Andrew McCallum. Chinese segmentation and new word detection using conditional random fields. In *Proceedings of the 20th International Conference on Computational Linguistics*, 2004.
45. Stefan Riezler and Yi Liu. Query rewriting using monolingual statistical machine translation. *Comput. Linguistics*, 36 (3): 569–582, 2010.
46. Knut Magne Risvik, Tomasz Mikolajewski, and Peter Boros. Query segmentation for web search. In *Proceedings of the Twelfth International World Wide Web Conference*, 2003.
47. Daniel E. Rose and Danny Levinson. Understanding user goals in web search. In *Proceedings of the 13th international conference on World Wide Web*, pages 13–19, 2004.
48. Milad Shokouhi. Learning to personalize query auto-completion. In *Proceedings of The 36th International ACM SIGIR conference on research and development in Information Retrieval*, pages 103–112, 2013.
49. Milad Shokouhi and Kira Radinsky. Time-sensitive query auto-completion. In *Proceedings of The 35th International ACM SIGIR conference on research and development in Information Retrieval*, pages 601–610, 2012.
50. Yang Song and Li-wei He. Optimal rare query suggestion with implicit user feedback. In *Proceedings of the 19th International Conference on World Wide Web*, pages 901–910, 2010.
51. Yang Song, Dengyong Zhou, and Li-wei He. Query suggestion by constructing term-transition graphs. In *Proceedings of the Fifth International Conference on Web Search and Data Mining*, pages 353–362, 2012.
52. Richard Sproat, Chilin Shih, William Gale, and Nancy Chang. A stochastic finite-state word-segmentation algorithm for Chinese. *Comput. Linguistics*, 22 (3): 377–404, 1996.
53. Xiangyan Sun, Haixun Wang, Yanghua Xiao, and Zhongyuan Wang. Syntactic parsing of web queries. In *Proceedings of the 2016 Conference on Empirical Methods in Natural Language Processing*, pages 1787–1796, 2016.
54. Xu Sun, Jianfeng Gao, Daniel Micol, and Chris Quirk. Learning phrase-based spelling error models from clickthrough data. In *Proceedings of the 48th Annual Meeting of the Association for Computational Linguistics*, pages 266–274, 2010.
55. Idan Szpektor, Aristides Gionis, and Yoelle Maarek. Improving recommendation for long-tail queries via templates. In *Proceedings of the 20th International Conference on World Wide Web*, pages 47–56, 2011.
56. Stewart Whiting and Joemon M. Jose. Recent and robust query auto-completion. In *Proceedings of the 23rd International Conference on International World Wide Web Conference*, pages 971–982, 2014.
57. Tom Young, Devamanyu Hazarika, Soujanya Poria, and Erik Cambria. Recent trends in deep learning based natural language processing [review article]. *IEEE Comput. Intell. Mag.*, 13 (3): 55–75, 2018.
58. Xiaohui Yu and Huxia Shi. Query segmentation using conditional random fields. In *Proceedings of the First International Workshop on Keyword Search on Structured Data*, pages 21–26, 2009.

Chapter 2
Query Classification

Jiafeng Guo and Yanyan Lan

Abstract Query classification, which is to assign a search query into a given target taxonomy, has been recognized as an important technique that can bring improvements in both efficiency and effectiveness of general Web search. Various classification taxonomies have been proposed in order to understand users' search query from different views, including intent taxonomy, topic taxonomy, performance taxonomy, and so on. Unlike traditional document classification tasks, query classification is much more difficult due to the short and ambiguous nature of queries as well as the demanding online computation requirement. In this chapter, we aim to provide a comprehensive review of the query classification methods in the literature to help readers have an idea of the development of this technique up till now.

2.1 Introduction

Understanding what the user is searching for is at the heart of designing successful Web search applications. One important technique toward this direction is query classification, i.e., to assign a Web search query to one or more predefined categories. Various classification taxonomies have been proposed in order to understand users' search query in different ways, which can be summarized into the following three perspectives:

- Why: to understand users' search intent/goal—they might search to locate a particular site or to access some Web services;
- What (or When or Where): to understand search query's topic, information type, geographic location, and time requirement;
- How: to understand how the search query performs—whether the results meet the users' expectations.

J. Guo (✉) · Y. Lan
Chinese Academy of Sciences, Beijing, China
e-mail: guojiafeng@ict.ac.cn; lanyanyan@ict.ac.cn

© Springer Nature Switzerland AG 2020
Y. Chang, H. Deng (eds.), *Query Understanding for Search Engines*,
The Information Retrieval Series 46, https://doi.org/10.1007/978-3-030-58334-7_2

There have been many examples where query classification can lead to significant improvement in Web search applications. For example, successful identification of user intent can help search engine select specialized ranking strategies to provide better search results [42]. By identifying search query topics, online advertisement services can promote different products more accurately. Moreover, if the query performance can be estimated in advance, or during the retrieval stage, remedial actions can be taken to ensure that users' information needs are satisfied by asking for refinement or by providing a number of different term expansion possibilities [33].

However, the computation of query classification is nontrivial. Different from the document classification tasks, users' search queries are usually short and ambiguous, with the meanings evolving over time. Therefore, query classification is much more difficult than traditional document classification tasks. Meanwhile, due to the demanding operational environment, each query classification approach has to be achievable in real time in order to aid in Web search applications. The efficiency requirement further increases the difficulty in designing query classification approaches.

In this chapter, we aim to provide a comprehensive review of the query classification methods in the literature. We group the existing works by the classification tasks, including intent classification (Sect. 2.2), topic classification (Sect. 2.3), performance classification (Sect. 2.4), and other classification "dimensions" including information type, geographic location, and time requirement (Sect. 2.5). In each section, we will focus on describing how the classification taxonomy is defined and evolves, what kinds of feature representations have been proposed, what types of models have been employed for different classification tasks, and how the proposed methods are evaluated.

2.2 Query Intent Classification

A major difference between Web search and classic IR (information retrieval) lies in that users' search need/goal is no longer restricted to acquiring certain information—they might search to locate a particular site or to access some Web services. Knowing the different intents associated with a query may benefit Web search in multiple ways. A direct application is to provide better search result pages using specialized ranking strategies for users with different intents [42]. For example, queries that express a need for reaching a particular site might rely more on URL and link information, while those involving open-ended research might weight content information more highly. Online advertisement services can also rely on the query intent classification results to place advertisements in the most appropriate time [24]. For example, the display of relevant advertising might be welcomed in a shopping commit phase but unwelcomed in a research phase.

Query intent classification, therefore, aims to identify the underlying goal of the user when submitting one particular query according to some predefined intent taxonomy. As a starting point, a Web search intent taxonomy with broad consensus was proposed by Broder [10] and refined by Rose and Levison [58] in early 2000, and some orthogonal taxonomies [24] have also been studied along the development of this area. Different classification methods have been leveraged for this task, from manual classification [47, 58] to automatic ones [3, 40, 42] such as decision tree and support vector machine. A majority of work in this area focuses on proposing effective features for query intent identification. Different kinds of features have been extracted mainly from three data resources, including search corpus, query strings, and user logs. Although the research community has consensus on the intent taxonomy, there is no standard benchmark data set constructed for this particular task. Most researchers conducted experiments on their own labeled data sets, with query size ranging from tens to thousands. Standard classification measures such as precision, recall, F1, and accuracy are used as major evaluation metrics.

As the review of different classification methods on search intent will be provided in Chap. 4, we will not cover those in this chapter.

2.3   Query Topic Classification

For successful web search systems, it is critical to understand what the user is searching for, because on this basis it could better provide some useful information. However, the above task is usually very challenging. On one hand, the information contained in the web data is often highly vague and incomplete; on the other hand, users' search intent are very subjective, sometimes they are even changing due to different scenarios and environments. To tackle these problems, we could resort to topic detection for help. That is to say, if a search engine could successfully map search queries to some specific topics, the search results will be improved. Previous works have shown that such topic mapping can significantly improve the retrieval performance. For example, we could alleviate the ambiguity issues (e.g., jaguar the animal versus jaguar the car), by well capturing their topics.

Query topic classification is, therefore, defined to identify the underlying topics of queries according to some pre-defined topic taxonomy. Typical topic taxonomies used in literature include that proposed in the KDD Cup 2005 [49], and a manually collected one from AOL [5]. Different methods have been leveraged for this task. Some are focusing to tackle the training data sparsity by introducing an intermediate taxonomy for mapping [43, 59, 69], some mainly considers the difficulty in representing the short and ambiguous query [4–8]. Some researchers also study the query topic classification in specific domains, such as product or ads [11, 62]. Standard classification measures such as precision, recall, F1, and accuracy are usually used as evaluation metrics for this task.

2.3.1 Topic Taxonomy

The taxonomy of topics is the foundation of query topic classification. It is usually defined as a hierarchical structure, which may cover many different topics, like education, economics, travel, sports, and so on.

The KDD Cup 2005 [49] provides a formal two-level taxonomy, with 67 second level nodes and 800,000 internet user search queries, as listed in Table 2.1. There are seven categories in the top level: Computers, Entertainment, Information, Living, Online Community, Shopping, and Sports. Then several second level subcategories are defined for each top level. For example, the top level category Computer has eight second level subcategories, i.e., Hardware, Internet & Intranet, Mobile Computing, Multimedia, Network & Telecommunication, Security, Software, and Others. We can see that these categories cover most topics meaningful in human's life, so the topic taxonomy is reasonable and provides a reliable foundation for the competition.

Another well-known topic taxonomy is based on a manually classified sample from one week's worth of queries from the AOL web search service. The taxonomy is one-level and contains 18 manually defined categories, as shown in Table 2.2. Since these data are collected from user's search log, most of these categories are also meaningful to human's real life. Therefore the search results will be significantly improved, if search queries are well classified to these pre-defined topic categories.

There have also been some related work talking about query topics for specific commercial taxonomy. For example, Broder et al. [11] proposed to classify queries onto a commercial taxonomy of web queries with approximately 6000 nodes, specifically for online advertising application. Since they are considering the matching problem between ads and queries, the taxonomy is required to provide some useful information to help discriminate different commercial topics. As a result, the taxonomy is also defined as a hierarchical structure with median depth 5 and maximum depth 9, and the distribution of different categories by taxonomy levels is shown in Fig. 2.1. Compared with the previous two taxonomies, this taxonomy is specifically useful for some commercial applications, such as web advertising.

2.3.2 Methods on Different Taxonomies

In this section, we introduce some representative research work on query topic classification under different topic taxonomies.

Table 2.1 The 67 Predefined Categories in KDD Cup 2005 (from [49])

Computers\Hardware	Computers\Internet & Intranet
Computers\Mobile Computing	Computers\Multimedia
Computers\Networks & Telecommunication	Computers\Security
Computers\Software	Computers\Other
Entertainment\Celebrities	Entertainment\Games & Toys
Entertainment\Humor & Fun	Entertainment\Movies
Entertainment\Music	Entertainment\Pictures & Photos
Entertainment\Radio	Entertainment\TV
Entertainment\Other	
Information\Arts & Humanities	Information\Companies & Industries
Information\Science & Technology	Information\Education
Information\Law & Politics	Information\Local & Regional
Information\References & Libraries	Information\Other
Living\Book & Magazine	Living\Car & Garage
Living\Career & Jobs	Living\Dating & Relationships
Living\Family & Kides	Living\Fashion & Apparel
Living\Finance & Investment	Living\Food & Cooking
Living\Furnishing & Houseware	Living\Gifts & Collectables
Living\Health & Fitness	Living\Landscaping & Gardening
Living\Pets & Animals	Living\Real Estate
Living\Religion & Belief	Living\Tools & Hardware
Living\Travel & Vacation	Living\Other
Online Community\Chat & Instant Messaging	Online Community\Forums & Groups
Online Community\Homepages	Online Community\People Search
Online Community\Personal Services	Online Community\Other
Shopping\Auction & Bids	Shopping\Stores & Products
Shopping\Buying Guides & Researching	Shopping\Lease & Rent
Shopping\Bargains & Discounts	Shopping\Other
Sports\American Football	Sports\Auto Racing
Sports\Baseball	Sports\Basketball
Sports\Hockey	Sports\News & Scores
Sports\Schedules & Tickets	Sports\Soccer
Sports\Tennis	Sports\Olympic Games
Sports\Outdoor Recreations	Sports\Other

Table 2.2 The 18 Predefined Categories in AOL Data (from [5])

Autos 3.46%	Personal Fin. 1.63%	Business 6.07%
Places 6.13%	Computing 5.38%	Porn 7.19%
Entertainment 12.60%	Research 6.77%	Games 2.38%
Shopping 10.21%	Health 5.99%	Sports 3.30%
Holidays 1.63%	Travel 3.09%	Home and Garden 3.82%
URL 6.78%	News and Society 5.85%	Orgs. and Insts. 4.46%

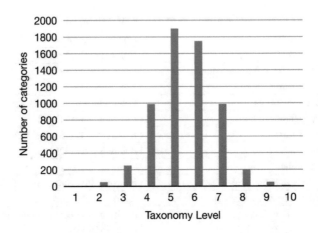

Fig. 2.1 Number of categories by level (from [11])

2.3.2.1   Representative Work on KDD Cup Taxonomy

Firstly, we introduce some typical work on KDD Cup 2005. The task of KDD Cup 2005 competition was to classify 800,000 internet user search queries into 67 predefined categories. This task was easy to understand, but brought some extra challenges compared with the traditionally defined query topic classification problem, as introduced in [42]. Firstly, there was no straight training data. KDD Cup 2005 only provided a small set of 111 queries with labeled categories, which were clearly not sufficient for direct supervised training. This was referred to training data sparsity problem. To tackle this problem, the competition allowed participants to acquire other rich open resources. For example, participants may resort to search engine, document repository, and knowledge base, to collect some extra information for better understanding and modeling. Furthermore, the competition did not provide detailed explanations for each topic category, so the topic semantics were implicit and not easy to understand, referred to implicit semantics problem. Besides, queries were very noisy because they were collected from real search query logs. For example, some words were misspelled when users typed the query into the search engine. At last, it was impossible to manually categorize these large scale queries. Therefore, participants need to design a scalable automatic classification strategy.

Facing these challenges, participants proposed different methods for the query topic classification. In [49], they summarized some major techniques adopted by most participants. The summarization was conducted from three aspects, i.e., preprocessing, gathering extra information, and modeling. As for preprocessing, the main benefit is to reduce the impact and workload of noisy queries, which was one typical challenge of this task. In the competition, most participants applied some typical text mining techniques in their algorithms, such as stop words filtering, stemming, and term frequency filtering for data preprocessing.

Some participants even tried some more advanced techniques, including spelling correction, compound word breaking, abbreviation expansion, and named entity detection, in their algorithms. The motivation to gather extra information is because queries were usually very short, and it was difficult to directly represent the query to a rich feature space, or infer the meaning of a query. Therefore, many participants used different ways to augment queries. For example, some participants used search result snippets, titles, and web pages to construct knowledge base, to expand query terms. As for modeling, participants mainly used two modeling approaches, based on three given data forms, i.e., search queries, words or phrases, and categories. Some participants used an alignment approach to build the model. For example, they directly mapped pre-defined directory structure to the target taxonomy, and produced required topics for each query. Some other participants proposed to construct the mappings between the target topic categories and words or descriptions, so that some bag-of-words modeling strategies could be used to produce the categories of search queries. As for specific methods, most participants adopted machine learning algorithms for this task, including SVM, KNN, Naive Bayesian classifier, Logistic Regression, and Neural Network. Some participants further used some ensemble methods, like Boosting and multiple model combination strategies, to improve their results.

Now we introduce some winner methods of KDD Cup 2005 in detail, including [43, 59] and [69]. Shen et al. [59] did a great job and won all the three awards, i.e., Query Categorization Precision Award, Query Categorization Performance Award, and Query Categorization Creativity Award. They designed a two phrase framework to tackle the two key difficulties of the KDD Cup 2005, i.e., implicit semantics problem and data sparsity problem. In phase I, they tackled the data sparsity problem by developing two kinds of base classifiers, a synonym-based classifier and a statistical classifier. Specifically, the synonym-based classifier was built by keyword matching between the enriched categories from search engine and the given category hierarchies in KDD Cup 2005. As a result, some training examples could be obtained by the mapping function. Then the statistical-based classifier, e.g., SVM, was trained based on these training examples and the manually labeled Web page directory, such as ODP. To tackle the feature sparsity problem, they used the search engine retrieved results to help represent a query, including the snippets, titles, URLs terms, and the category names in the directory. Phase II consisted of two stages. The first stage tackled the problem of lacking detailed query descriptions. Their strategy was to enrich queries by collecting their related web pages and category information through the use of multiple search engines, including Google (http://www.google.com), LookSmart (http://www.looksmart.com), and a search engine developed by the authors based on Lemur (http://www.lemurproject.org). In the second stage, the enriched queries were then classified through the trained base classifiers trained. Finally, two ensemble classifiers were utilized to improve the results. They also designed a demonstration system called Q2C@UST1, based on their algorithm.

Kardkoàcs et al. [43] won the runner-up of the Query Categorization Precision Award and Query Categorization Creativity Award, by using a proposed general solution to this problem, namely Ferrety Algorithm. Ferrety utilized different search engines, such as LookSmart (search.looksmart.com) and Zeal (www.zeal.com) (L&Z), to help understand the meaning of the given query. Therefore it could be treated as a meta-search engine. In this way, Ferrety could be able to create a basic dictionary and an ontology for the short queries. After that, a mapping between the target taxonomy and existing search engine taxonomies could be constructed to help identify the meaning of the query. In the training process, Ferrety used a neural network based learning algorithm named HITEC to find the category of each query. Experimental results showed that the parameters in HITEC, related to the TFIDF frequency scheme, were important for the feature selection and a good trade-off between evaluation measures, like precision and recall.

Vogel et al. [69] won the runner-up of Query Categorization Performance Award. They presented a classification system by using a Web directory to identify the subject context of query terms. The system consisted of three components. The first component searched a given query in the open web directory Dmoz.org to obtain a ranking list of the web directory category, by using Google. Since the web directory category may be different from the target topic taxonomy, a second component was designed to find the mapping between the web directory categories and the target taxonomy. In this process, the authors proposed to construct a semi-automatic mapping, because the web directory was too large. After that, the third component utilized the mapping to produce the topics for a query, based on the processed ranking list of categories. Specifically, a probability score was computed to select up to five nodes in the taxonomy, which maximized the evaluation metrics, such as the precision and the F-measure.

After the competition of KDD Cup 2005, there were also some following work to further improve the performances of query topic classification, including [13, 60, 61], and [62]. The key idea of [61] was to first build an offline bridging classifier on an intermediate taxonomy, and then finetune this classifier in an online mode. The advantage of their model was that they did not need to retrain their classifier, because they could use the similarity between the intermediate taxonomy to map each query to the target taxonomy. Furthermore, they proposed to introduce some category selection strategies to reduce the intermediate taxonomy cost. In this way, both effectiveness and efficiency could be achieved. Experimental results showed that the best result of the KDD Cup 2005 competition was outperformed by combining their algorithm with the winning solution of the KDD Cup 2005. Cao et al. [13] argued that most previous query classification methods did not consider the important context information for queries. So they introduced a conditional random field (CRF) model to incorporated the rich context information, such as the neighboring queries and their corresponding clicked URLs (Web pages) in search sessions, into query classification. Both local features (query terms, pseudo feedback, and implicit feedback) and context features (direct and taxonomy-based association between adjacent labels) were found useful in their CRF model. Finally, they conducted extensive experiments on real word search logs, and the results showed that their method significantly improved the query classification results, as compared with some state-of-the-art baselines, such as [61].

2.3.2.2   Representative Work on AOL Taxonomy

There are also some researches of query topic classification working on the topic taxonomy collected from AOL service. Representative works include [4–7]. Beitzel et al. [4, 5] examined three methods for query topic classification: the traditional information retrieval approach of exact matching against a large human-labeled query dataset, the machine learning approach of producing classifiers by some supervised learning methods from a large labeled dataset, and the data mining approach of designing some selectional preference rules [50] from a large unlabeled query logs. Their experimental results found that each approach had its advantages and disadvantages. For example, the exact matching approach had high precision, especially for high frequency queries, but the recall was low. The threshold of a supervised classifier needed to be carefully tuned, and may not do well on queries not exist in the training data. Therefore, they proposed to combine the three approaches, and experimental results showed that a better result was achieved.

The above works were quite different from the previous reviewed works on KDD Cup 2005. Since no straight training data was provided in KDD Cup 2005, participants had to resort to some external open sources to train their classifiers. However, in the work on AOL taxonomy such as [5, 6], and [7], they were able to develop some automatic topical classification methods without using any external information. Which one was the best remained a question. So Beitzel et al. [6, 8] analyzed various approaches of topical web query classification, from different aspects including features, taxonomy mapping strategies, classification methods, and combining methods. The experimental results showed that: (1) When using individual classifiers, there was almost no difference between the classifier that used only the query string and the one used the retrieved documents for features; while the latter one may further gain some improvement from the query log. These results indicated that it was not appropriate to treat query classification as a general text classification problem. (2) Combining different approaches did not always provide substantial improvement, but at least it would not hurt the best performance. These results provided some insights into the area of query topic classification.

2.3.2.3   Representative Work on Other Taxonomies

There are some representative work on other topic taxonomy or specific domains. For example, Broder et al. [11] proposed a methodology to build a practical robust query classification system, which was required to be both effective and efficient. Their target taxonomy was defined as a commercial taxonomy with 6000 nodes, as introduced before. Because they mainly cared about rare queries, whose observations were not sufficient in the query log, their method was to utilize search engine as a comprehensive repository to build knowledge, for better understanding the meaning of the query. Specifically, they employed the pseudo relevance feedback paradigm and used the top retrieved search results to gather more information for rare queries. Furthermore, elaborate voting schemes were utilized to filter some noisy results. The experimental results showed that the proposed method significantly improved the results of query classification.

Different from these works, Shen et al. [62] focused on product query classification, and studied two major questions in query topic classification, i.e., the impact of query expansion and the size of training data. As for the question of query expansion, they compared two enriching methods, i.e., the well studies method which enriched queries by search snippets and the method to expand queries by their similar queries in the click-through log data. Experimental results showed that both methods can improve the results, and the well studied method enriching queries by search results snippets performed better. As for the question of data augmentation, they compared three collection approaches, i.e., using labeled queries and their enriched representations, using labeled product names, translating the labeled product names to web queries. Experimental results showed that the second one performed much worse than the first one, but the gap would be bridged if we used the third method, which obtained the best result. Therefore, it is important to obtain a consistent representation between queries and their enriched data form, when conducting query enrichment/expansion.

2.3.3 Summary

In this section, we reviewed some literature work on query topic classification. Query topic classification attempts to determine the topical category for a query with a given topic taxonomy. Typical taxonomy includes that provided in the KDD Cup 2005 competition and that collected from the AOL service. Researchers may also use some specific topic taxonomy constructed in some target domains for commercial search engine. The KDD Cup 2005 is an important event in this area, since it provides an opportunity for researchers from different countries to develop techniques to enhance the task of query topic classification. In this competition, many methods have been proposed to tackle the main challenges of training data sparsity and feature sparsity problems. Even after the competition, there have been continuous research work to improve the performance of query topic classification. Despite from the setting in the KDD Cup 2005 that there is no explicit training data and participants need to use an intermediate taxonomy to conduct the classification, other research works study the case of directly learning the classifier on the target topic taxonomy.

2.4 Query Performance Classification

Query performance classification aims to categorize queries according to their *difficulty*, i.e., the likely quality of results returned by the search system for a query, in the absence of relevance judgments and without user feedback. In practice, query difficulty could be further specified in two ways, namely *system query difficulty* and *collection query difficulty* [2]. System query difficulty captures the difficulty of a query for a given retrieval system run over a given collection. In other words, the query is difficult for a *particular* system. System query difficulty is typically measured by the average precision of the ranked list of documents returned by the retrieval system when run over the collection using the query in question. Collection query difficulty captures the difficulty of a query with respect to a given collection. In this way, the difficulty of a query is meant to be largely *independent* of any specific retrieval system. Collection query difficulty can be measured by some statistics taken over the performance of a wide variety of retrieval systems run over the given collection using the query in question, e.g., the median average precision of all runs.

An accurate classification of query performance could be beneficial in many ways [76]:

- Feedback to the user: The user, alerted to the likelihood of poor results, could be prompted to reformulate their query to improve search effectiveness.
- Feedback to the search engine: The system, alerted to the difficult query, could automatically employ enhanced or alternate search strategies tailored to such difficult queries.
- Feedback to the system administrator: The administrator can identify the subjects related to the difficult queries and expand the collection of documents to better answer poorly covered subjects.
- For distributed information retrieval: Distributed retrieval systems could more accurately combine their input results if alerted to the difficulty of the query for each underlying (system, collection) pair.

The study of query performance classification is actually within the scope of a more general research topic, query performance prediction (estimation), which has been recognized by the IR community as an important capability for IR systems. The *Reliable Information Access* (RIA) [12] workshop was the first attempt to rigorously investigate the reasons for performance variability between queries and systems. One of the RIA workshop's conclusions was that the root cause of poor performance is likely to be the same for all systems. Later, the SIGIR workshop on Predicting Query Difficulty [15] brought together researchers and practitioners in query prediction to discuss and define the most relevant topics in this area, including the identification of reasons of query difficulty, prediction methods, evaluation methodology, potential applications, and practical tools and techniques. An acceleration for the research on query performance prediction was the Robust track of TREC 2004 and 2005 [70, 71], where systems were asked to rank testing topics by predicted difficulty. With the robust data set as a benchmark collection, many features and prediction methods have been proposed and compared during the past decade.

However, most existing studies on query performance prediction view the problem as a regression or ranking problem, rather than a classification problem. Features considered to be correlated to the retrieval performance for a query have been proposed to generate a difficulty score or used as a proxy to rank the queries. There have been only a few work that employed the proposed features to classify the queries into difficult/easy categories. Since this section focuses on the topic of query performance classification, we will first review those representative classification works on query difficulty and then briefly summarize the regression/ranking work to highlight the effective features that could be used in a classifier.

2.4.1 Representative Methods

Manual classification was first conducted in TREC-6 [72] to get an idea of how difficult the performance classification task is. A group of human experts were asked to classify a set of TREC queries into three categories, i.e., easy, middle, and hard, based on the query expression only. These judgments were compared to the collection difficulty measure of a query, the median of the average precision scores, as determined after evaluating the performance of all participating systems. The Pearson correlation between the expert judgments and the true values was very low (0.26). Moreover, the agreement between experts, as measured by the correlation between their judgments, was very low too (0.39). The low correlation with the true performance patterns, and the lack of agreement among experts, illustrates how challenging this task is.

Sullivan [66] proposed to classify very long queries (narratives) as easy or difficult based on similar queries. Similarity among queries was qualified using a cosine similarity coefficient, and the resulting query similarity matrix was processed using multidimensional scaling (MDS) method. In this way, they projected the queries into a two-dimensional space where similar queries were close to each other. Three performance measures were employed for search effectiveness (precision at 10, adjusted recall, and a composite measure), and the query difficulty was then defined as the collection difficulty measure using the average performance of six different search engines. 50 TREC queries were analyzed in their experiments. The top 25 queries on a given measure were treated as "easy," while the bottom 25 queries were treated as "difficult." For each effectiveness measure, each query was then classified using a cross-validated nonparametric discriminant analysis, based on its two nearest neighbors. The correct classification rates ranged from a low of 68% to a high of 92% on the difficult category. As we can see, this method relies on an existing set of queries whose search effectiveness has already been measured.

Cronen-Townsend introduced the *clarity score* [21] for query performance classification by measuring the "coherence" (clarity) of the language usage in the result list with respect to the corpus. The conjecture is that a common language of the retrieved documents, which is distinct from general language of the whole corpus is an indication for good results. In contrast, in an unfocused set of results, the language of retrieved documents tends to be more similar to the general language, and retrieval is expected to be less effective. Specifically, the clarity score is defined as the relative entropy, or Kullback–Leibler divergence, between the query and collection language models(unigram distributions) given by

$$\text{clarity score} = \sum_{w \in V} P(w|Q) \log_2 \frac{P(w|Q)}{P_{coll}(w)}, \tag{2.1}$$

where w is any term, Q the query, V is the entire vocabulary of the collection, $P(w|Q)$ denotes the query language model, and $P_{coll}(w)$ denotes the collection language model.

In this work, the query difficulty measure was system specific, which was defined by the average precision of a simple multinomial language modeling approach [65]. A strong positive association between the clarity score of a query and the average precision was found over several TREC test collections. The clarity score was further utilized to make a binary decision on each query, namely "good" (its performance is above a certain average precision threshold) or "bad" (its performance is below the same threshold). When relevance information is available for the queries, the average precision threshold was set based on kernel density estimation requiring half of the estimated probability density to be below the threshold. In this way, the probability of a good (bad) test query is 50%. With this class definition, they estimated the probability density functions for the clarity scores of queries and set the classification boundary as the intersection point of the two class-conditional distributions to minimize the classification error rate based on Bayes decision theory [28]. When relevance information is not available, they estimated the probability density over single term queries and set the classification threshold heuristically so that 80% of the probability density is below threshold. Experimental results showed that the heuristically set decision boundary agrees well with the previous optimal boundary obtained from Bayes decision theory.

Grivolla et al. [32] considered three types of features in automatic query performance classification, including empirical features, entropy and pairwise similarity, and retrieval scores. Empirical features refer to a number of features describing the query itself, such as the query length and different measures of ambiguity or specificity of the query terms (e.g., synonymy, number of senses, hyponymy). Entropy and pairwise similarity features are mainly based on the set of the K top-ranked documents for a query. The entropy of the K top-ranked documents can be computed using a statistical language model as proposed in [17].

$$H = - \sum_{w \in W} P(w) \cdot \log P(w), \tag{2.2}$$

where W is a lexicon of keywords and $P(w)$ is the probability of the word w in the document set. If the entropy of the set is high, the linguistic structure of the documents is highly variable. The conjecture is that a large linguistic variability is related with a higher risk that some retrieved documents are not relevant. They found good correlation between entropy and retrieval performance by limiting the vocabulary to the most frequent words from each document and also keeping the

K small. A score of the same type of entropy is the mean cosine similarity (MCS) of the documents. To compute the similarity, the documents are represented by the vector space model with the traditional TF.IDF weighting scheme.

Retrieval scores are among the best features, which are provided by the different systems for ranking the retrieved documents related to a given query. They used different transformations and normalizations of these scores, such as the mean score of the N top-ranked documents, the score of the n-th document, or the ratio of the scores assigned to the first and the n-th document. Their preliminary study showed that the correlation of these measures based on different retrieval scores in TREC 8 participates with average precision achieved on a query ranges from very strong to inexistent, independently of the performance of the corresponding document retrieval system.

Based on the average precision of the retrieved documents, each query was labeled as "easy" and "hard" using the median value of the average precision as the split point. Therefore, the query difficulty was defined as system specific. Each query was represented as a vector of features described above, and both support vector machines (SVMs) and decision trees were employed to perform the classification. Since there were only 50 queries from TREC 8 in experiments, they used the *leave-one-out* method for testing. The experiments conducted over a representative set of participant systems in TREC 8 showed that reliable prediction can be obtained, e.g., a precision of 84% for the Okapi system on medium length queries using decision trees. To assess the generalization capacity of their approach, they further trained the classifier with TREC 8 results and tested them with TREC 7 results. Very promising results (above 60% classification accuracy) were observed using classifiers trained on several systems, suggesting that their approach is not too dependent on a specific corpus and retrieval setting.

Zhou and Croft [82] considered query performance classification in Web search environments where collections are significantly heterogeneous and different types of retrieval tasks exist, such as content-based (ad hoc) retrieval and Named-Page (NP) finding task. They proposed three techniques to address these challenges. The first one, called *weighted information gain* (WIG), essentially measures the divergence between the mean retrieval score of top-ranked documents and that of the entire corpus. The hypothesis is that the more similar these documents are to the query, with respect to the query similarity exhibited by a general nonrelevant document (i.e., the corpus), the more effective the retrieval. Specifically, given query Q, corpus C, a ranked list L of documents, and the set of k top-ranked documents, $T_k(L)$, WIG is calculated as follows:

$$WIG(Q, C, L) = \frac{1}{K} \sum_{D \in T_k(L)} \sum_{t \in F(Q)} \lambda_t \log \frac{P(t|D)}{P(t|C)}, \qquad (2.3)$$

where t denotes a feature from the feature set $F(Q)$ and λ_t denotes the weight of the feature. $P(t|D)$ and $P(t|C)$ computed the conditional distribution of the feature, given a top-ranked document and the corpus, respectively, which were derived from the Metzler and Croft's Markov Random Field (MRF) model. Both single term and term proximity features could thus be utilized in the computation of WIG. WIG can well handle both content-based and NP queries by employing different estimation methods for $P(t|D)$ and $P(t|C)$ and setting different K values.

The second technique, called *query feedback* (QF), models the retrieval as a communication channel problem. The input is the query, the channel is the retrieval system, and the ranked list is the noisy output of the channel. By thinking about the retrieval process this way, the problem of performance prediction turns to the task of evaluating the quality of the channel. The main idea was to measure to what extent information on the input query could be recovered from the noisy output. Specifically, they used a decoder (clarity score based on ranked list language model) to translate the output list into a new query. Based on the new query, a second list of results is retrieved. The overlap between the two ranked lists is used as a similarity score between the new query and the original query. If the similarity is low, the noise in the channel is high; hence, the query is difficult.

The third feature, called the *first rank change* (FRC), is proposed for NP queries and derived from the ranking robustness technique [81]. FRC approximates the probability that the first ranked document in the original list will remain ranked first even after the documents are perturbed. The higher the probability is, the more confident the first ranked document becomes. In other words, the retrieval performance is more robust for that NP query.

The evaluation was conducted on the GOV2 collection using ad hoc topics from Terabyte Tracks of 2004, 2005, and 2006 as content-based queries, and Named-Page finding topics of the Terabyte tracks of 2005 and 2006 as NP queries. The average precision and reciprocal rank of the first correct answer was adopted as the performance measure of individual content-based and NP queries, respectively. Strong correlations were observed between WIG + QF and retrieval performance of content-based queries and between WIG + FRC and retrieval performance of NP queries. For classification, they divided each type of queries into two classes: "good" (better than 50% of the queries of the same type in terms of retrieval performance) and "bad" (otherwise). The *leave-one-out* method was adopted for testing. Each time one query was randomly selected from the pool, and the remaining queries were used as training data. A query classifier based on robustness score [81] was first applied to predict whether the query is content based or NP. Based on the predicted query type and the score computed for the query by a prediction technique, a binary decision was made about whether the query is good or bad by comparing the score threshold of the predicted query type obtained from the training data. The decision boundary was trained by maximizing the prediction accuracy on the training data similar as in [82]. Experimental results showed very promising results (above 60% classification accuracy) on automatic query performance classification in a Web search environment with mixed query types.

2.4.2   Effective Features in Performance Prediction

There have been extensive studies on the research problem of query performance prediction in the past decades. Since the performance score of each query can be directly evaluated based on ground-truth data, most existing works take the prediction task as a regression/ranking problem, where the correlation between the true retrieval effectiveness values/ranks and predicted difficulty scores/ranks is examined. Although the prediction problem is not directly formulated as a classification problem in these works, the proposed predictors are quite general and could be directly used as features in the classifier. Therefore, we briefly summarize the existing predictors related to query performance prediction for a comprehensive review.

Existing predictors for query performance prediction can be roughly categorized to pre-retrieval predictors and post-retrieval predictors [14]. Pre-retrieval predictors estimate the quality of the search results before the search takes place, thus only the raw query and statistics of the query terms gathered at indexing time can be exploited for estimation. In contrast, post-retrieval predictors can additionally analyze the search results. Pre-retrieval predictors are easy to compute but are usually inferior to post-retrieval predictors, since they do not take the retrieval method into account. The (usually short) query alone is often not expressive enough for reliable prediction of the quality of the search results.

Pre-retrieval predictors can be further classified into linguistic predictors and statistical predictors [14, 34]. Linguistic predictors apply morphological, syntactical, and semantical analysis over the query expressions in order to identify lexical difficulty of the query. In contrast, statistical predictors analyze the distribution of the query terms within the collection, which can be categorized into specificity-, similarity-, coherency-, and relatedness-based predictors. The specificity-based predictors predict a query to perform better with increased specificity. The similarity-based predictors measure the similarity between the query and the collection, assuming that queries that are similar to the collection are easier to answer since there might be many relevant documents to the query. Coherency-based predictors analyze the intersimilarity of documents containing the query terms and predict a query to be difficult if the retrieval algorithm cannot distinguish these documents. Finally, relatedness-based predictors consider the relationship between query terms, and a strong relationship between query terms suggests a well-performing query.

On the contrary, post-retrieval predictors analyze the search results, looking for coherency and robustness of the retrieved documents. According to [14], one can classify these methods into (1) clarity-based predictors that measure the coherency (clarity) of the result set and its separability from the whole collections of documents, (2) robustness-based predictors that estimate the robustness of the result set under different types of perturbations, and (3) score analysis-based predictors that analyze the score distribution of results.

Table 2.3 A taxonomy of predictors on query performance prediction

Pre-retrieval	Linguistic		*Morphological*, *syntactical*, and *semantical* [53]
	Statistical	Specificity	*Query scope (QS), simplified clarity score (SCS(q))*[36]
			avgIDF, avgICTF, maxIDF[55]
			maxICTF, varIDF, varICTF [55]
		Similarity	*Collection query similarity (SCQ)* [80]
		Coherency	*Coherence score (CS)* [37], *maxVAR, sumVAR* [80]
		Relatedness	*avgPMI, maxPMI* [33]
Post-retrieval	Clarity		*Clairty* [21], $Info_{DFR}$ [1]
			JSD [16], *Clarity variants* [20, 22, 35]
	Robustness	Query perturb	*Query Feedback (QF)* [82], *Sub-query overlap* [76]
		Doc perturb	*Robustness score* [81], *Sensitivity analysis* [68]
		Retrieval perturb	*JSD among distributions* [2]
		Cohesion	*Clustering tendency* [68], *Spatial autocorrelation* [25]
	Score analysis		*Highest or mean score* [67]
			Discriminative power [9]
			Weighted Information Gain (WIG) [82]
			Normalized Query Commitment (NQC) [64]
			Standard deviation [23]

We summarize several representative predictors according to the above taxonomy in Table 2.3. There have been comprehensive reviews [14, 34] and analyses [44, 45] of these predictors in the literature.

2.4.3 Summary

In this section, we review the work on query performance classification in the literature. We introduce the definition and the motivation of the task as well as the brief history in the development of this research direction. We then survey several representative works on query performance classification, from manual classification to automatic methods. For each method, we talk about the specific definition of query difficulty measure, the major predictive feature proposed, and how the evaluation was conducted. As mentioned before, query performance classification is actually within the scope of a more general research topic, query performance prediction. To make the survey on this direction comprehensive, we also discussed the effective features proposed for query performance prediction tasks, which could be made use in a classifier.

2.5   Other Query Classification Tasks

Beyond the previous major classification tasks on search queries, there has been research work paying attention to other "dimensions" in query classification, such as geographical location and time requirement.

2.5.1   Location-Based Classification

Many times a user's information need has some kind of geographic boundary associated with it. For example, "houses for sale nyc" explicitly showed are likely submitted by a user with the goal of finding house sale information in New York City, while "pizza" or "dentist" typically implies that the user is looking for information or services relevant to their current whereabouts. Location-based query classification thus aims to detect and categorize the geographic boundary/information in search queries. There are many uses of identifying geographic information in users' queries: we can provider better personalized search results and improve a user's search experience; we can also improve the sponsored advertisement matching for locally available goods and services that users may be interested in.

Although geographic information in search queries is the common target in this line of research, existing works have defined several location-based query classification tasks based on slightly different motivations or focuses. Accordingly, the features used to build the classifiers are also different in these works. Evaluation measures are similar in most work, including precision, recall, F measure, and accuracy. It is worth noting that precision is often emphasized over recall, and in particular, the accuracy of positive classification. The reason is that an incorrectly localized query may significantly hurt users' search experience.

Specifically, Gravano et al.'s [31] work on query locality classification was based on previous findings that Web pages (and resources, in general) can be characterized according to their *geographical locality*, where a *global* page was likely to be of interest to a geographically broad audience while a *local* page was likely to be of interest only to an audience in a relatively narrow region. Therefore, they defined queries as *local* if their best matches are likely to be "local" pages, or as *global*, if their best matches are likely to be "global" pages. Accordingly, they proposed their classification features on measures of frequency and dispersion of location names in the top search results produced by a query. Four types of state-of-the-art classification approaches were explored and evaluated based on 966 manually labeled queries from Excite search engine. Their empirical results indicated that for many queries locality can be determined effectively.

Wang et al. [73] introduced a slightly different task, i.e., detecting dominant locations from search queries. Here query's dominant location (QDL) refers to one or more geographical locations associated with a query in collective human knowledge, i.e., prominent location(s) agreed by majority of people who know the answer to the query. Based on this definition, they proposed to classify queries into four categories, including (1) queries without location keywords and do not have QDLs (Type-1), (2) queries with location keywords and have QDLs (Type-2), (3) queries without location keywords but have QDLs (Type-3), and (4) queries with location keywords but do not have QDLs (Type-4). Their major focus was the detection of Type-2 and Type-3 queries, where they calculated a QDL for each query from three information resources: queries, search results, and query logs. Experiments were conducted based on 10,000 manually labeled queries from MSN search log, and the empirical results showed that the best classification performance can be achieved by combing query and query log information.

Zhuang et al. [83] defined geo-sensitivity of a query as that, to answer the query, Web pages that either have association with certain geographical location(s) or are considered more relevant to users in certain geographical location(s) will be considered more relevant. To make it more concrete, they further defined four categories of geo-sensitivity for queries, namely *explicit*, *implicit*, *local*, and *nonsensitive*. Note that although the explicit, implicit, and local queries defined in this paper can be viewed as finer categories of local queries in [31], the classification task is quite different. In this work, they proposed a binary classification task by referring to the explicit or implicit query as *Geo-Sensitive Query(GSQ)*, and the rest as *Non-Geo-Sensitive Query(NGSQ)*. The geographical distributions of user clicks were taken as the major patterns to differentiate the two categories of queries. The evaluation based on 1000 manually labeled queries from *Yahoo! Search* logs showed the promising accuracy of the proposed method.

In [74], Welch and Cho proposed to identify *localizable* queries, where localizable queries are those search strings for which the user would implicitly prefer to see results prioritized by their geographical proximity. According to their definition, the localizable queries were similar to the local query category defined in [83]. To build the query classifier, they first identified localizable queries by finding previously issued queries that contain an explicit localization modifier, with the assumption that the "base" of these queries may be generally localizable. Based on the set of all base queries, they extracted relevant distinguishing features such as localization ratio, location distribution, click-through rates, frequency counts, and user distribution for classification. Multiple well-known supervised classifiers were evaluated for the task, and a meta-classifier comprised of three conventional classifiers performed the best.

Later, Yi et al. [75] focused on building models using city level geo information for detecting and discovering users' specific geo intent. A three-level classification scheme was proposed in their work. They first identified users' implicit geo intent and pinpointed the city corresponding to this intent. For queries with implicit city-level geo intent, they further classified them into three geo subcategories according to their different localization capabilities: (1) local geo queries, which consist of geo queries that imply a user's intention to find locally relevant information; (2) neighbor region geo queries, which contain geo queries that imply a user's intention to find related information from nearby regions; (3) remaining geo queries that do not fall into the above three categories and are not easily localized. Finally, they also predicted the city corresponding to the geo intent in a location-specific query. They proposed two different ways for extracting geo features: one is through building city-level geo language models and calculating a query's city generation posteriors, and the other one is through extracting rich geo information units (GIU) at the city level. They used click-through data as a surrogate for human labels to automatically obtain large-scale training and testing data set. Three types of classifiers were employed in their experiments, and the results demonstrated the effectiveness of using city-level language model features and GIU features for all three learning tasks.

2.5.2   Time-Based Classification

Many Web search queries have explicit or implicit time requirement over the relevant results. For example, the query "us election 2009" explicitly expresses the time (i.e., "2009") for the target results. For the query "SIGIR" (the name of an annual conference), although there is no explicit year information, related pages are expected to be time sensitive to the year when the query is submitted. Time-based classification, therefore, aims to classify search queries according to their time requirement. Since explicit time requirement is usually easy to detect, most of the time-based classifications focus on implicit time requirement detection. By detecting the implicit time requirement of search queries, the search quality can be largely improved by taking into account the time dimension beyond the topic similarity in relevance ranking.

Typically, we can classify search queries into two categories, one with time requirement, namely time-sensitive or temporal queries, and the rest, namely stable or atemporal queries. For the time-sensitive or temporal queries, two finer classes have been identified in the literature. One is recurrent/periodic query, which is about events that occur at regular, predictable time intervals, most often weekly, monthly, annually, bi-annually, etc. The other is newsworthy/burst query, which is about some breaking news or burst events. Note that newsworthy/burst queries may have multiple bursts at different time periods, e.g., "earthquake." Different features and approaches have been proposed in the past to differentiate one or two types of the time-sensitive queries from the rest.

For example, Jones and Diaz [41] defined three temporal classes of a query, namely temporal queries, temporally unambiguous queries, and temporally ambiguous queries. Note here the temporally unambiguous queries corresponded to the newsworthy/burst queries with one-time burst, while temporally ambiguous queries included newsworthy/burst queries with multiple bursts and recurrent queries. So their definition was a little bit different from other works in the literature. To automatically classify queries into the three classes, they introduced the temporal profiles of a query, which can be viewed as the temporal analogs of query language models, and proposed a set of features for discriminating between temporal profiles, such as KL divergence and autocorrelation. Supervised machine learning (i.e., decision tree) was then employed for the classification task. The evaluation based on TREC novelty and ad hoc queries demonstrated the effectiveness of temporal profiles in time prediction for queries.

In [26], Diaz trained a classifier to distinguish between newsworthy and non-newsworthy queries for better integration of news vertical into Web search results. The key idea is that there is a strong correlation between the click-through rate of a news display and the newsworthy of a query, and the click-through rate can be estimated by a set of nonlexicographic information (i.e., contextual features from search logs) of the query. A probabilistic model was further employed to estimate posterior mean of the click-through probability, given data from click feedback and related queries. Accuracy was tested for the classification method, and it achieved promising performance on detecting newsworthy queries by including both historic feedback and similarity information.

The detection of a special category of time-sensitive queries, namely implicitly year qualified queries (IYQQ), was considered in [52, 78]. An implicitly year qualified query is a query that does not actually contain a year, but yet the user may have implicitly formulated the query with a specific year in mind. The classification method of IYQQ proposed in [78] was simple and efficient. They built up an IYQQ dictionary by extracting all explicit YQQs from query log and removing the corresponding year stamp. In test, if a query can find an exact match in the dictionary, the query was regarded as an IYQQ. The classification method in [52] was slightly different, where a query was classified as IYQQ if it was qualified by at least two unique years, since they were mainly interested in temporally recurring events. Both classification methods were not directly evaluated but integrated as a component for reranking and evaluated by ranking performance.

In [79], Zhang et al. proposed to detect recurrent event queries (REQs) for Web search. They considered six types of features based on query log analysis, query reformulation, click log analysis, search engine result set, time-series analysis, and recurrent event seed word list. Three learning algorithms were employed for the classification task, including Naive Bayes method, SVM, and Gradient Boosted Decision Tree (GBDT). They collected 6000 manually labeled queries for training and evaluation. The best performance was achieved by the GBDT model.

Dong et al. [27] introduced a method to detect recency sensitive query (i.e., breaking-news queries) for recency ranking in Web search. The key idea of their method is to estimate two current language models, i.e., the content model and the query model, and compare them to the corresponding reference models, i.e., the language models in the past. Intuitively, if the query is more likely generated by the current model rather than the past model, it would be more likely to be recency sensitive. Therefore, a "buzziness" score was computed based on the differences between the current and reference models from both content and query views. A query was considered as a breaking-news one if its final buzz score exceeded some threshold. The evaluation was conducted based on 2, 000 manually judged queries, and a high precision score (0.87) can be achieved by their classifier.

Later, Shokouhi [63] proposed to detect recurrent queries based on time-series analysis. Chen et al. [18] also analyzed the time-series patterns to classify queries into four classes, namely stable query, one-time burst query, multitime burst query, and periodic query. Both methods were evaluated based on a small number of manually annotated queries.

2.6 Summary

An important way of understanding users' information needs in Web search is query classification. In this chapter, we discuss several different query classification tasks, from some major interests such as intent classification, topic classification, and performance classification to classification tasks in other "dimensions" such as geographic location and time requirement. For each classification task, there have been multiple classification taxonomies proposed in the past due to finer analysis of users' needs or specific application requests. Although different types of features have been proposed for different tasks, they are mainly from the resources such as query logs, click logs, retrieved documents, search corpus, and queries itself. Supervised, unsupervised, and semisupervised models have been employed in these tasks. However, except the topic classification task, which has a benchmark data set to compare different methods, most classification methods for the remaining tasks were evaluated on their own data set. Therefore, it is important for us to decide the effectiveness of these features not only by the relative performance improvement but also by the data size used in evaluation.

References

1. Giambattista Amati, Claudio Carpineto, and Giovanni Romano. Query difficulty, robustness, and selective application of query expansion. In *Proceedings of The 26th European Conference on IR Research*, volume 2997, pages 127–137, 2004.
2. Javed A. Aslam and Virgiliu Pavlu. Query hardness estimation using Jensen-Shannon divergence among multiple scoring functions. In *Proceedings of The 29th European Conference on IR Research*, volume 4425, pages 198–209, 2007.
3. Ricardo A. Baeza-Yates, Liliana Calderón-Benavides, and Cristina N. González-Caro. The intention behind web queries. In *Proceedings of The 13th International Conference on String Processing and Information Retrieval*, volume 4209, pages 98–109, 2006.
4. Steven M. Beitzel, Eric C. Jensen, Ophir Frieder, David A. Grossman, David D. Lewis, Abdur Chowdhury, and Aleksander Kolcz. Automatic web query classification using labeled and unlabeled training data. In *Proceedings of the 28th Annual International ACM SIGIR Conference on Research and Development in Information Retrieval*, pages 581–582, 2005a.
5. Steven M. Beitzel, Eric C. Jensen, Ophir Frieder, David D. Lewis, Abdur Chowdhury, and Aleksander Kolcz. Improving automatic query classification via semi-supervised learning. In *Proceedings of the 5th IEEE International Conference on Data Mining*, pages 42–49, 2005b.
6. Steven M. Beitzel, Eric C. Jensen, Abdur Chowdhury, and Ophir Frieder. Varying approaches to topical web query classification. In *Proceedings of the 30th Annual International ACM SIGIR Conference on Research and Development in Information Retrieval*, pages 783–784, 2007a.

7. Steven M. Beitzel, Eric C. Jensen, David D. Lewis, Abdur Chowdhury, and Ophir Frieder. Automatic classification of web queries using very large unlabeled query logs. *ACM Trans. Inf. Syst.*, 25 (2): 9, 2007b.
8. Steven M. Beitzel, Eric C. Jensen, Abdur Chowdhury, and Ophir Frieder. Analysis of varying approaches to topical web query classification. In *Proceedings of the 3rd International ICST Conference on Scalable Information Systems*, page 15, 2008.
9. Yaniv Bernstein, Bodo Billerbeck, Steven Garcia, Nicholas Lester, Falk Scholer, Justin Zobel, and William Webber. RMIT university at TREC 2005: Terabyte and robust track. In *Proceedings of the Fourteenth Text REtrieval Conference*, volume 500–266, 2005.
10. Andrei Z. Broder. A taxonomy of web search. *SIGIR Forum*, 36 (2): 3–10, 2002.
11. Andrei Z. Broder, Marcus Fontoura, Evgeniy Gabrilovich, Amruta Joshi, Vanja Josifovski, and Tong Zhang. Robust classification of rare queries using web knowledge. In *Proceedings of the 30th Annual International ACM SIGIR Conference on Research and Development in Information Retrieval*, pages 231–238, 2007.
12. Chris Buckley and Donna Harman. Reliable information access final workshop report. *ARDA Northeast Regional Research Center Technical Report*, 3, 2004.
13. Huanhuan Cao, Derek Hao Hu, Dou Shen, Daxin Jiang, Jian-Tao Sun, Enhong Chen, and Qiang Yang. Context-aware query classification. In *Proceedings of the 32nd Annual International ACM SIGIR Conference on Research and Development in Information Retrieval*, pages 3–10, 2009.
14. David Carmel and Elad Yom-Tov. *Estimating the Query Difficulty for Information Retrieval.* Morgan & Claypool Publishers, 2010.
15. David Carmel, Elad Yom-Tov, and Ian Soboroff. SIGIR workshop report: predicting query difficulty - methods and applications. *SIGIR Forum*, 39 (2): 25–28, 2005.
16. David Carmel, Elad Yom-Tov, Adam Darlow, and Dan Pelleg. What makes a query difficult? In *Proceedings of the 29th Annual International ACM SIGIR Conference on Research and Development in Information Retrieval*, pages 390–397, 2006.
17. Claudio Carpineto, Renato de Mori, Giovanni Romano, and Brigitte Bigi. An information-theoretic approach to automatic query expansion. *ACM Trans. Inf. Syst.*, 19 (1): 1–27, 2001.
18. Z Chen, H Yang, J Ma, J Lei, and H Gao. Time-based query classification and its application for page rank. *J Comput Info Sys*, 7: 3149–3156, 2011.
19. Nancy Chinchor. Appendix E: MUC-7 named entity task definition (version 3.5). In *Proceedings of the Seventh Message Understanding Conference*, 1998.
20. Kevyn Collins-Thompson and Paul N. Bennett. Predicting query performance via classification. In *Proceedings of the 32nd European Conference on IR Researches*, volume 5993, pages 140–152, 2010.
21. Stephen Cronen-Townsend, Yun Zhou, and W. Bruce Croft. Predicting query performance. In *Proceedings of the 25th Annual International ACM SIGIR Conference on Research and Development in Information Retrieval*, pages 299–306, 2002.
22. Steve Cronen-Townsend, Yun Zhou, and W. Bruce Croft. Precision prediction based on ranked list coherence. *Information Retrieval*, 9 (6): 723–755, 2006.
23. Ronan Cummins, Joemon M. Jose, and Colm O'Riordan. Improved query performance prediction using standard deviation. In *Proceeding of the 34th International ACM SIGIR Conference on Research and Development in Information Retrieval*, pages 1089–1090, 2011.
24. Honghua (Kathy) Dai, Lingzhi Zhao, Zaiqing Nie, Ji-Rong Wen, Lee Wang, and Ying Li. Detecting online commercial intention (OCI). In *Proceedings of the 15th international conference on World Wide Web*, pages 829–837, 2006.
25. Fernando Diaz. Performance prediction using spatial autocorrelation. In *Proceedings of the 30th Annual International ACM SIGIR Conference on Research and Development in Information Retrieval*, pages 583–590, 2007.
26. Fernando Diaz. Integration of news content into web results. In *Proceedings of the Second International Conference on Web Search and Data Mining*, pages 182–191, 2009.
27. Anlei Dong, Yi Chang, Zhaohui Zheng, Gilad Mishne, Jing Bai, Ruiqiang Zhang, Karolina Buchner, Ciya Liao, and Fernando Diaz. Towards recency ranking in web search. In *Proceed-*

ings of the Third International Conference on Web Search and Data Mining, pages 11–20, 2010.

28. Richard O. Duda and Peter E. Hart. *Pattern classification and scene analysis*. Wiley, 1973.

29. Hovy E., L. Gerber, U. Hermjakob, C.-Y. Lin, and D. Ravichandran. Towards semantic-based answer pinpointing. In *Proceedings of the DARPA Human Language Technology Conference*, 2001.

30. Nyberg E., T. Mitamura, J. Callan, J. Carbonell, R. Frederking, K. Collins-Thompson, L. Hiyakumoto, Y. Huang, C. Huttenhower, S. Judy, J.Ko, A. Kupsc, L.V.Lita, V.Pedro, D.Svoboda, and B.V.Durme. The javelin question-answering system at TREC 2003: A multi-strategy approach with dynamic planning. In *Proceedings of the 12th Text Retrieval Conference*, 2003.

31. Luis Gravano, Vasileios Hatzivassiloglou, and Richard Lichtenstein. Categorizing web queries according to geographical locality. In *Proceedings of the 2003 ACM CIKM International Conference on Information and Knowledge Management*, pages 325–333, 2003.

32. Jens Grivolla, Pierre Jourlin, and Renato de Mori. Automatic classification of queries by expected retrieval performance. In *Proceedings of the SIGIR workshop on predicting query difficulty*, 2005.

33. Claudia Hauff. Predicting the effectiveness of queries and retrieval systems. *SIGIR Forum*, 44 (1): 88, 2010.

34. Claudia Hauff, Djoerd Hiemstra, and Franciska de Jong. A survey of pre-retrieval query performance predictors. In *Proceedings of the 17th ACM Conference on Information and Knowledge Management*, pages 1419–1420, 2008a.

35. Claudia Hauff, Vanessa Murdock, and Ricardo Baeza-Yates. Improved query difficulty prediction for the web. In *Proceedings of the 17th ACM Conference on Information and Knowledge Management*, pages 439–448, 2008b.

36. Ben He and Iadh Ounis. Inferring query performance using pre-retrieval predictors. In *Proceedings of the 11th International Conference on String Processing and Information Retrieval*, volume 3246, pages 43–54, 2004.

37. Jiyin He, Martha A. Larson, and Maarten de Rijke. Using coherence-based measures to predict query difficulty. In *Proceedings of the 30th European Conference on IR Research*, volume 4956, pages 689–694, 2008.

38. David A. Hull. Xerox TREC-8 question answering track report. In *Proceedings of The Eighth Text REtrieval Conference*, volume 500–246, 1999.

39. Abraham Ittycheriah, Martin Franz, Wei-Jing Zhu, Adwait Ratnaparkhi, and Richard J. Mammone. IBM's statistical question answering system. In *Proceedings of The Ninth Text REtrieval Conference*, volume 500–249, 2000.

40. Bernard J. Jansen, Danielle L. Booth, and Amanda Spink. Determining the informational, navigational, and transactional intent of web queries. *Inf. Process. Manag.*, 44 (3): 1251–1266, 2008.

41. Rosie Jones and Fernando Diaz. Temporal profiles of queries. *ACM Trans. Inf. Syst.*, 25 (3): 14, 2007.

42. In-Ho Kang and Gil-Chang Kim. Query type classification for web document retrieval. In *Proceedings of the 26th Annual International ACM SIGIR Conference on Research and Development in Information Retrieval*, pages 64–71, 2003.

43. Zsolt Tivadar Kardkovács, Domonkos Tikk, and Zoltán Bánsághi. The ferrety algorithm for the KDD cup 2005 problem. *SIGKDD Explorations*, 7 (2): 111–116, 2005.

44. Oren Kurland, Anna Shtok, David Carmel, and Shay Hummel. A unified framework for post-retrieval query-performance prediction. In *Proceedings of the Third International Conference on Information Retrieval Theory*, volume 6931, pages 15–26, 2011.

45. Oren Kurland, Anna Shtok, Shay Hummel, Fiana Raiber, David Carmel, and Ofri Rom. Back to the roots: a probabilistic framework for query-performance prediction. In *Proceedings of the 21st ACM International Conference on Information and Knowledge Management*, pages 823–832, 2012.
46. Kyung-Soon Lee, Jong-Hoon Oh, Jin-Xia Huang, Jae-Ho Kim, and Key-Sun Choi. TREC-9 experiments at KAIST: QA, CLIR and batch filtering. In *Proceedings of The Ninth Text REtrieval Conference*, volume 500–249, 2000.
47. Uichin Lee, Zhenyu Liu, and Junghoo Cho. Automatic identification of user goals in web search. In *Proceedings of the 14th international conference on World Wide Web*, pages 391–400, 2005.
48. Xin Li and Dan Roth. Learning question classifiers. In *Proceedings of the 19th International Conference on Computational Linguistics*, pages 1–7, 2002.
49. Ying Li, Zijian Zheng, and Honghua (Kathy) Dai. KDD CUP-2005 report: facing a great challenge. *SIGKDD Explorations*, 7 (2): 91–99, 2005.
50. Chris Manning and Hinrich Schütze. *Foundations of Statistical Natural Language Processing*. MIT Press, Cambridge, 1999.
51. Donald Metzler and W. Bruce Croft. Analysis of statistical question classification for fact-based questions. *Inf. Retr.*, 8 (3): 481–504, 2005.
52. Donald Metzler, Rosie Jones, Fuchun Peng, and Ruiqiang Zhang. Improving search relevance for implicitly temporal queries. In *Proceedings of the 32nd Annual International ACM SIGIR Conference on Research and Development in Information Retrieval*, pages 700–701, 2009.
53. Josiane Mothe and Ludovic Tanguy. Linguistic features to predict query difficulty. In *ACM Conference on research and Development in Information Retrieval, SIGIR, Predicting query difficulty-methods and applications workshop*, pages 7–10, 2005.
54. Marius Pasca and Sanda M. Harabagiu. High performance question/answering. In *Proceedings of the 24th Annual International ACM SIGIR Conference on Research and Development in Information Retrieval*, pages 366–374, 2001.
55. Vassilis Plachouras, Ben He, and Iadh Ounis. University of Glasgow at TREC 2004: Experiments in web, robust, and terabyte tracks with terrier. In *Proceedings of the Thirteenth Text REtrieval Conference*, volume 500–261, 2004.
56. John M. Prager, Dragomir R. Radev, Eric W. Brown, Anni Coden, and Valerie Samn. The use of predictive annotation for question answering in TREC8. In *Proceedings of The Eighth Text REtrieval Conference*, volume 500–246, 1999.
57. Dragomir R. Radev, Weiguo Fan, Hong Qi, Harris Wu, and Amardeep Grewal. Probabilistic question answering on the web. In *Proceedings of the Eleventh International World Wide Web Conference*, pages 408–419, 2002.
58. Daniel E. Rose and Danny Levinson. Understanding user goals in web search. In *Proceedings of the 13th international conference on World Wide Web*, pages 13–19, 2004.
59. Dou Shen, Rong Pan, Jian-Tao Sun, Jeffrey Junfeng Pan, Kangheng Wu, Jie Yin, and Qiang Yang. Q^2c@ust: our winning solution to query classification in KDDCUP 2005. *SIGKDD Explorations*, 7 (2): 100–110, 2005.
60. Dou Shen, Rong Pan, Jian-Tao Sun, Jeffrey Junfeng Pan, Kangheng Wu, Jie Yin, and Qiang Yang. Query enrichment for web-query classification. *ACM Trans. Inf. Syst.*, 24 (3): 320–352, 2006a.
61. Dou Shen, Jian-Tao Sun, Qiang Yang, and Zheng Chen. Building bridges for web query classification. In *Proceedings of the 29th Annual International ACM SIGIR Conference on Research and Development in Information Retrieval*, pages 131–138, 2006b.
62. Dou Shen, Ying Li, Xiao Li, and Dengyong Zhou. Product query classification. In *Proceedings of the 18th ACM Conference on Information and Knowledge Management*, pages 741–750, 2009.
63. Milad Shokouhi. Detecting seasonal queries by time-series analysis. In *Proceeding of the 34th International ACM SIGIR Conference on Research and Development in Information Retrieval*, pages 1171–1172, 2011.

64. Anna Shtok, Oren Kurland, David Carmel, Fiana Raiber, and Gad Markovits. Predicting query performance by query-drift estimation. *ACM Trans. Inf. Syst.*, 30 (2): 11:1–11:35, 2012.
65. Fei Song and W. Bruce Croft. A general language model for information retrieval. In *Proceedings of the 1999 ACM CIKM International Conference on Information and Knowledge Management*, pages 316–321, 1999.
66. Terry Sullivan. Locating question difficulty through explorations in question space. In *Proceedings of the 2001 ACM/IEEE Joint Conference on Digital Libraries*, pages 251–252, 2001.
67. Stephen Tomlinson. Robust, web and terabyte retrieval with hummingbird search server at TREC 2004. In *Proceedings of the Thirteenth Text REtrieval Conference*, volume 500–261, 2004.
68. Vishwa Vinay, Ingemar J. Cox, Natasa Milic-Frayling, and Kenneth R. Wood. On ranking the effectiveness of searches. In *Proceedings of the 29th Annual International ACM SIGIR Conference on Research and Development in Information Retrieval*, pages 398–404, 2006.
69. David S. Vogel, Steffen Bickel, Peter Haider, Rolf Schimpfky, Peter Siemen, Steve Bridges, and Tobias Scheffer. Classifying search engine queries using the web as background knowledge. *SIGKDD Explorations*, 7 (2): 117–122, 2005.
70. Ellen M Voorhees. Overview of the trec 2004 robust retrieval track. In *Proceedings of 13th Text Retrieval Conference*, 2004.
71. Ellen M. Voorhees. Overview of the TREC 2005 robust retrieval track. In *Proceedings of the Fourteenth Text REtrieval Conference*, volume 500–266, 2005.
72. Ellen M. Voorhees and Donna Harman. Overview of the sixth text retrieval conference (TREC-6). *Inf. Process. Manag.*, 36 (1): 3–35, 2000.
73. Lee Wang, Chuang Wang, Xing Xie, Josh Forman, Yansheng Lu, Wei-Ying Ma, and Ying Li. Detecting dominant locations from search queries. In *Proceedings of the 28th Annual International ACM SIGIR Conference on Research and Development in Information Retrieval*, pages 424–431, 2005.
74. Michael J. Welch and Junghoo Cho. Automatically identifying localizable queries. In *Proceedings of the 31st Annual International ACM SIGIR Conference on Research and Development in Information Retrieval*, pages 507–514, 2008.
75. Xing Yi, Hema Raghavan, and Chris Leggetter. Discovering users' specific geo intention in web search. In *Proceedings of the 18th International Conference on World Wide Web*, pages 481–490, 2009.
76. Elad Yom-Tov, Shai Fine, David Carmel, and Adam Darlow. Learning to estimate query difficulty: including applications to missing content detection and distributed information retrieval. In *Proceedings of the 28th Annual International ACM SIGIR Conference on Research and Development in Information Retrieval*, pages 512–519, 2005.
77. Dell Zhang and Wee Sun Lee. Question classification using support vector machines. In *Proceedings of the 26th Annual International ACM SIGIR Conference on Research and Development in Information Retrieval*, pages 26–32, 2003.
78. Ruiqiang Zhang, Yi Chang, Zhaohui Zheng, Donald Metzler, and Jian-Yun Nie. Search engine adaptation by feedback control adjustment for time-sensitive query. In *Human Language Technologies: Conference of the North American Chapter of the Association of Computational Linguistics*, pages 165–168, 2009.
79. Ruiqiang Zhang, Yuki Konda, Anlei Dong, Pranam Kolari, Yi Chang, and Zhaohui Zheng. Learning recurrent event queries for web search. In *Proceedings of the 2010 Conference on Empirical Methods in Natural Language Processing*, pages 1129–1139, 2010.
80. Ying Zhao, Falk Scholer, and Yohannes Tsegay. Effective pre-retrieval query performance prediction using similarity and variability evidence. In *Proceedings of the 30th European Conference on IR Research*, pages 52–64, 2008.

81. Yun Zhou and W. Bruce Croft. Ranking robustness: a novel framework to predict query performance. In *Proceedings of the 2006 ACM CIKM International Conference on Information and Knowledge Management*, pages 567–574, 2006.
82. Yun Zhou and W. Bruce Croft. Query performance prediction in web search environments. In *Proceedings of the 30th Annual International ACM SIGIR Conference on Research and Development in Information Retrieval*, pages 543–550, 2007.
83. Ziming Zhuang, Cliff Brunk, and C. Lee Giles. Modeling and visualizing geo-sensitive queries based on user clicks. In *Proceedings of the First International Workshop on Location and the Web*, pages 73–76, 2008.

Chapter 3
Query Segmentation and Tagging

Xuanhui Wang

Abstract Query tagging is an important step for query understanding. It applies traditional natural language processing techniques on query strings. Specific challenges are raised due to the shortness of query strings. In this chapter, we describe techniques proposed in the existing literature on how to achieve meaningful query tagging in the following areas: query segmentation, query syntactic tagging, and query semantic tagging.

3.1 Introduction

Query tagging is an important step for query understanding. It is a process that works with query strings more closely based on Natural Language Processing (NLP) techniques [19]. Traditionally, NLP techniques are developed for documents with well-formed sentences and can be used for Information Retrieval (IR). For example, phases in documents can be identified and used in document index [37]. Thus, it is important to segment queries to match phrases in documents to boost retrieval accuracy. Furthermore, Part-Of-Speech (POS) tags and linguistic structures carry meaningful information to match queries and documents. They are also important for search engines to improve result relevance. However, the keyword-based queries are usually short and lack of sentence structures. It raises challenges to apply NLP on queries directly. In this chapter, we describe techniques proposed in the existing literature on how to overcome these challenges to achieve meaningful query tagging in the following areas: query segmentation, query syntactic tagging, and query semantic tagging.

X. Wang (✉)
Google Research, Mountain View, CA, USA
e-mail: xuanhui@gmail.com

© Springer Nature Switzerland AG 2020
Y. Chang, H. Deng (eds.), *Query Understanding for Search Engines*,
The Information Retrieval Series 46, https://doi.org/10.1007/978-3-030-58334-7_3

3.2 Query Segmentation

Search engines usually provide a search box as the user interface and a few keywords can be used to search web pages to satisfy users' information needs. Due to the simplicity for users to formulate search queries, such a user interface gains popularity and becomes a standard for search engines. However, queries formulated in this interface are generally not complete natural language sentences, but consist of a bunch of keywords. Thus it becomes harder to apply NLP techniques directly on queries. For example, a sentence like "Where can I find Pizza Hut in New York" is likely tagged well by NLP tools than a query "pizza hut new york."

Query segmentation is one of the first steps towards query understanding. It does not involve heavy NLP processes such as Part-Of-Speech (POS) tagging or Named Entity Recognition (NER). Its goal is to split a query string into a few segments. The basic bag-of-words (BOW) model can be thought as segmenting queries based on individual words. Such an approach is simple but can be less meaningful. For Chinese language, most of the individual words have little meaning by themselves and the meaning of a sentence is carried by a sequence of words. However, there are no natural boundaries such as spaces in Chinese language and segmentation is a necessary step for Chinese documents and queries [24, 28]. For English language, spaces are presented inside sentences and individual words obtained in the BOW model are more meaningful compared with Chinese language. However, the BOW model can still be less effective because the meaning of a phrase can be totally different from its individual words. For example, knowing that "new york " is a city name and treating them as a whole is better than treating them as two individual words "new" and "york."

An advanced operator provided by many search engines is the double quotation. A user can enclose several words together by double quotation to mandate that they appear together as an inseparable sequence in retrieved documents. Such an operator is usually used by skilled users and may not be known widely. It also requires additional efforts from end users. For example, when users search for unfamiliar topics, they may not know where to put the double quotation. A search engine that can automatically split a query into meaningful segments is highly likely to improve its overall user satisfaction.

To improve retrieval accuracy and search engine utility, it is necessary to go beyond the BOW model. At a minimum, it is beneficial to know whether some words comprise an entity like an organization name, which makes it possible to enforce word proximity and ordering constraints on document matching, among other things. In this section, we discuss different query segmentation techniques.

3.2.1 Problem Formulation

The problem of query segmentation is to find boundaries to segment queries into a list of semantic blocks. In general, given a query of n words, $x_1 \ldots x_n$, query segmentation is to find boundaries of these n words, $[x_1 \ldots x_{s_1}][x_{s_1+1} \ldots x_{s_2}] \ldots [\ldots x_n]$, with each segment as a well-defined "concept." For example, given query "new york times subscription," a good segmentation is "[new york times] [subscription]," but not "[new york] [times subscription]" because "times subscription" is less meaningful.

For an n-word query, there are $n-1$ possible places for boundaries and thus a total of 2^{n-1} possible segmentations. The goal of query segmentation is to find the most meaningful segmentations, e.g., "[new york times] [subscription]" in the example above. In many cases, there are several possible segmentations for a query that are equally meaningful due to ambiguity. For example, the "two man power saw" example used in [4] can have four different interpretations from Google returned documents and these lead to the following valid segmentations: "[two man power saw]," "[two man] [power saw]," [two] [man] [power saw], and "[two] [man power] [saw]." Thus the problem of query segmentation is usually formulated to find a few good ones.

Due to short length of queries, external resources are commonly used in query segmentation, including web corpora [26, 30], query logs [22], click-through data [18], Wikipedia titles [13, 30], etc. The methods proposed in this area can be classified as heuristic-based, supervised learning, and unsupervised learning approaches. In the following, we use "segment" to represent a semantic segmented block and "segmentation" to represent a valid split of a query with non-overlapping segments.

3.2.2 Heuristic-Based Approaches

Heuristic-based approaches are based on statistics obtained from external resources. They do not rely on any sophisticated learning and have the following two types: one type is to decide whether to put a boundary between two adjacent words and the other is to quantify the connectedness of a segment and break queries by maximizing the overall connectedness.

3.2.2.1 Pointwise Mutual Information

Given an n-word query, the most direct way for query segmentation is to decide whether a boundary should be put at the $n-1$ places. The Pointwise Mutual Information (PMI) approach is to make this decision locally based on the surrounding words. For example, given a query "free computer wallpaper downloads," we would like to decide whether to put a break between "free" and "computer," between "computer" and "wallpaper," etc. More formally, we would like to decide a break at the place between word x_i and x_{i+1} for $1 \leq i < n$. Intuitively, if two words always appear together in a corpus, it is better to not put a break but keep them in a single segment.

PMI is an information-theoretic measure [4, 8] on term associations. Given any two objects u and v, their PMI is defined as:

$$PMI(u, v) = \log \frac{Pr(u, v)}{Pr(u) \cdot Pr(v)}, \tag{3.1}$$

where $Pr(u, v)$ is the probability of observing u and v appearing together, $Pr(u)$ and $Pr(v)$ are the probability of observing u and v in the given corpus, respectively.

Let us assume that we have a web corpus that has been tokenized into word sequences. We can count the raw frequency denoted as $\#(x_i, x_{i+1})$, $\#(x_i)$, and $\#(x_{i+1})$ from the corpus. Let N denote the total number of words in this corpus. Then we have

$$Pr(x_i, x_{i+1}) = \frac{\#(x_i, x_{i+1})}{N}$$

$$Pr(x_i) = \frac{\#(x_i)}{N} \tag{3.2}$$

$$Pr(x_{i+1}) = \frac{\#(x_{i+1})}{N}.$$

PMI between two adjacent words can be used for query segmentation by setting a threshold κ. Apparently, how to choose the parameter κ needs some validation data. For example, Jones et al. [14] used a threshold $\kappa = \log 8$ on Yahoo! search logs. They reported that the PMI method was quite effective in their experiments.

3.2.2.2 Connexity

The above PMI method only concerns about two adjacent words. It can also be used in n-gram level to measure the connectedness of a segment. Risvik et al. [26] defined a measure called *connexity* based on the following properties for a segment s:

- s is significantly frequent in all resources.
- s has a "good" mutual information.

In their approach, a segment is essentially an n-gram where $2 \leq n \leq 4$. We denote it by $s = x_i \ldots x_j$ and its connexity is defined as

$$connexity(s) = \begin{cases} frequency(s) \cdot PMI(x_i \ldots x_{j-1}, x_{i+1} \ldots x_j) & \text{if } |s| \geq 2 \\ frequency(s) & \text{otherwise}, \end{cases} \tag{3.3}$$

Table 3.1 Query segmentations and their connexity scores for an example query. Segmentations are sorted by the aggregated connexity scores that are computed as summation over all segment scores, as shown by scores in parentheses. The single word segments contribute 0 to the aggregated scores

Connexity	Query: msdn library visual studio
34,259	[msdn library] (5110) [visual studio] (29149)
29,149	msdn (47658) library (209682) [visual studio] (29149)
5110	[msdn library] (5110) visual (23873) studio (53622)
41	[msdn library visual studio] (41)
7	msdn (47658) [library visual studio] (7)
0	msdn (47658) library (209682) visual (23873) studio (53622)

where the mutual information is on the longest but complete subsequences and can be computed similarly as for words in Eqs. (3.1) and (3.2).

Based on query logs and web corpora, the connexity of an arbitrary segment s can be computed. The number of possible s becomes exponentially large as n goes larger. In practice, n is capped to a number such as 4 in [26]. Segments with higher connexity are more likely to be coherent concepts. To make the number of segments manageable, thresholds were used on frequency as a pre-processing and thresholds on connexity as post-processing filtering in [26].

The connexity was computed from web corpora offline and stored as a lookup table used for query segmentation. On a high level, the non-overlapping segments can be identified as segmentation candidates to be scored. An example used by Risvik et al. [26] is shown in Table 3.1. The aggregated scores are computed as the summation of the connexity scores over all segments that have at least 2 words. While a brute force way is to enumerate all possible segmentations, the top segmentations can be found based on a dynamic programming approach similar to the one presented in Sect. 3.2.4.1.

3.2.2.3 Naive Segmentation

The connexity measures how coherent a segment is. Another method proposed by Hagen et al. [13] is based on simple statistics of segment frequency and length only. They call this method "Naive Segmentation." The score of a segment s in this method is defined as

$$
Score(s) = \begin{cases} 0 & \text{if } |s| = 1 \\ |s|^{|s|} \cdot frequency(s) & \text{if } frequency(s) > 0 \text{ for } |s| \geq 2 \\ -1 & \text{if } frequency(s) = 0 \text{ for } |s| \geq 2. \end{cases} \tag{3.4}
$$

A valid segmentation S contains a list of segments that completely cover q without any overlapping. The score of a segmentation is defined as

$$
Score(S) = \begin{cases} -1 & \text{if } \exists s \in S, Score(s) < 0 \\ \sum_{s \in S, |s| \geq 2} Score(s) & \text{else .} \end{cases} \tag{3.5}
$$

A single word segment has a 0 score and this is implicit in Eq. (3.5). Such a method is purely hand-crafted but was shown to be effective in [13]. The exponential component on the segment length boosts scores of longer segments. It is justified empirically by the connection with the power-law distribution of n-gram frequencies for n-grams that are longer than bigrams. Conversely, the exponential component still favors bigrams compared with the empirical bigram frequency and directly using empirical frequencies for all n-grams dropped by the segmentation accuracy significantly. Favoring bigrams was also observed in the human-generated segmentations [13]. In addition, they further extended this method to leverage Wikipedia titles in the following way:

$$
weight(s) = \begin{cases} |s| + \max_{s' \in s, |s'|=2} frequency(s') & \text{if } s \text{ is a title in Wikipedia} \\ frequency(s) & \text{otherwise.} \end{cases} \tag{3.6}
$$

And the weight is used to compute the $Score(S)$ for segmentations as follows:

$$
Score(S) = \begin{cases} -1 & \text{if } \exists s \in S, weight(s) = 0, |s| \geq 2 \\ \sum_{s \in S, |s| \geq 2} |s| \cdot weight(s) & \text{else .} \end{cases} \tag{3.7}
$$

Since the $Score(S)$ is a summation of its components, the top segmentations can also be found through a dynamic programming similar to the one in Sect. 3.2.4.1.

3.2.2.4 Summary

There are two types of heuristic-based approaches. The PMI method is to measure how easy it is to insert a break between two adjacent words and is of the first type. This can be done efficiently. Along the same line, Zhang et al. [38] proposed the eigenspace similarity as a similar measure as PMI and the method belongs to the first type as well. The connexity and naive segmentation methods belong to the second type. In this type, a score that measures coherence of a segment is defined based on a few factors such as segment frequency, length, mutual information between the longest but complete subsequences, and the appearance of the segment in Wikipedia titles. Segment scores are then used to define scores for segmentations that can be used to select the top segmentations. There are a few additional methods that belong to the second type. For example, Mishra et al. [22] proposed a way to define segment scores to identify the so-called Multi-Word Expression (MWE) and then score segmentations similarly.

3.2.3 Supervised Learning Approaches

Query segmentation based on supervised learning approaches was introduced by Bergsma and Wang [4]. In the supervised learning setting, segmentation is formulated as a function that takes a query q as input and outputs a segmentation $\mathbf{y}$:

$$S : q \rightarrow \mathbf{y}, \tag{3.8}$$

where $\mathbf{y}$ is a $n-1$ dimensional vector with binary values and $y_i = 1$ means that there is break between word x_i and x_{i+1}. Such a setting has a similar flavor as the PMI approach. The difference is that supervised learning approaches learn segmentation function S from training data, while the PMI approach is based on hand-crafted heuristics.

The training data for supervised learning consists of a collection of pairs $\{(q, \mathbf{y})\}$. A set of features $\Phi(q, \mathbf{y})$ can be defined for each training instance. The score of a segmentation $\mathbf{y}$ is

$$Score(q, \mathbf{y}; \mathbf{w}) = \mathbf{w} \cdot \Phi(q, \mathbf{y}). \tag{3.9}$$

The training is thus to find the best $\mathbf{w}^*$ on the training data so that for q,

$$Score(q, \mathbf{y}; \mathbf{w}^*) \geq Score(q, \mathbf{z}; \mathbf{w}^*), \forall \mathbf{z} \neq \mathbf{y}. \tag{3.10}$$

Such a $\mathbf{w}^*$ is usually not existent and slack variables can be used in the Support Vector Machine (SVM) setting. After the parameter $\mathbf{w}^*$ is learnt, the segmentation function gives the output for an input q:

$$\hat{\mathbf{y}} = \arg\max_{\mathbf{y}} Score(q, \mathbf{y}; \mathbf{w}^*). \tag{3.11}$$

The above formulation can be solved by structured classifiers [32] where all the $n - 1$ decisions are jointly made. However, in reality, a simpler classification framework, where each binary decision was made for each position i for $1 \leq i < n$ based on its context, was shown to be not only efficient, but also effective. Specifically, at each position i, the following context was considered:

$$\{\ldots, x_{L_2}, x_{L_1}, x_{L_0}, x_{R_0}, x_{R_1}, x_{R_2}, \ldots\}, \tag{3.12}$$

where L_i and R_i are the indexes on the left and right side of the position i, respectively. Based on the context, a set of features were defined in [4]:

- Decision-boundary features. The set of features in this category concern about x_{L_0} and x_{R_0} from indicator functions such as is_free (e.g., 1 is fired for this feature if x_{L_0} is word "free" and 0 otherwise.), to POS tags (e.g., DT JJ is fired as a feature when POS of x_{L_0} is DT and POS of x_{R_0} is JJ.). In additional, the PMI between (x_{L_0}, x_{R_0}) in Eq. (3.1) or its raw counts in Eq. (3.2) were also used as features.
- Context features. This set of features concern about n-grams in the context. For x_{L_1} and x_{R_1}, they collected token-level features using indicator functions, POS tags on bigram $[x_{L_1}x_{L_0}]$ and $[x_{R_0}x_{R_1}]$, counts on trigram $[x_{L_1}x_{L_0}x_{R_0}]$ and $[x_{L_0}x_{R_0}x_{R_1}]$. If context tokens were not available at this position, a feature was fired to indicate this. Furthermore, if tokens x_{L_2} and x_{R_2} were available, token-level, bigram, trigram, and fourgram counts from web or a query database were also included.
- Dependency features. A feature in this category is motivated by the work in noun phrase parsing to capture whether x_{L_0} is more likely to modify a later token such as x_{R_1}. For an example of "female bus driver," we might not wish to segment "female bus" because "female" has a much stronger association with "driver" than with "bus." Thus as features, the pairwise counts between x_{L_0} and x_{R_1} and then x_{L_1} and x_{R_0} were included. Features from longer range dependencies did not improve performance in their evaluation.

3.2.3.1 Summary

There are other supervised learning methods. Kale et al. [15] formulated query segmentation as the same classification problem as above. However, they did not use hand-crafted features. Rather, they directly use the low-dimensional word embedding vectors that were pre-trained from query logs. Yu et al. [36] proposed a query segmentation method based on Conditional Random Fields (CRF).

The advantage of supervised learning approaches lies in that they can incorporate any information as features and then learn a function to combine them. For example, the raw counts used in the PMI approach can be used as features. Their combination formula is automatically determined from training data, while the formula is pre-defined in the heuristic-based approach. Supervised learning approaches give better segmentation accuracy; however, the prerequisite is training data that is usually manually segmented by human annotators.

3.2.4 Unsupervised Learning Approaches

Unsupervised learning approaches do not rely on human annotated training data and are more sophisticated than the heuristic-based approaches. A representative work of this line is by Tan and Peng [30]. In their work, a generative model was proposed for query segmentation in which a query is generated by repeatedly sampling well-formed segments (called "concepts") in a probabilistic manner.

Formally, let $P(s)$ be the probability of a segment s and S be a segmentation for a query. The likelihood of S is

$$P(S) = P(s_1)P(s_2|s_1)\dots. \tag{3.13}$$

Under the Independent and Identically Distributed (IID) assumption for all s, we have a unigram-like model

$$P(S) = \prod_i P(s_i) \tag{3.14}$$

since $P(s_i|s_1, \dots) = P(s_i)$. Assume that we know $P(s)$ for any segment s, $P(S)$ can be used to select the top segmentations for a query. Given a query, we can enumerate all different segmentations and score them. However, this is not feasible for longer queries given that there are 2^{n-1} segmentations for an n-word query. An efficient dynamic programming is presented in the following section.

3.2.4.1 Dynamic Programming for Top Segmentations

In practice, segmentation enumeration is infeasible except for short queries. However, the IID assumption of the unigram model makes it possible to use dynamic programming to compute the top k segmentations [30]. The algorithm is summarized in Algorithm 1. In this algorithm, for any i, the best k segmentations for partial query $x_1 \dots x_i$ are stored in $B[i]$. $B[n]$ stores the best k segmentations for the n-word query and is constructed by comparing the options when the last break in the query is placed at different positions of $[1..n - 1]$, together with the default segmentation that treats the whole query as the single segment. The complexity of this algorithm is $O(n \cdot k \cdot m \cdot \log(k \cdot m))$, where n is the query length, m is the maximum allowed segment length, and k is the number of best segmentations to keep. It is clear that $m \leq n$. Also, m is implicit in the algorithm and is related to the variable j. To be more accurate, j should range in $[i - m, i - 1]$ in Algorithm 1 because a segment longer than m has $P(s) = 0$.

Such a dynamic programming is generic and can be easily adapted to the connexity and naive segmentation methods in Sect. 3.2.2 by changing the computed scores that are stored in $B[i]$.

Algorithm 1 Find top segmentations

Input: query $x_1...x_n$, segment probability distribution $P(s)$.
Output: top k segmentations for query.
 1: Let $B[i]$ be the top k segmentations for the partial query $x_1...x_i$.
 2: For $b \in B[i]$,
 3: $b.segs$: list of segments for the partial query.
 4: $b.prob$: likelihood of $segs$ for the partial query.
 5: **for all** $i \in [1..n]$ **do**
 6:    Let $s = x_1...x_i$
 7:    **if** $P(s) > 0$ **then**
 8:       Let $new.segs = \{s\}$, $new.prob = P(s)$
 9:       $B[i] = \{new\}$
10:    **end if**
11:    **for all** $j \in [1..i - 1]$ **do**
12:       **for all** $b \in B[j]$ **do**
13:          Let $s = x_j..x_i$
14:          **if** $P(s) > 0$ **then**
15:             Let $new.segs = b.segs \cup \{s\}$, $new.prob = b.prob \times P(s)$
16:             $B[i] = B[i] \cup \{new\}$
17:          **end if**
18:       **end for**
19:    **end for**
20:    Sort $b \in B[i]$ by $b.prob$ and truncate $B[i]$ to size k
21: **end for**
22: **return** B[n]

3.2.4.2 Parameter Estimation

The main question is how to estimate $P(s)$. This can be done based on some of the heuristic-based approaches in Sect. 3.2.2 or just raw frequencies of n-grams. Though raw frequencies for longer n-grams (e.g., $n > 5$) are very sparse and hard to compute, Tan and Peng [30] proposed a way to estimate lower bounds of raw frequencies for any n-gram and that can be used to estimate $P(s)$. However, as noted in [13], the lower bound can become loose and regress to 0. This effectively excludes too long n-grams from being segments. In general, only n-grams up to a cap (e.g., 5) are considered as potential segments.

One drawback of using raw frequency is that such a method may favor partial segmentation. For example, the frequency for n-gram "york times" is larger than or equal to the frequency of "new york times." Thus $P(\text{york times}) \geq P(\text{new york times})$. However, "york times" is unlikely to appear alone; $P(\text{york times})$ should be very small.

Tan and Peng [30] proposed an expectation–maximization (EM) algorithm for the parameter estimation. The EM algorithm is an iterative procedure that starts with a random guess of parameters and refines them in each iteration. The E-step can be thought as automatically segmenting the texts in a probabilistic manner using the current set of estimated parameter values. Then in the M-step, a new set of parameter values are calculated to maximize the complete likelihood of the data which is augmented with segmentation information. The two steps alternate until a termination condition is reached.

The EM algorithm can be applied to any collection of texts to give an estimation of $P(s)$. This is infeasible to the web corpus. In [30], a query-dependent pseudo corpus was constructed for every query by counting all the matched n-grams of the query in a corpus:

$$D = \{(x, c(x)) | x \in q\}. \tag{3.15}$$

D is enhanced with a dummy n-gram z with count $c(z) = N - \sum_i c(x_i)|x_i|$, where N is the corpus length. Note the difference between n-grams and segments in this context.

Given D, EM uses the minimum description length principle to find the optimal parameters $P(s)$. We use a shorthand θ to represent all parameters. Given the current parameter θ, the description length of an n-gram x is $-\log P(x|\theta)$ and

$$P(x|\theta) = \sum_{S_x} P(S_x|\theta), \tag{3.16}$$

where S_x varies over all possible segmentations of x. All S_x's are the hidden variables in the EM algorithm. The description length of D is

$$-\log P(D|\theta) = -\sum_{x \in q} c(x) \cdot \log P(x|\theta) - c(z) \log(1 - \sum_{x \in q} P(x|\theta)). \tag{3.17}$$

EM algorithm is to find the optimal $\hat{\theta}$:

$$\hat{\theta} = \arg\min(-\log P(D|\theta)) = \arg\max \log P(D|\theta) = \arg\max P(D|\theta). \tag{3.18}$$

The concrete EM algorithm used to find a local optimal θ is the variant Baum–Welch algorithm from [9]. In the E-step, it uses a dynamic programming called the *forward–backward* algorithm that can efficiently compute the probability of forming a segment $[x_i, \ldots x_j]$ between the i-th and j-th positions in an n-gram x, denoted as $P([x_i, \ldots x_j]|x)$. Concretely, let the *forward probability* $\alpha_i(x)$ be the probability of generating any complete segmentation such that the first i words are $x_1 \ldots x_i$. Then $\alpha_0(x) = 1$ and

$$\alpha_i(x) = \sum_{j=0}^{i-1} \alpha_j(x) P(s = [x_{j+1} \ldots x_i]). \tag{3.19}$$

Similarly, let the *backward probability* $\beta_i(x)$ be the probability of generating any complete segmentation such that the last i words are $x_{n-i+1} \ldots x_n$. Then

$\beta_n(x) = 1$ and

$$\beta_i(x) = \sum_{j=i+1}^{n} \beta_j(x) P(s = [x_i \ldots x_{j-1}]). \qquad (3.20)$$

Notice that $P(x|\theta) = \alpha_n(x) = \beta_0(x)$ and

$$P([x_i, \ldots x_j]|x) = \frac{\alpha_{i-1}(x) P(s = [x_i \ldots x_j]) \beta_{j+1}(x)}{P(x|\theta)}. \qquad (3.21)$$

Then the M-step can reestimate

$$P(s) \propto \sum_{x \in D} c(x) \sum_{i=0}^{|x|} \sum_{j=i}^{|x|} P([x_i \ldots x_j]|x) \mathbf{I}\{s = [x_i \ldots x_j]\}, \qquad (3.22)$$

where $\mathbf{I}$ is an indicator function. The forward–backward algorithm is more efficient than directly estimating $P(S_x|x)$ for all S_x and x, given that only $\alpha_i(x)$ and $\beta_i(x)$ are needed to be computed.

The EM algorithm can be extended to handle Maximum A Posteriori (MAP) estimation with a prior $P(\theta)$. Then the learning is to find

$$\hat{\theta} = \arg\max P(D|\theta) P(\theta) = \arg\max(\log P(D|\theta) + \log P(\theta)), \qquad (3.23)$$

where

$$\log P(\theta) = \gamma \sum_{s:P(s|\theta)>0} \log P(s|\theta) \qquad (3.24)$$

and γ is a hyper-parameter to the model. Techniques like lexicon deletion proposed in [9] are used in [30] when the objective can be increased if a segment s is deleted from the parameters $P(s)$.

3.2.4.3 External Sources

The main problem of a purely unsupervised approach is that it only tries to optimize the statistical aspects of the concepts; there is no linguistic consideration involved to guarantee that the output concepts are well-formed. For example, the query "history of the web search engine" favors the "[history of the] [web search engine]." This is because "history of the" is a relatively frequent pattern in the corpus. To address this issue, external resources like Wikipedia titles and anchor texts/aliases were used as well-formed concepts to address the problem in the previous example.

In [30], the above EM algorithm is extended to incorporate Wikipedia as a regularization term

$$\lambda \sum_{s \in Wikipedia} count(s) \log P(s), \tag{3.25}$$

where the summation is over all the Wikipedia titles or anchors and $count(s)$ is the count of s in titles or anchors. Technically, such a variant belongs to semi-supervised learning.

3.2.4.4 Summary

Unsupervised learning approaches have a unique advantage that no labeled data is needed. Existing approaches mainly use EM as their main algorithms. For example, Peng et al. [24] used it on Chinese language segmentation. Li et al. [18] leveraged clicked documents to bias the estimation of query segmentation towards bigrams appeared in clicked documents. These demonstrated the flexibility of unsupervised learning approaches in different applications and the ability to incorporate different external resources.

3.2.5 Applications

Query segmentation can be used to improve retrieval accuracy in the n-gram model or term-dependency model [21]. In particular, Bendersky et al. [2] compared using simple n-grams or query segmentation in the term-dependency model and found that query segmentation can reduce the number of term-dependency relations. It in turn reduced the query latency while still maintaining the retrieval effectiveness.

Query segmentation provides phrases that can be used as units in IR models. Wu et al. [34] combined the BOW model and query phrase model together to derive ranking features. A learning-to-rank model was trained based on the enlarged set of features. Such a model was shown to be able to improve relevance ranking.

It should be noted that most of the above methods assume flat segmentations for queries. More advanced nested segmentation was proposed to segment queries into tree structures [27], where a hierarchical segmentation was built up by recursively merging smaller segments to bigger ones for a query. Such a tree structure was used to define a proximity factor in document scoring. We direct interested readers to [27] for more details.

3.3   Query Syntactic Tagging

Syntactic analysis is usually conducted over complete sentences in NLP. Its goal is to understand a sentence's grammatical constituents, POS of words, and their syntactic relations. The task of query syntactic tagging is to apply NLP techniques to search queries and is depicted by the examples in Fig. 3.1 that was used by Sun et al. [29]. In this figure, we have 3 queries, the POS tags of each word in the queries and the syntactic relations among words (e.g., head-modifier relations in noun phrases). Specifically, for query "cover iphone 6 plus," the relation tells us that the head token is "cover," indicating its intent is to shop for iphone covers, instead of iphones; for query "distance earth moon," the head is "distance," indicating its intent is to find the distance between the earth and the moon; for query "faucet adapter female," the intent is to find a female faucet adapter. Such knowledge is crucial for search engines to show relevant pages because correctly identifying the head of the queries (e.g., covers instead of iphones) in the examples can boost pages with matched topics [29].

Syntactic analysis of search queries is important for a variety of tasks such as better query refinement and improved query-document matching [1]. However, search queries are different from well-formed sentences in the following aspects. First, search queries are short and have only keywords. Second, capitalization is in general missing. Third, word order in a query is fairly free. All these are important sentence characteristics that syntactic parsing relies on. Thus significant challenges arise when applying syntactic parsing NLP techniques on search queries. In this section, we review how different methods proposed in the literature overcome these challenges for query syntactic tagging.

Fig. 3.1 Examples of query syntactic tagging used by Sun et al. [29]. For each query example, the POS tag for each word is shown below the word. The syntactic relation is denoted by arrows that point from heads to modifiers. Search queries are not well-formed, compared with natural language sentences

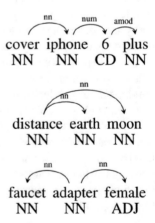

3.3.1   Syntactic Structures for Search Queries

Barr et al. [1] sampled a few thousand queries from the Yahoo! search engine logs in August 2006 and asked human annotators to label POS tags of these queries. They compute the statistics of the tags and the results are shown in Table 3.2. As shown in this table, they are very different from the Brown or Penn tag sets given that many standard POS tags are extremely sparse in web search queries. For example, there are about 90 tags in the Brown tag set, but there are only 19 unique classes for Web search queries. There are 35 types of verbs and 15 types of determiners in the Brown tag set, but there is only a single label of verbs that accounts for 2.35% of the tags and a single determiner that accounts for 0.7% in the web queries. Furthermore, the most common tag in Table 3.2 is proper-noun, which constitutes 40% of all query terms, and proper nouns and nouns together constitute 71% of query terms. By contrast, in the Brown corpus, the most common tag is noun and it constitutes about 13% of terms.

Barr et al. [1] also showed examples of different ways of capitalization used in web search queries and reported that capitalization in queries was inconsistent. On a sample of 290, 122 queries, only 16.8% contained some capitalization, while 3.9% of them are all capitalized. Though capitalization is an important clue to identify proper nouns in NLP, it becomes noisy to use when tagging queries.

Table 3.2   Tags used for labeling POS of words in web search queries from [1]. The counts are for the number of tokens appearing in the sampled queries

POS tag	Example	Count	Percentage
Proper-noun	texas	3384	40.2%
Noun	pictures	2601	30.9%
Adjective	big	599	7.1%
URI	ebay.com	495	5.9%
Preposition	in	310	3.7%
Unknown	y	208	2.5%
Verb	get	198	2.4%
Other	conference06-07	174	2.1%
Comma	,	72	0.9%
Gerund	running	69	0.8%
Number	473	67	0.8%
Conjunction	and	65	0.8%
Determiner	the	56	0.7%
Pronoun	she	53	0.6%
Adverb	quickly	28	0.3%
Possessive	?s	19	0.2%
Symbol	(	18	0.2%
Sentence-ender	?	5	0.1%
Not	n?t	2	0.0%

3.3.2   Supervised Learning Approaches

In NLP, POS taggers for complete sentences are trained in a supervised manner based on a set of labeled data. The trained taggers for a language can be generally applied to any texts in that language. For example, the Brill Tagger [7] and the Stanford Tagger [31] are freely available and can be used to tagger English texts. Barr et al. [1] took these taggers off the shelf and applied them on their human annotated queries. They found that the accuracy from these standard taggers was well below a simple baseline that tags a query term based on the most frequent POS tag obtained from their own labeled queries. Their findings highlighted the need to train a specific POS tagger for web queries.

Based on the queries with labeled POS tags, the most basic supervised learning approach is called the Most Common Tag in [1]. In this method, a mapping between a word and a tag is constructed. The tag for a word is the most common tag counted from the labeled query data. In the prediction phase, the POS tags for a query are just a simple lookup from the mapping for each individual words. Though fairly simple, this method was shown to be better than the standard taggers [1].

Barr et al. [1] also proposed to train a Brill Tagger using the labeled query data, instead of the standard Treebank data. They found that the trained tagger outperformed the Most Common Tag one, showing the promise of more advanced supervised learning approaches. Due to the difference between queries and sentences, some commonly useful features are not available for queries. A promising direction for supervised learning approaches is to craft those missing features to improve the tagging accuracy. For example, capitalization information is noisy in query data. Barr et al. [1] proposed an automatic query term capitalization method based on their capitalization statistics in search results. They found that this can boost the Brill tagger significantly given that proper nouns are the most frequent in web queries and capitalization is an indicative feature to tag proper nouns.

3.3.3   Transfer Learning Approaches

Supervised learning approaches need labeled data. Given the vast amount of search queries, creating a labeled data set with sufficient coverage and diversity is challenging. However, tagging well-formed sentences is well-studied. This motivates many tagging methods based on the transfer learning principle. The common strategy in the existing approaches is to leverage top retrieved results or clicked ones to help query tagging. We review them in this section.

3.3.3.1 Simple Transfer Methods

Bendersky et al. [3] proposed a pseudo-relevance feedback approach to tag queries. In this approach, a pre-trained tagger is used to tag both query terms and sentences from top retrieved documents. For each term, there are two multinomial distributions over POS tags: one based on the tagging results of the given query and the other based on the POS tag counts from the top retrieved documents. The two distributions are interpolated to give the final distribution of POS tags for each individual query term.

Keyaki et al. [16] used a similar methodology to the one used by Bendersky et al. [3], but proposed to precompute the tags for web documents offline. This can reduce the heavy computation needed in the pseudo-relevance feedback approach used in [3]. Specifically, the proposed method has the following two steps:

Offline. Given a web corpus, morphological analysis is conducted on every sentence in the corpus based on standard NLP methods. The POS tag of each term in a sentence is obtained. The output of this step is a large collection of sentences with POS tags on all terms. This is a pre-computing step and conducted offline.

Online. When a query is issued, sentences (with POS tag for each term) that contain two or more query terms are retrieved from the sentence collection created during offline computation. Then appropriate POS tags of query terms are obtained based on the POS tags of terms appearing in the retrieved sentences. With regard to a single term query, the most frequently appearing POS tag in the web corpus is tagged to the query term.

It can be seen that this method is designed to work with the following two properties: (1) capitalization information in query is not used and (2) word order in queries does not matter. In fact, they relied on the sentences in the web corpus to provide a high accuracy tagging. The shortcoming of this method is on the online retrieval part given that sentences are used as retrieval units for queries. The retrieval accuracy could be lower due to the short length of sentences and this can affect the query tagging accuracy in turn.

3.3.3.2 Learning Methods

Ganchev et al. [11] employed a more complete transfer learning method based on search logs. Search logs consist of both queries and "relevant" search results that are either retrieved by a search engine or clicked by end users. The training data in the "source" domain was human annotated sentences. A supervised POS tagger was trained based on the "source" training data and applied to the search result snippets. The POS tags on these snippets were then transferred to queries. In this process, the tag of a query term was the most frequent tag of the term in the tagged snippets. This simple transfer process produced a set of noisy labeled queries. Then a new query tagger was trained based on the combination of the "source" training data and the noisy labeled query data. The pre-trained tagger can be used by itself to tag input queries. Ganchev et al. [11] compared using clicked documents and the top retrieved results and found that both methods performed similarly.

Sun et al. [29] proposed to transfer both POS tags and dependency parsing results from clicked sentences to queries. A click sentence is a well-formed sentence that (1) contains all query tokens and (2) appears in the top clicked documents of the query. For each sentence, both POS tags of individual terms and dependency between terms were constructed. While it is simple to transfer POS tags from sentences to queries similarly as previous methods, it is challenging to transfer the dependency relations because not all words in a sentence appear in queries. Sun et al. [29] proposed heuristics to handle the following cases and an uninformative "dep" relation was also introduced:

- Directly connected (46%)
- Connected via function words (24%)
- Connected via modifiers (24%)
- Connected via a head noun (4%)
- Connected via a verb (2%)

Sun et al. [29] also proposed methods to infer a unique dependency tree for a query and refine dependency labels for the placeholder "dep." All these resulted in a query treebank without additional manual labeling. A syntactic parser was then trained from the web query treebank data and shown to be more accurate than standard parsers.

3.3.4 Summary

For query syntactic tagging, the majority of existing approaches transfer information from sentences in search results or snippets to search queries. POS tags of queries and documents can also be used to define matching features to improve ranking accuracy [1]. In contrast to the POS tagging, dependency parsing is not fully exploited for web search. Recent work by Tsur et al. [33] and Pinter et al. [25] focused identifying queries with question intents and their syntactic parsing. A query treebank is created and can be used to further study query syntactic tagging.

3.4 Query Semantic Tagging

The problem of query semantic tagging is to assign labels, from a set of pre-defined semantic ones, at word level. Such labels are usually domain-specific. An example from [20] of query semantic tagging is in the following where the labels are in parentheses and all the labels are in the *product* domain.

> **cheap** (SortOrder) **garmin** (Brand) **steetpilot** (Model) **c340** (Model) **gps** (Type)

Semantic labels can be used to provide users with more relevant search results. For example, many specialized search engines build their indexes directly from a relational database where structured information or labels are available in the documents (e.g., Brand = "garmin"). Query semantic labels can thus be used to match documents more accurately. In this section, we discuss named entity recognition on a coarse level and grammar-based approaches in a fine-grained domain-specific level.

3.4.1 Named Entity Recognition

As shown in [12], about 71% of search queries contain named entities. Given their high percentage, identifying named entities, as known as Named Entity Recognition (NER), becomes an important task for web search. For named entities, the classes of labels include "Game," " Movie," "Book," "Music," etc. Given a query, the tasks of NER are to identify which words in the query represent named entities and classify them into different classes.

For NER tasks, Guo et al. [12] found that only 1% of the named entity queries contain more than 1 entity and the majority of named entity queries contain exactly a single one. Thus a named entity query can be thought as containing two parts: entities and contexts. For example "harry porter walkthrough" contains entity "harry porter" and context "walkthrough" and the context indicates "harry porter" should be labeled as "Game." Without this context, the query "harry porter" can also be a "Book" or "Movie." This shows that the classes for named entities can be ambiguous and its context in the query helps disambiguate them.

Traditional NER is mainly performed on natural language texts [6] and a supervised learning approach based on hand-crafted features is exploited (e.g., whether the word is capitalized or whether "Mr." or "Ms." is before the word). These features can be extracted and utilized in the NER tasks for natural language texts. However, directly applying them on queries would not perform well, because queries are very short and are not necessarily in standard forms. In the current literature, weakly supervised methods are proposed for NER on queries.

3.4.1.1 Template-Based Approach

A template-based approach was proposed by Paşca [23] that aimed to extract named entities from search logs based on a small set of seeds. This method does not need hand-crafted extraction patterns nor domain-specific knowledge. An example of the procedure is displayed in Fig. 3.2. The procedure starts with a set of seed instances in a category ("Drug" in the example) and proceeds with the following steps:

Step 1   Identify query templates that match the seed instances. For each seed instance, all queries containing this instance are located. The prefix and suffix of each matched query become one template and templates from all matched queries of all the seed instances become a collection of templates.

Step 2   Identify candidate instances. Based on the collection of templates from Step 1, this step is to match the template against all queries in the search logs. The non-template parts of the matched queries become the candidates. The assumption of this step is that instances belonging to the target category should share the templates.

Step 3   Internal representation of the candidate instances. For each candidate, each template matched in Step 2 becomes a dimension in the template vector used as the internal representation. All templates form a signature vector for the candidate.

Step 4   Similarly, internal representation of the seed instances is created. These vectors are aggregated together as the reference vector for the target category.

Step 5   All the candidate instances are then ranked by the similarity between its signature vector and the reference vector for the category.

All the steps for the category "Drug" are shown in Fig. 3.2. The seed instances are {*phentermine, viagra, vicodin, vioxx, xanax*} and the output of the method is an enlarged set of list {*viagra, phentermine, ambien, adderall, vicodin, hydrocodone, xanax, vioxx, oxycontin, cialis, valium, lexapro, ritalin, zoloft, percocet, ...* }.

As seen in the data flow, this method only needs a very small number of seed instances and is thus weakly supervised. Paşca [23] used tens of target categories and tens of seed entities in each target category. The method, though simple, is shown to be effective in discovering more named entities in target categories.

3.4.1.2 Weakly Supervised Learning Approach

The approach in [23] is based on heuristics. Inspired by it, Guo et al. [12] formulate a topic model based learning approach in a more principled manner. It follows the same staring points as [23] where a set of seed instances of each target class is provided. We thus call such an approach weakly supervised learning approach.

In this approach, a query having one named entity is represented as a triple (e, t, c), where e denotes named entity, t denotes context of e, and c denote class of e. Note that t can be empty (i.e., no context). Then the goal of NER here becomes to find the triple (e, t, c) for a given query q, which has the largest joint probability $Pr(e, t, c)$. The joint probability is factorized:

$$Pr(e, t, c) = Pr(e)Pr(c|e)Pr(t|e, c) = Pr(e)Pr(c|e)Pr(t|c). \tag{3.26}$$

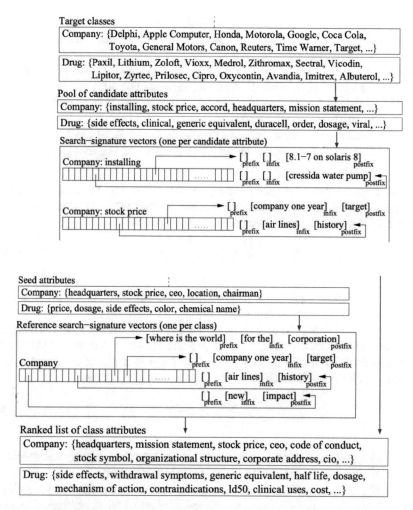

Fig. 3.2 Data flow overview of the template-based approach for named entity recognition in [23]

It is assumed that context only depends on class, but not on any specific named entity. This is similar to [23] where the reference vector of a target category only depends on templates.

In search logs, only query strings are available: contexts and name entities are not explicitly labeled, nor classes of entities. Guo et al. [12] took a weakly supervised approach where a set of named entities are collected and labeled as seeds.

$$S = \{(e, c)\} \tag{3.27}$$

Starting from the seed S, a list of training instances $\{(e, t)\}$ are obtained as follows:

Step 1   For each $e \in S$, collect all queries that contain e from search logs. All the queries obtained thus have entities and contexts separated and form a data set $D_1 = \{(e, t)\}$.

Step 2   Estimate $Pr(c|e)$ and $Pr(t|c)$ based on S and D_1 using the Weakly Supervised LDA (WS-LDA) model described below.

Step 3   For each $t \in D_1$, collect all queries that contain t from search logs and form $D_2 = \{(e, t)\}$ for all t.

Step 4   With $Pr(t|c)$ fixed, estimate $Pr(c|e)$ based on WS-LDA for all $\{e : e \notin S\}$. $Pr(e)$ is also estimated as proportional to the empirical frequency of e in D_2.

The proposed WS-LDA model is based on the traditional LDA model [5]. Given a data set of $D = \{(e, t)\}$, we can treat e as the "document" and t as the "words" in LDA model. Class c becomes the hidden variable and then

$$Pr(e, t) = Pr(e) \sum_c Pr(c|e) Pr(t|c) \tag{3.28}$$

Such a formulation is easy to be mapped to the LDA framework and the parameter $Pr(c|e)$ and $Pr(t|c)$ can be estimated by fitting the model to the data D.

The WS-LDA model leverages the seed S data set as weakly supervised signals to serve two purposes: (1) the set of classes are pre-defined in WS-LDA; (2) the estimated $Pr(c|e)$ should be close to S. The latter is achieved by introducing a regularization term in the LDA objective function to be maximized:

$$\sum_{(e,c) \in S} Pr(c|e). \tag{3.29}$$

In this way, $Pr(c|e)$ and $Pr(t|c)$ estimated from WS-LDA optimize the fitness on the search logs and stay closely to the seed labels in S as well.

The WS-LDA model also provides a natural way to give prediction for an input query. For an input query q, it can enumerate all possible segmentations of (e, t) of q and label q with class c based on the parameters estimated from WS-LDA:

$$(e, t, c)^* = \arg \max_{(e,t,c)} Pr(q, e, t, c) = \arg \max_{(e,t,c):(e,t)=q} Pr(e, t, c). \tag{3.30}$$

The WS-LDA approach was further extended to incorporated search sessions [10] in which the adjacent queries in a search session were used to improve the class label prediction for the named entities. Furthermore, building a taxonomy of named entities search intents based on unsupervised learning approaches such as hierarchical clustering was proposed by Yin and Shah [35].

3.4.2   Fine-Grained Tagging

Fine-grained query semantic tagging has a strong NLP flavor than the methods for NER above. For example, Manshadi and Li [20] defined a context-free grammar for queries in the "product" domain. The design choice of being context-free is to accommodate the loose order property of words in queries. Based on the grammar, a parse tree was constructed for an input query and the nodes in the parse tree (e.g., Brand or Model) were the semantic tags for the queries. Standard tagging methods such as Conditional Random Fields (CRF) [17] have a strong assumption on the order of the input sentences and is thus less effective for query tagging. Manshadi and Li [20] compared their grammar-based approach with CRF models and found that their methods performed better. This demonstrates the unique challenges of query semantic tagging and special design choices such as context-free grammar are critical for this task.

3.5   Conclusions

In this chapter, we reviewed the existing literature on query tagging. We classified them into query segmentation, query syntactic tagging, and query semantic tagging. We reviewed a few representative methods for each category and discussed their pros and cons. This chapter is just a starting point for the work in query tagging. It is by no means exhaustive in the research area. Our hope is to give an introduction to this exciting but challenging areas and an overview of the existing work. There are a few future directions for query tagging. (1) There is still considerable room to improve the accuracy of each query tagging task. For example, more and more user interaction data is accumulated over time for search engines. How to explore this huge amount of data as external resources to boost each tagging task is worth studying. (2) The recent development of deep learning techniques has advanced the NLP techniques. How to leverage the newly developed NLP techniques on query tagging is also an interesting direction. (3) Query tagging can benefit other IR tasks such as query suggestion. It looks promising to study how to leverage query tagging on these related tasks.

References

1. Cory Barr, Rosie Jones, and Moira Regelson. The linguistic structure of English web-search queries. In *Proceedings of the 2008 Conference on Empirical Methods in Natural Language Processing*, pages 1021–1030, 2008.
2. Michael Bendersky, W. Bruce Croft, and David A. Smith. Two-stage query segmentation for information retrieval. In *Proceedings of the 32nd Annual International ACM SIGIR Conference on Research and Development in Information Retrieval*, pages 810–811, 2009.

3. Michael Bendersky, W. Bruce Croft, and David A. Smith. Structural annotation of search queries using pseudo-relevance feedback. In *Proceedings of the 19th ACM Conference on Information and Knowledge Management*, pages 1537–1540, 2010.
4. Shane Bergsma and Qin Iris Wang. Learning noun phrase query segmentation. In *Proceedings of the 2007 Joint Conference on Empirical Methods in Natural Language Processing and Computational Natural Language Learning*, pages 819–826, 2007.
5. David M. Blei, Andrew Y. Ng, and Michael I. Jordan. Latent Dirichlet allocation. *J. Mach. Learn. Res.*, 3: 993–1022, 2003.
6. Andrew Eliot Borthwick. *A Maximum Entropy Approach to Named Entity Recognition*. PhD thesis, 1999.
7. Eric Brill. Transformation-based error-driven learning and natural language processing: A case study in part-of-speech tagging. *Comput. Linguistics*, 21 (4): 543–565, 1995.
8. Kenneth Ward Church and Patrick Hanks. Word association norms, mutual information, and lexicography. *Comput. Linguistics*, 16 (1): 22–29, 1990.
9. Carl de Marcken. *Unsupervised language acquisition*. PhD thesis, Massachusetts Institute of Technology, Cambridge, MA, USA, 1996.
10. Junwu Du, Zhimin Zhang, Jun Yan, Yan Cui, and Zheng Chen. Using search session context for named entity recognition in query. In *Proceeding of the 33rd International ACM SIGIR Conference on Research and Development in Information Retrieval*, pages 765–766, 2010.
11. Kuzman Ganchev, Keith B. Hall, Ryan T. McDonald, and Slav Petrov. Using search-logs to improve query tagging. In *Proceedings of the 50th Annual Meeting of the Association for Computational Linguistics*, pages 238–242, 2012.
12. Jiafeng Guo, Gu Xu, Xueqi Cheng, and Hang Li. Named entity recognition in query. In *Proceedings of the 32nd Annual International ACM SIGIR Conference on Research and Development in Information Retrieval*, pages 267–274, 2009.
13. Matthias Hagen, Martin Potthast, Benno Stein, and Christof Bräutigam. Query segmentation revisited. In *Proceedings of the 20th International Conference on World Wide Web*, pages 97–106, 2011.
14. Rosie Jones, Benjamin Rey, Omid Madani, and Wiley Greiner. Generating query substitutions. In *Proceedings of the 15th international conference on World Wide Web*, pages 387–396, 2006.
15. Ajinkya Kale, Thrivikrama Taula, Sanjika Hewavitharana, and Amit Srivastava. Towards semantic query segmentation. *CoRR*, abs/1707.07835, 2017.
16. Atsushi Keyaki and Jun Miyazaki. Part-of-speech tagging for web search queries using a large-scale web corpus. In *Proceedings of the Symposium on Applied Computing*, pages 931–937, 2017.
17. John D. Lafferty, Andrew McCallum, and Fernando C. N. Pereira. Conditional random fields: Probabilistic models for segmenting and labeling sequence data. In *Proceedings of the Eighteenth International Conference on Machine Learning*, pages 282–289, 2001.
18. Yanen Li, Bo-June Paul Hsu, ChengXiang Zhai, and Kuansan Wang. Unsupervised query segmentation using clickthrough for information retrieval. In *Proceeding of the 34th International ACM SIGIR Conference on Research and Development in Information Retrieval*, pages 285–294, 2011.
19. Christopher D. Manning and Hinrich Schütze. *Foundations of Statistical Natural Language Processing*. MIT Press, Cambridge, MA, USA, 1999. ISBN 0-262-13360-1.
20. Mehdi Manshadi and Xiao Li. Semantic tagging of web search queries. In *Proceedings of the 47th Annual Meeting of the Association for Computational Linguistics and the 4th International Joint Conference on Natural Language Processing*, pages 861–869, 2009.
21. Donald Metzler and W. Bruce Croft. A Markov random field model for term dependencies. In *Proceedings of the 28th Annual International ACM SIGIR Conference on Research and Development in Information Retrieval*, pages 472–479, 2005.
22. Nikita Mishra, Rishiraj Saha Roy, Niloy Ganguly, Srivatsan Laxman, and Monojit Choudhury. Unsupervised query segmentation using only query logs. In *Proceedings of the 20th International Conference on World Wide Web*, pages 91–92, 2011.

23. Marius Pasca. Weakly-supervised discovery of named entities using web search queries. In *Proceedings of the Sixteenth ACM Conference on Information and Knowledge Management*, pages 683–690, 2007.
24. Fuchun Peng, Fangfang Feng, and Andrew McCallum. Chinese segmentation and new word detection using conditional random fields. In *Proceedings of the 20th International Conference on Computational Linguistics*, pages 562–568, 2004.
25. Yuval Pinter, Roi Reichart, and Idan Szpektor. Syntactic parsing of web queries with question intent. In *Proceedings of the 2016 Conference of the North American Chapter of the Association for Computational Linguistics: Human Language Technologies*, pages 670–680, 2016.
26. Knut Magne Risvik, Tomasz Mikolajewski, and Peter Boros. Query segmentation for web search. In *Proceedings of the Twelfth International World Wide Web Conference*, 2003.
27. Rishiraj Saha Roy, Anusha Suresh, Niloy Ganguly, and Monojit Choudhury. Improving document ranking for long queries with nested query segmentation. In *Proceedings of the 38th European Conference on IR Research*, pages 775–781, 2016.
28. Richard Sproat, Chilin Shih, William Gale, and Nancy Chang. A stochastic finite-state word-segmentation algorithm for Chinese. *Comput. Linguistics*, 22 (3): 377–404, 1996.
29. Xiangyan Sun, Haixun Wang, Yanghua Xiao, and Zhongyuan Wang. Syntactic parsing of web queries. In *Proceedings of the 2016 Conference on Empirical Methods in Natural Language Processing*, pages 1787–1796, 2016.
30. Bin Tan and Fuchun Peng. Unsupervised query segmentation using generative language models and Wikipedia. In *Proceedings of the 17th International Conference on World Wide Web*, pages 347–356, 2008.
31. Kristina Toutanova, Dan Klein, Christopher D. Manning, and Yoram Singer. Feature-rich part-of-speech tagging with a cyclic dependency network. In *Human Language Technology Conference of the North American Chapter of the Association for Computational Linguistics*, 2003.
32. Ioannis Tsochantaridis, Thorsten Joachims, Thomas Hofmann, and Yasemin Altun. Large margin methods for structured and interdependent output variables. *J. Mach. Learn. Res.*, 6: 1453–1484, 2005.
33. Gilad Tsur, Yuval Pinter, Idan Szpektor, and David Carmel. Identifying web queries with question intent. In *Proceedings of the 25th International Conference on World Wide Web*, pages 783–793, 2016.
34. Haocheng Wu, Yunhua Hu, Hang Li, and Enhong Chen. A new approach to query segmentation for relevance ranking in web search. *Inf. Retr. J.*, 18 (1): 26–50, 2015.
35. Xiaoxin Yin and Sarthak Shah. Building taxonomy of web search intents for name entity queries. In *Proceedings of the 19th International Conference on World Wide Web*, pages 1001–1010, 2010.
36. Xiaohui Yu and Huxia Shi. Query segmentation using conditional random fields. In *Proceedings of the First International Workshop on Keyword Search on Structured Data*, pages 21–26, 2009.
37. ChengXiang Zhai. Fast statistical parsing of noun phrases for document indexing. In *Proceedings of the 5th Applied Natural Language Processing Conference*, pages 312–319, 1997.
38. Chao Zhang, Nan Sun, Xia Hu, Tingzhu Huang, and Tat-Seng Chua. Query segmentation based on eigenspace similarity. In *Proceedings of the 47th Annual Meeting of the Association for Computational Linguistics and the 4th International Joint Conference on Natural Language Processing of the AFNLP*, pages 185–188, 2009.

Chapter 4
Query Intent Understanding

Zhicheng Dou and Jiafeng Guo

Abstract Search engines aim at helping users find relevant results from the Web. Understanding the underlying intent of queries issued to search engines is a critical step toward this goal. Till now, it is still a challenge to have a scientific definition of query intent. Existing approaches attempting to understand query intents can be classified into two categories: (1) query intent classification: mapping queries into categories and (2) query intent mining: finding subtopics covered by the queries. For the first group of work, the mapping between queries and categories can be conducted in various ways, including classifying based on navigational, informational, or transactional intent, based on geographic locality, temporal intent, topical categories, or available vertical services. For query intent mining, the output can be a list of explicit subqueries, or some implicit representation of subintent, such as a list of document clusters, a list of entities, etc. In this chapter, we will introduce these query intent prediction approaches in detail.

4.1 Introduction to Query Intent Understanding

Search engines aim at helping users find relevant results from the Web. In most existing Web search engines, users' information needs are represented by simple keyword queries. Studies have shown that the vast majority of queries issued to search engines are short, usually comprised of two to three keywords [19, 28, 45, 52, 53]. How to precisely understand the complex search intent implicitly represented by such short queries is a critical and challenging problem and has received much attention in both IR academic and industry communities.

Z. Dou (✉)
Renmin University of China, Beijing, China
e-mail: dou@ruc.edu.cn

J. Guo
Chinese Academy of Sciences, Beijing, China
e-mail: guojiafeng@ict.ac.cn

© Springer Nature Switzerland AG 2020
Y. Chang, H. Deng (eds.), *Query Understanding for Search Engines*,
The Information Retrieval Series 46, https://doi.org/10.1007/978-3-030-58334-7_4

Query intent itself is an ambiguous word, and it is still a challenge to have a scientific definition of query intent. Intent itself means the perceived need for information that leads to a search, but how to describe or classify the need is still in an exploratory stage. Till now, different kinds of query intent understanding tasks have been explored toward discovering the implicit factors related to real user information needs. These tasks include but are not limited to identifying the type of search goals and demanded resources required by a user, identifying the topical categories a query belongs to, selecting vertical services a query might be relevant to, and mining subintents for an ambiguous or broad query. Basically, query intent understanding is mainly for the purpose of recovering the hidden aspects that belong to the original user information need but is lost within the short and simple keyword queries issued to search engines.

Existing approaches attempting to understand query intents can be roughly grouped into two categories as follows:

Intent classification   This is basically a task that maps queries into categories. The mapping between queries and categories can be conducted in various ways, such as classifying based on user goals like navigational, informational, or transactional intent, classifying based on topical categories, classifying based on vertical services, classifying based on geographic locality, or classifying based on temporal intent.

Intent mining   The task is mainly for broad or ambiguous queries. It aims to find subtopics covered by a query. The output can be a list of explicit subqueries, or some implicit representation of subintent such as a list of document clusters, a list of entities, etc.

In this chapter, we will introduce existing query intent understanding approaches in detail.

4.2   Intent Classification Based on User Goals

A major difference between Web search and classic IR (information retrieval) lies in that users' search need/goal is no longer restricted to acquiring certain information—they might search to locate a particular site or to access some Web services. Therefore, the first type of query intent understanding tasks we discuss is identifying the underlying goal of a user when submitting one particular query. More specifically, it aims to classifying user goals into navigational, informational, transactional, etc. For instance, when a user issues the query "amazon", he or she could be trying to reach the specific website http://www.amazon.com; while a user submitting "Olympic history" is most likely to be interested in finding information on that topic but not concerned about the particular website. The query "adobe photoshop download" might indicate that the user is finding a Web page where he or she can find a link to download the desired software. In this case, the query is more likely to be an transactional query, other than informational or navigational.

4.2.1   Taxonomies of User Goals

Basically, user goals can be classified based on the type of demanded resources users are seeking for by issuing a query. Several taxonomies of user goals have been proposed since Broder [10] introduced this concept. In the first part of this subsection, we will briefly introduce these taxonomies.

4.2.1.1   Broder's Intent Taxonomy

The first and most popular taxonomy of query intent (here intent means user goal) on the Web was proposed by Broder [10]. According to Broder, there are three classes of queries: informational, navigational, and transactional, which are introduced in detail as follows.

Navigational Navigational intent means that a user's immediate intent is to reach a particular website for browsing. The website could be a website the user has visited it in the past. The user uses a navigational query to reach this website because it is more convenient for his or her to input a short navigational query other than typing the URL. A user may also issue a navigational query to find a website he or she never visited in the past, but she assumes that there should be such a website. Example navigational queries are

- `Renmin University of China`. The target website of the user who submits this query is likely to be http://www.ruc.edu.cn, the homepage of Renmin University of China.
- `jd.com`. Users may want to use this URL-like query to directly reach the website http://www.jd.com.
- `apple store`. Most users might use this query to find http://store.apple.com.

As shown by the previous examples, the most typical navigational queries are those homepage-finding queries. A navigational query has usually one "perfect" result, which is exactly the website the user is looking for. But in some rare cases, a navigational query could be ambiguous, and different users might use the same query to find their particular websites. For example, a user might use "aa" to reach https://www.aa.com, whereas another might use the same query to navigate to http://www.aa.org.

Informational For informational queries, the user wants to obtain some information assumed to be available on the Web. The information could be present on one or multiple Web pages. Broder emphasized that the information could be found on these Web pages in a *static* form, which means that "no further interaction is predicted, except reading" [10]. Example informational queries include

- `how to cook beef`. Users are finding more ways to cook beef.
- `Beijing tourist attractions`. Users use this query to find a list of tourist attractions in Beijing and detailed introduction to them.
- `deep learning`. Users might use this query to learn information about deep learning, such as the definition, architectures, algorithms, or applications.

Transactional The goal of a transactional query is to find a Web page where he or she can then perform some interactive tasks such as downloading a software, listening to music, or playing a game online. Example transactional queries are

- `7zip download`. The goal is to find a link for downloading the file compression software 7zip.
- `currency converter`. Users use this query to find a currency converter and then calculate live currency and foreign exchange rates with this currency converter.

Broder studied the statistics of these types of queries by doing a survey of 3,190 valid AltaVista users. The survey results indicated that about 24.5% of queries are navigational queries. He also found that it is not easy use a single question to distinguish between transactional and informational queries by the survey. Alternatively, by asking users whether they are shopping or want to download a file, he estimated that at least 22% of queries are transactional queries. Broder further manually assessed 400 queries from the AltaVista log, and found about 20% are navigational, 48% are informational, and 30% are transactional queries, leaving 2% of queries undetermined in their intents.

4.2.1.2 Rose and Levinson's Taxonomy

Rose and Levinson [47] further improved Broder's intent classification and proposed a hierarchy of query goals with three top-level categories. They developed a framework for manual classification of search goals and introduced subcategories for some classes. Specifically, Rose and Levinson divided informational intent into five sub classes as follows:

- **Directed**: directly answering open or closed questions,
- **Undirected**: undirected requests to simply learn more about a topic,
- **Advice**: requests for advice,
- **Location**: the desire to locate something in the real world,
- **List**: simply getting a list of suggestions for further research.

At the same time, they replaced the transactional intent with the "resource" intent, which represents the goal of obtaining something other than information from the Web. The resource intent is comprised of four specific interactive tasks including "download," "entertainment," "interact," and "obtain."

Table 4.1 Intent taxonomy proposed by Rose and Levinson [47]

Search goal	Minor classes	Percentage	Broder's
Navigational	/	13–16%	Navigational
Informational	Directed, undirected, advice, locate, list	61–63%	Informational
Resource	Download, entertainment, interact, obtain	21–27%	Transactional

Rose and Levinson [47] studied the distribution of different types of queries by manually classifying queries from AltaVista query logs. They found that about 61% to 63% of queries are informational queries, and 13% to 16% are navigational. More details are shown in Table 4.1.

4.2.1.3   Taxonomy Proposed by Baeza-Yates et al.

Different from the above two taxonomies that classify queries into navigational, informational, and transactional (or resource), Baeza-Yates et al. [4] established a slightly different classification system of user goals. They classify queries into **Informational**, **Not informational**, and **Ambiguous**. Based on their definition, the informational intent is similar to the informational intent defined by Broder [10] and Rose and Levinson [47]. Differently, they merged navigational queries and transactional queries into a single category: "Not informational" queries, because both types of queries are issued to find other resources other than information on the Web. Baeza-Yates et al. further introduced the third category: ambiguous queries. An ambiguous query means that its user goal cannot be easily inferred based on the query string without additional resources. More information about query ambiguity will be introduced in Sect. 4.4.

Baeza-Yates et al. [4] studied the distribution of queries based on a log sample containing about 6,000 queries from the Chilean Web search engine TodoCL.[1] They manually classified these queries and found that 61% of queries are informational queries, 22% are not informational queries, and about 17% are ambiguous.

4.2.1.4   Taxonomy Proposed by Jansen et al.

Jansen, Booth, and Spike [30] presented a three-level hierarchical taxonomy based on existing taxonomies, with the top most level being informational, navigational, and transactional. They also provided a comprehensive reviews and evaluation of the different query intent taxonomies proposed in the literature by aligning prior work to their categorizations. Their studies showed that about 81% of queries are informational, 10% are navigational, and about 9% are transactional queries, based

---

[1]TOdoCL, http://www.todocl.com.

Table 4.2 Distribution of query intents in existing studies

Intent type	Broder	Rose and Levinson	Baeza-Yates et al.	Jansen et al.
Navigational	20%	13%–16%	/	10%
Informational	40%	61%–63%	61%	81%
Transactional	30%	/	/	9%
Resource	/	21%–27%	/	/
Not informational	/	/	22%	/
Ambiguous	/	/	17%	/

on automatic and manual analysis over the Dogpile[2] search engine transaction log. Note that the proportion of informational queries is much higher than those reported in previous works. They believed that the variation in the reported percentage may be related to the small-size samples used in prior studies and the power log distribution of Web queries. Readers who are interested in this taxonomy can read [30] for more details.

4.2.1.5 Summarization

We summarize the major intent types defined in existing studies, together with the distributions of queries belonging to these intents according to the original studies. The statistics is shown in Table 4.2. The table indicates that although a large percentage of queries issued to search engines are for information seeking (informational queries), there are still many queries that are issued for other intents, such as seeking a particular website or performing an interactive task.

All these studies have provided deeper understanding on users' search goals with more specific and detailed definitions on intent taxonomy. However, from a review of the existing literature, Broder's taxonomy is the most widely adopted one in automatic query intent classification work probably due to its simplicity and essence. Besides, it is worth to note that not the full taxonomy of Broder has been utilized in all the intent classification works. There are studies trying to identify navigational and informational queries [32, 34], or differentiating transactional or navigational queries from the rest. Different features have been designed according to the specific classification tasks as we will show in Sect. 4.2.3.

4.2.2 Methods Used for Predicting User Goals

Although various kinds of taxonomies are proposed to classify different underlying goals of the user when submitting one particular query, a common premise is that

---

[2]http://www.dogpile.com/.

when users use search engines to seek information, their goals are diverse. With the classification of different intentions driving user queries, search engines can utilize different ranking mechanisms to support different types of queries and to improve user experience. For example, for software downloading queries, search engines can provide a direct download link in the search result page.

Early work on query intent classification performed manual classification to establish the intent taxonomy [10, 47] and verified the feasibility of automatic intent classification [34]. Labeling tools with carefully designed questionnaire were utilized to facilitate the manual classification process. Later, automatically identifying such intents became the mainstream in this research community, starting from heuristically constructed classifiers. In this section, we will briefly review these approaches. As we just mentioned, although different taxonomies have been proposed as we introduced in the previous section, Broder's taxonomy is most received by IR community. Furthermore, Broder's study has shown that transactional queries are usually hard to be identified from navigational queries and informational queries. Hence, most effort on automatically identifying user goals focused on simply dividing queries into navigational and informational.

User goals can be automatically identified by either unsupervised methods (rule-based methods) or supervised learning-based methods. For unsupervised methods, one or multiple rules are manually created for identifying query types. For example, Kang et al. [32] utilized a linear function to generate a score based on four measures to decide the query intent. Lee et al. [34] adopted a similar linear combination approach and used the threshold derived from the goal-prediction graph to classify query intents. Brenes et al. [8, 9] ranked queries based on three types of features to detect navigational queries. Jansen et al. [29, 30] implemented an automatic classifier based on handcrafted rules by identifying the linguistic characteristics of queries with respect to different intents (these features will be introduced in Sect. 4.2.3.1). All of these methods relied on "*ad hoc*" thresholds and parameters.

To avoid such heuristics, some researchers turned to supervised learning-based methods, and different models have been used in existing approaches. Among these models, linear regression, SVM, and decision tree are widely used. Linear regression and decision tree can generate interpretable models and illustrate the usefulness of each feature studied, while SVM is shown to be useful for processing high-dimensional vectors, especially those text-based features. For example, Kang and Kim [32] and Lee et al. [34] used the linear regression model to classify queries. Nettleton et al. [42] employed Kohonen self-organized maps (SOM) and C4.5 decision trees to classify user sessions into informational, navigational, and transactional. Liu et al. [37] also used C4.5 decision tree model for query intent classification. Baeza-Yates et al. [4] and Lu et al. [40] employed SVM for intent classification.

To better model users' search sessions, Hu et al. [25] proposed to use skip-chain Conditional Random Field (CRF) to predict commercial query intent. The skip-chain CRF can model the correlation between nonconsecutive similar queries in users' search sessions via skip edges to improve the prediction accuracy. Similarly, Deufemia et al. [18] employed both CRF and Latent Dynamic Conditional Random

Field (LDCRF) to model sequential information between queries within a user session and showed that CRF can achieve better performance than SVM on informational query identification. Multitask learning has also been used in query intent classification. In [7], Bian et al. proposed to learn both ranking functions and query intent classifier simultaneously. A logistic model is utilized to predict the probability of query intents. The ranking function jointly learned with query categorization was demonstrated to be more effective than that learned with predefined query categorization.

Furthermore, Lu et al. [40] compared several machine learning methods, including naive Bayes model, maximum entropy model, SVM, and stochastic gradient boosting tree (SGBT), for navigational query identification. They found that SGBT coupled with linear SVM feature selection is most effective. Zamora et al. [64] studied decision trees, SVM, and ensemble methods for query intent classification with respect to the taxonomy of Broder. They found the use of ensembles allows to reach significant performance improvements.

Beside these classification models, Baeza-Yates et al. [4] employed Probabilistic Latent Semantic Analysis (PLSA), an unsupervised method to cluster queries into informational, not informational, and ambiguous categories. They also applied the supervised learning method SVM and found that the combination of supervised and unsupervised learning is a good alternative to find user's goals, rather than the sole use of each method.

4.2.3   Features

As discussed, user goals can be identified by either unsupervised methods (rule-based methods) or supervised learning-based methods. Both types of methods rely on one or multiple well-designed features, which reflect characteristics of different types of queries. There are a large number of features proposed by existing works. These features, can be extracted from query string itself, document corpus, query logs, anchor texts, or summaries of top search results. Some features were proposed according to specific classification tasks, such as for classifying intent into navigational/navigational/transactional, into navigational/non-navigational, or into informational/non-informational. We think that most features can be assumed to be independent of the taxonomy used, although they are originally proposed for a specific classification task. Hence here we mainly categorize the features into three groups according to the data resources and the types of the features:

- **Features extracted from query strings**: linguistic features defined based on the surface strings of the query;
- **Features extracted from the corpus**: features defined on the corpus to be retrieved or the top retrieved documents, typically using document content, anchor texts, or URL information.

- **Features extracted from query log**: features defined on the user interaction logs recorded by search engines/toolbars, typically using information such as click-through, sessions, and eye/mouse movement.

In the remaining part of this section, we will briefly introduce some commonly used features within each category. At the end of the section, we will briefly summarize where the features are used and what classification task they are used for.

4.2.3.1   Features Extracted from Query Strings

The simplest features used for identifying query intent are linguistic character-istics of query terms or query strings, for example, whether the query string contains specific characters, URLs, or entity names. Jansen et al. [29, 30] tried to classify query intent into informational, navigational, and transactional based on characteristics of queries and query terms. They used some simple features extracted from query strings, such as query length (they assumed that a navi-gational query has less than three terms). They identified key characteristics of different categories of queries based on an analysis of queries from three different Web search engines. For example, navigational queries are queries containing company/business/organization/people **names**, or queries **containing domain suf-fixes**. Transactional queries are identified by checking whether queries contain **specific terms** (for example, "lyrics," "download," "images," "audio," "buy" for transactional intent, "ways to," "how to," "list" for informational). A simple rule-based classifier was implemented to identify query categories based on the above characteristics. They then used this classifier to categorize a million real queries and found that more than 80% of Web queries are informational, with about 10% each being navigational and transactional.

Kang and Kim [32] also used linguistic features. They assumed that navigational queries are usually proper names, whereas some informational queries may include a **verb**. They simply classify the queries that have a verb (except the "be" verb) into informational queries.

4.2.3.2   Features Extracted from the Corpus

Kang and Kim [32] employed the WT10g[3] dataset to build two document subsets, namely DBHOME and DBTOPIC, to identify intent types. DBHOME is comprised of those documents acting as entry points for a particular website within WT10g, while DBTOPIC includes the remaining Web pages in WT10g. Kang and Kim pro-

---

[3]http://ir.dcs.gla.ac.uk/test_collections/wt10g.html.

posed several search corpus-based features that consider the following information contained in both sets:

- the distribution of query terms in both subsets,
- the mutual information of query term pairs in both subsets.

They further assumed that terms of navigational queries appear in titles and anchor texts more frequently than informational queries. They utilized the probability that a query appear in anchor text and page titles as a feature for predicting user goals. They combined the above three types of features and the query string-based feature we just introduced (i.e., containing verb) to classify query intent into informational and.

Kang [31] then proposed to explore hyperlink information for transactional intent detection. Specifically, he clustered hyperlinks according to the extension of a linked object (e.g., site, music, or file) with the assumption that some types of hyperlinks are more likely to be linked to transactional activities (for example, if the linked object is a binary file, its possible activity is downloading). He then extracted cue expressions (i.e., short definition or explanation) for each hyperlink type based on titles and anchor texts. Based on this information, Kang proposed a new set of features called *link scores* for each query. The basic idea was to calculate the proportion of candidate expressions (i.e., the whole expression, the first and last term, and the first and last biterm of the query) in the collection of cue expressions that represent each hyperlink type. The experimental dataset consisted of 495 navigational and informational queries from TREC and 100 transactional queries manually extracted from a Lycos[4] log file. Using the proposed features as well as those in [32], he achieved the overall performance of 78% in both precision and recall for the identification of transactional queries.

Lee et al. [34] defined anchor-link distribution in the search corpus as a feature for intent classification. They checked the destinations of the links with the same anchor text as the query. For a navigational query, a single authoritative website exists (i.e., a dominating portion of links with the query as the anchor text point to this website). On the contrary, for an informational query, because of lack of a single authoritative site, the links with the query as anchor text may point to a number of different destinations. Lee et al. located all the anchor links that have the same text as the query, extracted their destination URLs, counted the number of links for each distinct URL, sorted the URLs in the descending order of link numbers, and finally calculated the distribution of links over these distinct URLs. The anchor-link distribution of a navigational query is expected to be highly skewed toward the most frequent URL, whereas the anchor-link distribution for an informational query should be more flat. They used mean, median, skewness, and kurtosis to measure the skewness of anchor-link distribution and used them as features for query intent classification. Anchor-link distribution can be considered as an alternative of query-click distribution (which will be introduced later) when

---

[4]http://lycos.com.

click-through data is unavailable or sparse. Liu et al. [37] and Lu et al. [40] also used the anchor-link distribution for identifying navigational queries.

Herrera et al. [24] studied search corpus features (including anchor text-based features and page content-based features). Beside those previously proposed features, they included the use of some new features. One of the new features is based on the idea that statistics about the occurrence of the query terms across different domains are useful for determining the user goal. They used this assumption to include two new features, namely density of domains in the top similar anchor texts and density of domains in the top similar texts, which compute the ratio of distinct domains in top K answers in top similar anchor texts and top retrieved pages, respectively. Another feature is the popularity of the query. They utilized the WT10g query set the same as [32] and additional 600 queries from the WBR03 collection, 200 queries for each intent category. By using all the features, they achieved an accuracy of 82.5% on WBR03 queries and 77.67% on WT10g queries. They showed that the query popularity feature is effective when combined with other features, increasing their discriminative nature.

4.2.3.3   Features Based on Query Log

Query log is one of the effective data sources for search ranking and intent understanding. It has been well utilized in existing works on query goal identification. Lee et al. [34] and Liu et al. [37] investigated the problem of separating navigational queries from informational based on click-through data. Both approaches computed the click distribution from click-through data for each query. Given a query, its click distribution is constructed as follows:

1. count the times each document is clicked by all users under the query;
2. sort all clicked documents in the descending order of the total number of clicks made on the documents by all users;
3. normalize click frequencies so that all values add up to 1 and get the distribution.

Basically, similar to the anchor-link distribution we just introduced, if the click distribution of a query is highly skewed toward one or just a few domains or Web pages, the query is more likely to be a navigational query. In contrast, when the click distribution is relatively flat, the query tends to be informational. To summarize click distribution into a single numeric feature that captures how skewed the distribution is, different statistical measurements, such as mean, median, skewness, and kurtosis, can be used. Click entropy, which was proposed by Dou et al. [19, 20], can also be used to quantifying a click distribution. Wang and Agichtein [60] revisited the classification problem with respect to clear (navigational)/informational/ambiguous proposed by Baeza-Yates et al. [4]. They proposed entropy-based metrics of the click distributions of individual searchers, which is better than entropy of all result clicks of a query in distinguishing informational and ambiguous queries. They also involved domain entropy as a backoff to the URL entropy to deal with the sparsity problem. Using the 150 manually labeled queries from MSN search query log, they showed user-based click entropy features can improve the classification performance as compared with overall entropy features.

In addition, Lee et al. assumed that navigational queries are usually associated with fewer clicks than informational ones; hence, they used the average number of clicks of a query as another feature to identify navigational queries. Liu et al. [37] also observed that navigational queries usually have fewer clicks than informational or transactional queries. Differently, they use "n Clicks Satisfied (nCS)" to quantify this. nCS is the proportion of sessions containing a given query in which the user clicked at most n results. They further assumed that users tend to click on the top results of navigational queries. Based on this, they proposed to use "top n Results Satisfied (nRS)," the proportion of sessions containing a given query in which the user clicked at most top n results. Given a small n value (e.g., two), navigational queries tend to have higher nCS and nRS values than informational or transactional queries.

Brenes and Gayo-Avello [8] proposed three user log features, each associated with a Navigational Coefficient (NC), to identify navigational queries. The first NC is the rate of visits to the most visited result in the query. It is equal to the click probability of the rank no. 1 result (i.e., the maximum click probability) in the click distribution we have introduced. The second NC is defined as $1 - \frac{\text{number of distinct results}}{\text{number of visits to all results}}$. The third and last value, *percentage of navigational sessions*, computes the ratio of one-query one-click sessions to all the sessions containing that query. Each NC was then used to rank the queries from AOL search logs, and only case studies were conducted for evaluation.

Nettleton et al. [42] used number of clicks, click position, and used browsing time on clicked documents as features for predicting user goals. Deufemia et al. [18] introduced several new interaction features based on user behaviors during the exploration of Web pages associated to the links of the SERP. They not only considered the absolute and effective dwell time on a Web page but also measured the amount of reading of a Web page and the number of words during the browsing. There were also some interaction features designed for transactional queries, such as *AjaxRequestsCount* that represents the number of AJAX requests originated during browsing. The basic assumption is that capturing interaction features on specific portions of Web pages conveys a better accuracy in the evaluation of user actions. They collected 129 labeled search sessions from 13 subjects for evaluation. Using the proposed interaction features together with traditional query, search, and context features, they achieved 0.84, 0.88, and 0.86 for transactional, informational, and navigational query identification, respectively. They also demonstrated the effectiveness of the transactional interaction features for transactional queries.

Guo and Agichtein [22] explored mouse movements for inferring informational and navigational intents. The features included average trajectory length, average vertical range, and average horizontal range. Based on 300 labeled queries from the MSN search engine, they showed that using these simple features can achieve an accuracy of 70.28% for intent classification.

4.2.3.4 Features Leveraging Multiple Sources

Baeza-Yates et al. [4] proposed to use terms from the documents clicked by the query to construct the feature vector and group the queries into clusters. Using a dataset of 6042 manually labeled queries according to informational, non-informational, or ambiguous intentions, they constructed feature vectors from a query log from the Chilean Web search engine TodoCL.[5] Evaluation results demonstrated that such term-based features are good at detecting informational queries (approximately 80% precision with recall above 80%) but less effective on non-informational (close to 60% precision with 40% recall) and ambiguous queries (less than 40% precision with recall lower than 20%). In [41], Mendoza and Zamora further extended this vector representation by considering the time users take to review the documents they select, leading to *tf-idf-time* and *tf-idf-pop-time* weighting schemes. The basic idea is that the time spent in each query differs by query intent (for example, an informational query may take more time for the user to review the result pages). Based on 2000 labeled queries, they showed that vector representation based on *tf-idf-time* weighting scheme is the most effective (above 90% in F-measure) in identifying informational/navigational/transaction intents as compared with that based on *tf-pop* and *tf-idf-pop-time* schemes.

Liu et al. [39] proposed to leverage Web page forms to generate useful query patterns for transactional query identification. Specifically, they first analyzed the distribution of form clicks and obtained a group of high-quality transactional queries by mining toolbar log. With these transactional queries as training data, they matched them with the information contained in forms to help generalize these queries into patterns. These transactional query patterns along with a confidence score were used as basic features to classify new queries. Note that in this work, the authors used both corpus-based features (Web page forms) and query log-based features (toolbar log).

4.2.3.5 Summary of Features Used

Table 4.3 summarizes some main features used in existing approaches. Brenes et al. [9] did a survey and evaluation of query intent detection methods. They found that the combination of features extracted from query terms, anchor text, and query log performed the best. Beside these approaches, there also exists some effort on feature engineering over a large number of features for query intent identification. For example, Lu et al. [40] studied both search corpus and user log features for navigational query detection. For each query, the top 100 URLs were recorded and 100 query–URLs were generated for features construction. For each query–URL pair, they extracted a total of 197 features, among which 29 features are query log features using click information, and the rest are search corpus features based on

---

[5]http://www.todocl.com.

Table 4.3 Features used for query intent classification

Source	Feature	Work
Query string	Containing entities (company, business, organization, people names)	Jansen et al. [30]
	Containing domain suffixes	
	Containing clue words (lyrics, download, image, etc.)	
	POS, containing verb	Kang and Kim [32]
Corpus	Anchor-link distribution (mean, median, skewness, kurtosis, etc.)	Lee et al. [34], Liu et al. [37], Lu et al.[40]
	Query term distribution of subdocument sets (HOME and TOPIC), etc.	Kang and Kim [32],
	The usage rate of query term as anchor texts and page titles	Kang [31]
	Link scores	Kang [31]
Query log	Average number of clicks	Lee et al. [34], Liu et al. [37], Nettleton et al. [42]
	Click distribution (mean, median, skewness, kurtosis, etc.)	Lee et al. [34], Liu et al. [37], Lu et al. [40]
	Click probability of the most clicked result, i.e., click distribution (max)	Brenes and Gayo-Avello [8], Lu et al. [40]
	n Clicks Satisfied (nCS)	Liu et al. [37]
	top n Results Satisfied (nRS)	
	Click entropy	Dou et al. [19], Lu et al. [40]
	Click position	Nettleton et al. [42]
	Browsing time	
	Mouse movements	Guo et al. [22]

URL itself and anchor texts pointed to the URL. Feature integration operators such as normalized ratio, mean, and entropy were then utilized to calculate statistics of the raw features. In this way, the combination of selected features yield the best classification result.

4.2.4 Summary

Query intent classification based on user goals attempts to categorize the underlying goal of users' search. Broder's taxonomy and its simplified variants have been widely adopted as the major intent taxonomies. Researchers have developed different types of features in order to enrich the query representation for the classification tasks, from simple query string features using surface term characteristics, to corpus-based features leveraging Web content information, to query log features capturing user interactive behaviors. This line of research started in early 2000 and reached its peak in around 2008–2009, with diverse models and features emerging in the research community. However, the lack of a benchmark dataset devoted to the task makes it difficult to fairly compare existing work. One may refer to the work from Brenes et al. [9], which partially addressed this problem by comparing several previous methods based on a large query set (6624 queries) from MSN Query Log.

4.3 Vertical Intent Classification

With the emergence of numerous vertical search services (e.g., job search, product search, image search, map search, news search, weather search, or academic search), it is becoming popular in search engines to present aggregated results from multiple verticals through the standard general Web search interface. This is so-called aggregated search or federated search. An example aggregated search result page from Bing search engine (http://www.bing.com) is shown in Fig. 4.1. A customized region containing latest weather forecast information of Beijing city is directly shown in the search result of query "Beijing weather." Directly showing this more specialized answer region in SERP will benefit most users, hence they do not need to spend extra effort on opening normal Web search results to browse the detailed information again. Furthermore, with this kind of aggregated search, users do not have to identify his or her intent in advance and decide which vertical service to choose to satisfy his or her intention. This usually reduces user efforts and hence can greatly improve user satisfaction.

At the same time, irrelevant vertical results within the search engine result page (SERP) may disturb users. For example, providing image search results in SERP for query "Beijing weather," or displaying weather vertical results for query "weather forecasting method" is useless or even detrimental to user experience. Therefore, it is critical to have query vertical intent classifiers in a general or aggregated search engine that can predict whether a query should trigger respective vertical search services. This is also called vertical selection problem [3, 25]. Note that a query may implicitly cover more than one intent or vertical.

4.3.1 Topical Intent Classification

Some verticals are genre specific [2]. Therefore, some prior work in topical intent classification is relevant to vertical selection. The main target of topical intent classification is to classify a query into a ranked list of n categories (e.g., assigning the query "Transformers" to the category "Entertainment/Movies" and "Entertainment/Games").

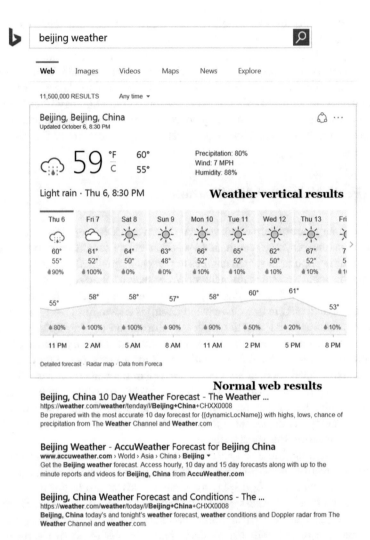

Fig. 4.1 An example aggregated search result page for the query "Beijing weather" from Bing (http://www.bing.com). A region containing latest weather forecast information of Beijing city is shown in the search result. Users can directly get this information without extra effort for viewing normal search results or opening corresponding vertical search engines

The main challenge of classifying Web queries is the sparseness of query features due to the limitation of information provided by short Web queries. To solve this problem, most topical query classification approaches leverage external data sources, in addition to the original query strings, to enrich features. One typical way is to extract features from search engine results, including the document content, titles, URLs, and snippets. For example, Shen et al. [50] used the titles, the snippets, and the full plain text of the documents returned by search engines and ODP taxonomies[6] to generate textual features for classifying queries into 67 target topical categories, based on support vector machine (SVM) classifiers. Broder et al. [11] used retrieved search results to classify queries into a commercial taxonomy comprised of approximately 6000 nodes within the sponsored search environment. Given a query, they issued the query to a general Web search engine, classified the returned Web pages, and then used the page classification results to classify the original query. Beitzel et al. [6] found that a classifier trained using snippets from the retrieved documents performs merely 11% better than using only query lexical features (mainly query terms).

In addition to the work primarily focusing on enriching feature representation, some other approaches aim at obtaining more training data from query logs by semi-supervised learning. For example, Beitzel et al. [5] leveraged unlabeled data to improve supervised learning. They developed a rule-based automatic classifier produced using selectional preferences mined from the linguistic analysis of a large-scale query log. They used this unsupervised classifier to mine a large number of unlabeled queries from query logs as training data, together with some manually classified queries, to improve the supervised query classification models.

As the Query Topic Classification task has been discussed in Sect. 4.3 of the Query Classification chapter, we will not cover those again in this chapter.

4.3.2   Vertical Intent Classification

In addition to detecting the topical categories, some other vertical intent classification methods have been proposed by utilizing more resources, which are summarized as follows.

(1) Content of vertical corpus. Vertical intent can be classified by evaluating whether the query is relevant to the content of each vertical or whether the vertical can return sufficient amount of information.
(2) Query strings. Vertical services specialize on identifiable domains and types of media. This enables users to possibly express interest in vertical content explicitly [2], using keywords such as "news" for the news vertical or "weather"

---

[6]http://www.dmoz.org.

for the weather vertical. Therefore, another potentially useful source of evidence for vertical intent classification is the query string itself.

(3) Characteristic of normal Web search results. Characteristic of search results returned from the normal search service (i.e., the Web vertical) is also helpful for detecting vertical type of the query. For example, if many shopping websites are returned for a query, it is likely that the query has a commercial intent.

(4) User behaviors on verticals and the aggregated search page. Some verticals have a search interface through which users directly search for vertical content. For example, Bing search engine (http://www.bing.com) has a separated search service (http://www.bing.com/images) for image vertical and http://www.bing. com/news for news vertical. Vertical intent of a query can be estimated by evaluating whether users actively use this query in the vertical, or other user behaviors gathered from these search services. At the same time, some users prefer the default Web search interface, other than separated vertical services. Furthermore, some verticals do not have a separated interface. The rich user behaviors made on the default search page can be utilized for vertical intent classification. For example, whether users click image answers more frequently than normal Web pages for query "tom cruise" is an important implicit feedback for judging the image vertical intent of "tom cruise."

Details of the features will be introduced in the remaining part of this section.

4.3.2.1 Corpus-Based Features

As Arguello et al. introduced, we may view vertical intent classification (vertical selection) analogous to resource selection in federated search [2, 3], if we consider verticals as external collections. Corpus-based features are derived from document rankings obtained by issuing the query to different verticals. Arguello et al. proposed constructing smaller, representative corpora of vertical content rather than using the original vertical index. The representative corpora can be a sample from the vertical or a sample from surrogate corpora like Wikipedia.

Simple corpus-based features may include the number of relevant documents returned by verticals and ranking scores of the top ranked documents.

Another batch of features are those used for predicting query performance. One representative feature is Clarity proposed by Cronen-Townsend et al. [16]. Clarity is the relative entropy, or Kullback–Leibler divergence, between the language of the top ranked documents and the language of the collection. More specifically, Clarity of a query to a vertical v is calculated as follows:

$$Clarity(q, v) = \sum_w P(w|\theta_q) \log_2 \frac{P(w|\theta_q)}{P(w|\theta_{C_v})}. \tag{4.1}$$

Here w is a term from the vocabulary generated based on the document collection C_v of vertical v. $P(w|\theta_q)$ and $P(w|\theta_{C_v})$ are the query and collection language models, respectively. $P(w|\theta_q)$ is usually estimated by averaging the language models of the top retrieved documents of q. A low Clarity score usually means that random results are returned from the vertical, hence the query has low probability belonging to the vertical.

Another representative corpus-based feature is ReDDE, which is originally proposed by Si and Callan [51] for solving the resource selection problem. ReDDE is a resource-ranking algorithm, which estimates the distribution of relevant documents across the set of available verticals. It scores a target vertical based on the retrieval of an index that combines documents sampled from every target verticals. Given this retrieval, ReDDE accumulates a vertical's score from its document scores, taking into account the difference between the number of documents contained in the vertical and the number of documents sampled from the vertical. More specifically,

$$ReDDE(q, v) = |D_v| \sum_{d \in R} I(d \in S_v) P(q|\theta_d) P(d|S_v), \tag{4.2}$$

where $|D_v|$ is the number of documents in vertical v and S_v is the documents sampled from v. This feature is used by Arguello et al. [2] for vertical intent classification.

4.3.2.2 Query String-Based Features

Query string-based features aim to model the explicit expression of queries issued to search engines for seeking vertical contents. For each vertical, we can generate a list of handcrafted rules that can directly identify possible vertical intent of a query. For example, "[location] `weather` → weather" for weather intent identifies that each query comprised of a location name and the term "weather" has an explicit weather intent.

Tsur et al. [56] investigated the problem of detecting queries with a question intent. They called these queries as CQA-intent queries, since answers to them are typically found in community question answering (CQA) sites. As CQA-intent queries are usually long, they proposed to take the structure of queries into consideration for detecting CQA-intent queries. They extracted the following query string-based features: (1) the position of WH words in the query; (2) the number of tags the specific tags appear in the part-of-speech (POS) tagging result of the query.

4.3.2.3 Query Log-Based Features

Query log contains rich information about users' preferences on verticals. The vertical of a query can be estimated by evaluating the similarity between the query and all clicked documents within the vertical.

Arguello et al. [2] used the query likelihood given by a unigram language model constructed from the vertical's query log as a feature for classifying query vertical intent. Given a query q, the probability it belongs to a vertical v is defined by

$$QL(q, v) = \frac{P(q|\theta_v)}{\sum_{v' \in V} P(q|\theta_{v'})},$$

(4.3)

where θ_v is vertical v's language model generated based on query log and V is a set of candidate verticals.

Kanhabua et al. [33] used query logs for detecting event-related queries (such as queries related to political elections, sport competitions, or natural disasters). More specifically, they used the normalized query volume aggregated across all users over time and the normalized click frequency for the query accumulated from all URLs and users as daily time series. In addition to these two data sources, they further used the temporal distribution of number of top-K search results retrieved from an external document collection as the third time series. For each time series, they extracted a list of features, including but not limited to: (1) Seasonality, which is a temporal pattern that indicates how periodic is an observed behavior over time. They used Holt–Winters adaptive exponential smoothing to decompose the time series and generated the seasonality component. Then they used trending scope and trending amplitude as features. (2) Autocorrelation, which is the cross correction of a signal with itself or the correlation between its own past and future values at different times. (3) Click entropy, which is proposed by Dou et al. [19], is used to model the temporal content dynamics. (4) Other features, including burstiness, kurtosis, and temporal KL-divergence. Information about more features can be found in [33].

Zhou et al. [67] used the query log-based features together with the query string-based features for vertical intent classification. They first identified vertical intent for a set of queries based on query string-based features we introduced in Sect. 4.3.2.2. For example, "Beijing weather" is predicted to have a weather intent because it contains the explicit keyword "weather." Queries containing "images," "picture," or "photo" are related to image vertical. Then, they classified URLs using the same rule-based method. For example, an URL containing a word "images" will be classified into image vertical. All clicked URLs made on a vertical query are also assumed to belong the same vertical. Finally, for a given query q and a vertical v, they calculated the fraction of clicks that linked to pages in the vertical, compared to the number of total clicks for the query, and used a threshold to identify whether q is related to vertical v.

4.3.2.4 Search Results-Based Features

In addition to the corpus-based features, which mainly rely on the documents returned from the verticals or representative corpora of verticals, we can also develop features based on characteristic of search results returned by the general Web search.

The first type of information we can utilize is the statistics of websites within the results. If the results of a query contain many websites, which are typical websites of a vertical, the query is possibly relevant to the vertical.

The second type of information is the keywords or phrases contained in the snippets or the content of the search results. For example, if the snippets of search results of a query contain the keywords "film" or "movie" frequently, the query may have a movie intent.

4.3.2.5 Vertical Intent Classification Models

Similar to topical intent classification, most existing vertical intent classification (or vertical selection) approaches [2, 33, 56] are based on supervised learning-based algorithms, such as Logistic Regression, SVM, Random Forest, and Gradient Boosted Decision Tress (GBDT). Studies have shown that when trained using a large set of labeled data, a machine learned vertical selection model outperforms baselines that require no training data [3].

One problem of the supervised classifiers is that whenever a new vertical is introduced, a costly new set of editorial data must be gathered. To solve this problem, Arguello et al. [3] proposed methods for reusing training data from a set of existing verticals to learn a predictive model for a new vertical. Their experiments showed the need to focus on different types of features when maximizing portability (the ability for a single model to make accurate predictions across multiple verticals) than when maximizing adaptability (the ability for a single model to make accurate predictions for a specific vertical). Hu et al. [25] also revealed that it is a big challenge to create training data for statistical machine learning-based query vertical classification approaches. They proposed a general methodology to discover large quantities of intent concepts by leveraging Wikipedia, which required very little human effort. Within this framework, each intent domain is represented as a set of Wikipedia articles and categories, and the intent of a query is identified through mapping the query into the Wikipedia representation space. Based on their study on three different vertical classification tasks, i.e., travel, job, and person name, this approach achieved much better coverage than previous approaches to classify queries in an intent domain even through the number of seed intent examples is very small. Li et al. [35, 36] used click graphs to automatically infer class memberships of unlabeled queries from those of labeled ones based on the co-click behaviors of users. They then used these automatically labeled queries to train content-based query classification models using query terms as features. Their experimental results on product intent classification and job intent classification indicated that by using a large amount of training queries obtained in this way, classifiers using only query term or lexical features (without the use of features from search results) can outperform those using augmented features from external knowledge.

4.4 Query Intent Mining

A large percentage of queries issued to search engines are broad or ambiguous [19, 20, 28, 45, 52]. By submitting one query, users may have different intents or information need. For an ambiguous query, users may seek for different interpretations; whereas for a query on a broad topic, users may be interested in different subtopics. For example, by issuing the ambiguous query [apple], one user might be searching for information about the IT company Apple, whereas another user might be looking for information about apple fruit. By issuing a broad query [harry potter], a user may want to seek content covering various aspects, such as [harry potter movie], [harry potter book], or [harry potter characters] within this broad topic. Without accurately understanding users' underlying intents of a query, search engines may fail to return enough results that can cover major intents in the top ranks, hence may affect search experience of some users. So it is critical to mine underlying intents of a query.

Query intent mining, which is called **subtopics mining** sometimes, is an essential step to search result diversification, which aims to solve the problem of query ambiguity. Search result diversification aims to return diverse search results that cover as many user intents as possible. It has received a lot of attention in recent years. Many search result diversification algorithms [1, 12, 13, 17, 21, 43, 45, 46, 49, 63, 68] have been developed to improve search result diversity. A common characteristic of most existing explicit diversification algorithms is that they assume the existence of a flat list of independent subtopics [17, 21, 49]. Table 4.4 shows the manually created subtopics for query "defender" (topic number 20) in TREC 2009 [14]. There are five distinct subtopics for the query. For subtopics s_1, s_3, and s_5, users are all looking for different information about a software "Windows Defender". For subtopic s_2, users are interested in general information about a brand of car "Land Rover Defender." For subtopic s_4, users are finding specific information about playing a "Defender arcade game" online.

The Subtopic Mining subtask in NTCIR-9 Intent task [54] and NTCIR-10 Intent-2 task [48] aimed to have an evaluation of intent mining approaches. In the Subtopic Mining subtask, systems were required to return a ranked list of subtopic strings in response to a given query. A subtopic could be a specific interpretation of an

Table 4.4 Subtopics of query "defender"

No.	Subtopic description
s_1	I'm looking for the homepage of Windows Defender, an antispyware program
s_2	Find information on the Land Rover Defender sport-utility vehicle
s_3	I want to go to the homepage for Defender Marine Supplies
s_4	I'm looking for information on Defender, an arcade game by Williams. Is it possible to play it online?
s_5	I'd like to find user reports about Windows Defender, particularly problems with the software

ambiguous query (e.g., "Microsoft windows" or "house windows" in response to "windows") or an aspect of a faceted query (e.g., "windows 7 update" in response to "windows 7"). The subtopics collected from participants were pooled and manually assessed. The Subtopic Mining subtask received 42 Chinese runs and 14 Japanese runs in NTCIR-9. INTENT-2 attracted participating teams from China, France, Japan, and South Korea—12 teams for Subtopic Mining, and it received 34 English runs, 23 Chinese runs, and 14 Japanese runs. More details about these evaluation tasks can be found in [54] and [48]. A similar task is the I-Mine task [38, 61] in NTCIR-11 and NTCIR-12.

In the remaining part of this section, we will briefly introduce existing approaches for mining query intent or subtopics.

4.4.1   Mining Intent from Query Logs

Query log data contain much useful information about user intents, as queries are directly issued by real-world users. When a user issues the query that may be ambiguous or underspecified and does not get expected results, she often refines the query and resubmits a new query to search engines. So by analyzing the query strings, reformulation, follow-up, and co-click behavior in query logs, it is able to identify user intents.

4.4.1.1   Mining Intent from Query Strings and Sessions

The most simple way to mine intents for a query is directly retrieving longer queries started or ended with the original query. A longer query containing the original query usually stands for a narrower intent, hence it is reasonable to directly take the longer queries as subintents. As there might be a large number of queries containing a short query, usually only the top n extended queries with the highest frequencies are selected.

Strohmaier et al. [55] obtained similar queries from search sessions, filtered out noisy queries using click-through data, and then grouped the remaining queries based on random walk similarity. They also estimated the popularity of each intent based on the number of observations in the query logs.

4.4.1.2   Mining Intent Based on Reformulation Behavior

Radlinski and Dumais [43] proposed to use the reformulation behavior of users within query logs to find likely user intents. Dou et al.[21] refined this method and used it to generate subtopics from query log for search result diversification.

Suppose for each query q_i, n_i is the number of times the query was issued. For a pair of queries (q_i, q_j), let n_{ij} be the number of times q_i was followed by q_j. The empirical probability of q_i being followed by q_j can be defined as follows:

$$p_{ij} = \frac{n_{ij}}{n_i}. \tag{4.4}$$

The problem of directly using the empirical follow-up probability p_{ij} is that follow-up queries are usually dominated by top user intents. For example, top three follow-up queries for query "defender" are "windows defender download," "Microsoft defender," and "windows defender" in a real search engine. These queries are actually talking about the same intent related to "windows defender." To retrieve more diverse intents, an MMR-like [12] measure can be used to greedily select the set of queries that are related to the given query yet different from each other.

Suppose $R(q_i)$ is the set of queries (subtopics) already selected, the next best query, namely q^n, is selected by:

$$q^n = \arg\max_{q_j} \left[\lambda \cdot p_{ij} - (1 - \lambda) \cdot \max_{q_k \in R(q_i)} sim(q_j, q_k) \right], \tag{4.5}$$

where λ is a parameter to control the similarity between returned intents (queries). $sim(q_j, q_k)$ is the similarity between two queries q_j and q_k.

We assume that the two queries q_j and q_k are similar if:

- q_j and q_k are frequently co-issued in the same query sessions. The probability of two queries being issued together in the same query sessions can be evaluated by the measurement $p_{jk}^* = \sqrt{p_{jk} p_{kj}}$ proposed by Radlinski and Dumais [43]. A high p_{jk}^* value means that q_j and q_k are frequently issued in the same sessions.
- The results by searching q_j and q_k are similar. Suppose $Docs(q_j)$ and $Docs(q_k)$ are top ten search results returned for query q_j and q_k. Dou et al. [21] used $\frac{|Docs(q_j) \cap Docs(q_k)|}{|Docs(q_j) \cup Docs(q_k)|}$ to evaluate the result similarity of these two queries.
- The words contained in q_j and q_k are similar. Dou et al. used $\frac{|q_j \cap q_k|}{|q_j \cup q_k|}$ to measure the text similarity between these two queries.

Dou et al. [21] then used a linear combination of these factors as follows and used it in Eq. (4.5) to rank queries as subtopics:

$$sim(q_j, q_k) = \frac{1}{3} \left\{ p_{jk}^* + \frac{|Docs(q_j) \cap Docs(q_k)|}{|Docs(q_j) \cup Docs(q_k)|} + \frac{|q_j \cap q_k|}{|q_j \cup q_k|} \right\}. \tag{4.6}$$

Example subtopics mined from query logs for the query "defender" are shown in Table 4.5.

Table 4.5 Subtopics of query "defender" mined from query logs

Subtopic	Rank	Subtopic	Rank
Windows defender download	1	Defender marine supply	6
Defender arcade game	2	Install Microsoft defender	7
Defender antivirus	3	Defender for XP	8
Land rover defender	4	Microsoft defender review	9
Free windows defender beta	5	Defender pro	10

4.4.1.3   Mining Intent from Click Graph

Radlinski et al. [44] proposed to combine reformulation and click information within query logs to find likely user intents.

To mine query intent, they first identified a set of possibly related queries to a query q by retrieving the k most frequent valid reformulations of q, and the k most frequent valid reformulations of these direct reformulations. Here "valid" means that the formulation is made by enough users (e.g., at least 2 users in [44]), and the probability of this formulation made among all formulations is larger than a threshold (Radlinski et al. used 0.001 as the threshold in [44]). They then removed queries less related to the original query by using a two-step random walk on the bipartite query-document click graph. Only those queries that have similar clicks with the original queries can be kept. Last, the left queries are clustered based on their similarities within the click graph based on random walk.

Hu et al. [27] employed both expanded queries and click graph to mine query intents. The entire solution is similar to Radlinski et al. [44]. They assumed that documents clicked in a specific search are likely to represent the same underlying intent. They grouped the URLs associated with a query and its expanded queries into clusters and then used expanded queries associated with the clusters to describe the intents.

4.4.2   Mining Intent from Search Results

A typical way for mining intent from search results is search result clustering [59, 65]. Zeng et al. [65] reformalized the search result clustering problem as a supervised salient phrase ranking problem. Given a query, they first extracted and ranked salient phrases as candidate cluster names, based on a regression model learned from human-labeled training data. The documents are assigned to relevant salient phrases to form candidate clusters, and the final clusters are generated by merging these candidate clusters.

Dou et al. [21] treated each cluster as an implicit subtopic/intent. They assumed that a cluster (subtopic), denoted by $cluster_1$, is more important than another cluster, denoted by $cluster_2$, if: (1) $cluster_1$ is ranked higher than $cluster_2$ in terms of salient phrases; and (2) the best document within the cluster $cluster_1$ is ranked higher than that in $cluster_2$. They then employed the following equation based on the above two assumptions to evaluate the importance of a cluster subtopic:

$$w(q, c) = 0.5 \times \frac{K - \text{clstRank}_c + 1}{K} + 0.5 \times \frac{1}{\text{bestDocRank}_c}, \qquad (4.7)$$

where clstRank_c is the rank of the cluster among all clusters, and bestDocRank_c is the highest rank of the documents within the cluster, i.e., $\text{bestDocRank}_c = \min_{d \in c} \text{rank}_d$. They used the same settings $N = 200$ and $K = 10$ as those in [65].

Wang et al. [57] used surrounding text of query terms in top retrieved documents to mine intent. They first extracted text fragments containing query terms from different parts of documents. Then they grouped similar text fragments into clusters and generated a readable subtopic for each cluster. Based on the cluster and the language model trained from a query log, they calculated three features and combined them into a relevance score for each subtopic. Subtopics were finally ranked by balancing relevance and novelty. Their evaluation experiments with the NTCIR-9 INTENT Chinese Subtopic Mining test collection show that the proposed method significantly outperformed a query log-based method proposed by Radlinski et al. [44] and a search result clustering-based method proposed by Zeng et al. [65] in terms of the official evaluation metrics used at the NTCIR-9 INTENT task. Moreover, the generated subtopics were significantly more readable than those generated by the search result clustering method.

4.4.3 Mining Intent from Anchor Texts

Anchor texts created by Web designers provide meaningful descriptions of destination documents. They are usually short and descriptive, which share the similar characteristics with Web queries. Given a query, anchor texts that contain the query terms usually convey the information about the query intents, hence it is reasonable to use these kinds of related anchor texts as query intents or subtopics.

Dou et al. [21] mined query intent from anchor text for search result diversification. For a given query q, they retrieved all anchor texts containing all query terms of q, weighted them, and selected the most important ones as subtopics. They assumed that the importance of an anchor text is usually proportional to its popularity on the Web, i.e., how many times it is used in Web sites or pages. However, a shorter anchor text usually matches the query better than a longer anchor text. The subtopic of the longer anchor text may be overspecified or drifted from the original query. Based on these observations, they design the following ranking function to evaluate

Table 4.6 Subtopics of query "defender" mined from anchor text in ClueWeb09 document corpus

Subtopic	Rank	Subtopic	Rank
Castle defender	1	Reputation defender	6
Public defender	2	Star defender	7
Cosmic defender	3	Chicago defender	8
Windows defender	4	Base defender	9
Brewery defender	5	Doodle defender	10

the importance of an anchor text c:

$$f(q, c) = \text{freq}(c) * \text{rel}(q, c)$$

$$= \left[\text{nsite}_c + \log(\text{npage}_c - \text{nsite}_c + 1) \right] * \frac{1 + \text{len}(q)}{\text{len}(c)}. \tag{4.8}$$

The first term $\text{freq}(c) = \text{nsite}_c + \log(\text{npage}_c - \text{nsite}_c + 1)$ evaluates the popularity of anchor text c, in which npage_c denotes the number of source pages that contain the anchor text c, and nsite_c denotes the number of unique source sites of these links. As it is easy to create a large number of source pages within the same source site to boost the anchor text, in the above equation, each source site just counts once. Additional pages containing the anchor text (totally $\text{npage}_c - \text{nsite}_c$ pages) from these sites are assigned lower weights by discounting their votes using the log function. Obviously an anchor text used by a larger number of different websites will get a high value of $\text{freq}(c)$.

The second term $\text{rel}(q, c) = \frac{1 + \text{len}(q)}{\text{len}(c)}$ punishes the anchor texts that contain too many words. Note that $\text{len}(q)$ is the count of query terms, and $\text{len}(c)$ is the number of terms contained in c. For the query q, an anchor text $q + t_1$ with an additional term t_1 gets as high $\text{rel}(q, c)$ as one, because it is a perfect subtopic of the query; whereas, another one $q + t_1 + t_2$ containing two additional terms gets lower $\text{rel}(q, c)$.

Table 4.6 shows the top 10 anchor texts with their weights for the query "defender" mined from the ClueWeb09 [15] collection.

4.4.4 Mining Intent from Query Suggestions

Another data source for mining intents is query suggestions. Query suggests are widely used resources for mining intent. Some search result diversification approaches directly utilized query suggestions as query intents or subtopics [17, 21, 49]. Search engines generate query suggests to users, to let them simply navigate to a better query when they are not satisfied by the current results. The query suggestions can be directly extracted from the search result page, and this is the reason why they are widely used in academic when there is no query log data.

4.4.5   Mining Complex Intents

All the above intent mining approaches assume the existence of a flat list of independent subtopics. However, it is hard to say these subtopics could reflect the complex information needs of users. Furthermore, most intent lists are mined from a single data source, whereas different data sources may help reflect the uncertainty of a query from different perspectives. For example, query logs reflect the popular requirements of real-world users, whereas anchor texts give an overview of the possible meanings of a query that is less biased by users and search engines. At the same time, the sole use of one data source or one mining algorithm may fail to satisfy the various requirements of different users, for example, when they are used for search result diversification [19]. Query logs are not available for new queries, and they have bias toward background rankings. Anchor texts can conquer these shortcomings instead. Query logs and anchor texts are applicable for short and popular queries; whereas subtopics mined from search results may work for both popular and tail queries.

As different types of subtopics are complimentary to each other, combining them together can potentially help the applications (such as search result diversity). Dou et al. [21] proposed a general framework of diversifying search results based on multiple dimensions of subtopics.

Hu et al. [26] revealed that user intents covered by a query can be hierarchical. They leveraged hierarchical intents and proposed hierarchical diversification models to promote search result diversification. Similar to previous works [17, 49], they used query suggestions extracted from Google search engine as subtopics. For each query, we collected its query suggestions from Google as the first-level subtopics. To generate subtopic hierarchy, they further issued the first-level subtopics as queries to Google and retrieved their query suggestions as the second-level subtopics. Finally, they collect 1696 first-level subtopics and 10,527 second-level subtopics for 194 TREC Web track queries. They assumed a uniform probability distribution for all the first-level subtopics and assumed a uniform probability distribution for the second-level subtopics with respect to their parent subtopics. Experimental results showed that using the hierarchical intent structures outperformed the use of flat intent list.

Wang et al. [58] also investigated the problem of hierarchical intents. They modeled user intents as intent hierarchies and used the intent hierarchies for evaluating search result diversity. They proposed several diversity measures based on intent hierarchies and demonstrated that in some cases, the new measures outperformed the original corresponding measures.

4.5   Other Kinds of Intent Classification

In addition to the general intent classification task, researchers also investigated solutions for classifying specific intents, such as temporal intent [33, 66] and geographic intent [62].

4.5.1   Temporal Intent Classification

Kanhabua et al. [33] studied the problem of detecting event-related queries. They used seasonality, autocorrelation, click entropy, kurtosis, and many other features to model the patterns of the time series extracted from query logs and document corpus. Differently, Zhao et al. [66] explored the usage of time-series data derived from Wikipedia page views, a freely available data source, for temporal intent disambiguation. They also used seasonality, autocorrelation, and other time-series-based features. Hasanuzzaman et al. [23] used 11 independent features extracted from the temporal information contained in the query string, its issuing date, and the extra data collected.

4.5.2   Geographic Intent Classification

Yi et al. [62] addressed the geo intent detection problem. They created a city language model, which is a probabilistic representation of the language surrounding the mention of a city in Web queries. They used several features derived from these language models to identify users' implicit geo intent or predict cities for queries that contain location-related entities.

References

1. Rakesh Agrawal, Sreenivas Gollapudi, Alan Halverson, and Samuel Ieong. Diversifying search results. In *Proceedings of the Second International Conference on Web Search and Data Mining9*, pages 5–14, 2009.
2. Jaime Arguello, Fernando Diaz, Jamie Callan, and Jean-François Crespo. Sources of evidence for vertical selection. In *Proceedings of the 32nd Annual International ACM SIGIR Conference on Research and Development in Information Retrieval*, pages 315–322, 2009.
3. Jaime Arguello, Fernando Diaz, and Jean-François Paiement. Vertical selection in the presence of unlabeled verticals. In *Proceeding of the 33rd International ACM SIGIR Conference on Research and Development in Information Retrieval*, pages 691–698, 2010.
4. Ricardo A. Baeza-Yates, Liliana Calderón-Benavides, and Cristina N. González-Caro. The intention behind web queries. In *Proceedings of the 13th International Conference on String Processing and Information Retrieval*, pages 98–109, 2006.

5. Steven M. Beitzel, Eric C. Jensen, Ophir Frieder, David D. Lewis, Abdur Chowdhury, and Aleksander Kolcz. Improving automatic query classification via semi-supervised learning. In *Proceedings of the 5th IEEE International Conference on Data Mining*, pages 42–49, 2005.
6. Steven M. Beitzel, Eric C. Jensen, Abdur Chowdhury, and Ophir Frieder. Varying approaches to topical web query classification. In *Proceedings of the 30th Annual International ACM SIGIR Conference on Research and Development in Information Retrieval*, pages 783–784, 2007.
7. Jiang Bian, Tie-Yan Liu, Tao Qin, and Hongyuan Zha. Ranking with query-dependent loss for web search. In *Proceedings of the Third International Conference on Web Search and Data Mining*, pages 141–150, 2010.
8. David J. Brenes and Daniel Gayo-Avello. Automatic detection of navigational queries according to behavioural characteristics. In *Proceedings of the LWA 2008 - Workshop-Woche: Lernen, Wissen & Adaptivität*, pages 41–48, 2008.
9. David J. Brenes, Daniel Gayo-Avello, and Kilian Pérez-González. Survey and evaluation of query intent detection methods. In *Proceedings of the 2009 workshop on Web Search Click Data*, pages 1–7, 2009.
10. Andrei Z. Broder. A taxonomy of web search. *SIGIR Forum*, 36 (2): 3–10, 2002.
11. Andrei Z. Broder, Marcus Fontoura, Evgeniy Gabrilovich, Amruta Joshi, Vanja Josifovski, and Tong Zhang. Robust classification of rare queries using web knowledge. In *Proceedings of the 30th Annual International ACM SIGIR Conference on Research and Development in Information Retrieval*, pages 231–238, 2007.
12. Jaime G. Carbonell and Jade Goldstein. The use of MMR, diversity-based reranking for reordering documents and producing summaries. In *Proceedings of the 21st Annual International ACM SIGIR Conference on Research and Development in Information Retrieval*, pages 335–336, 1998.
13. Harr Chen and David R. Karger. Less is more: probabilistic models for retrieving fewer relevant documents. In *Proceedings of the 29th Annual International ACM SIGIR Conference on Research and Development in Information Retrieval*, pages 429–436, 2006.
14. Charles L. A. Clarke, Nick Craswell, and Ian Soboroff. Overview of the TREC 2009 web track. In *Proceedings of The Eighteenth Text REtrieval Conference*, volume 500–278, 2009.
15. ClueWeb09. The clueweb09 dataset. http://boston.lti.cs.cmu.edu/Data/clueweb09/.
16. Stephen Cronen-Townsend, Yun Zhou, and W. Bruce Croft. Predicting query performance. In *Proceedings of the 25th Annual International ACM SIGIR Conference on Research and Development in Information Retrieval*, pages 299–306, 2002.
17. Van Dang and W. Bruce Croft. Diversity by proportionality: an election-based approach to search result diversification. In *Proceedings of the 35th International ACM SIGIR conference on research and development in Information Retrieval*, pages 65–74, 2012.
18. Vincenzo Deufemia, Massimiliano Giordano, Giuseppe Polese, and Luigi Marco Simonetti. Exploiting interaction features in user intent understanding. In *Proceedings of the 15th Asia-Pacific Web Conference*, pages 506–517, 2013.
19. Zhicheng Dou, Ruihua Song, and Ji-Rong Wen. A large-scale evaluation and analysis of personalized search strategies. In *Proceedings of the 16th International Conference on World Wide Web*, pages 581–590, 2007.
20. Zhicheng Dou, Ruihua Song, Ji-Rong Wen, and Xiaojie Yuan. Evaluating the effectiveness of personalized web search. *IEEE Trans. Knowl. Data Eng.*, 21 (8): 1178–1190, 2009.
21. Zhicheng Dou, Sha Hu, Kun Chen, Ruihua Song, and Ji-Rong Wen. Multi-dimensional search result diversification. In *Proceedings of the Forth International Conference on Web Search and Data Mining*, pages 475–484, 2011.
22. Qi Guo and Eugene Agichtein. Exploring mouse movements for inferring query intent. In *Proceedings of the 31st Annual International ACM SIGIR Conference on Research and Development in Information Retrieval*, pages 707–708, 2008.
23. Mohammed Hasanuzzaman, Sriparna Saha, Gaël Dias, and Stéphane Ferrari. Understanding temporal query intent. In *Proceedings of the 38th International ACM SIGIR Conference on Research and Development in Information Retrieval*, pages 823–826, 2015.

24. Mauro Rojas Herrera, Edleno Silva de Moura, Marco Cristo, Thomaz Philippe C. Silva, and Altigran Soares da Silva. Exploring features for the automatic identification of user goals in web search. *Inf. Process. Manage.*, 46 (2): 131–142, 2010.

25. Jian Hu, Gang Wang, Frederick H. Lochovsky, Jian-Tao Sun, and Zheng Chen. Understanding user's query intent with Wikipedia. In *Proceedings of the 18th International Conference on World Wide Web*, pages 471–480, 2009.

26. Sha Hu, Zhicheng Dou, Xiao-Jie Wang, Tetsuya Sakai, and Ji-Rong Wen. Search result diversification based on hierarchical intents. In *Proceedings of the 24th ACM International Conference on Information and Knowledge Management*, pages 63–72, 2015.

27. Yunhua Hu, Ya-nan Qian, Hang Li, Daxin Jiang, Jian Pei, and Qinghua Zheng. Mining query subtopics from search log data. In *Proceedings of the 35th International ACM SIGIR conference on research and development in Information Retrieval*, pages 305–314, 2012.

28. Bernard J. Jansen, Amanda Spink, and Tefko Saracevic. Real life, real users, and real needs: a study and analysis of user queries on the web. *Inf. Process. Manag.*, 36 (2): 207–227, 2000.

29. Bernard J. Jansen, Danielle L. Booth, and Amanda Spink. Determining the user intent of web search engine queries. In *Proceedings of the 16th International Conference on World Wide Web*, pages 1149–1150, 2007.

30. Bernard J. Jansen, Danielle L. Booth, and Amanda Spink. Determining the informational, navigational, and transactional intent of web queries. *Inf. Process. Manag.*, 44 (3): 1251–1266, 2008.

31. In-Ho Kang. Transactional query identification in web search. In *Proceedings of the Second Asia Information Retrieval Symposium*, pages 221–232, 2005.

32. In-Ho Kang and Gil-Chang Kim. Query type classification for web document retrieval. In *Proceedings of the 26th Annual International ACM SIGIR Conference on Research and Development in Information Retrieval*, pages 64–71, 2003.

33. Nattiya Kanhabua, Tu Ngoc Nguyen, and Wolfgang Nejdl. Learning to detect event-related queries for web search. In *Proceedings of the 24th International Conference on World Wide Web*, pages 1339–1344, 2015.

34. Uichin Lee, Zhenyu Liu, and Junghoo Cho. Automatic identification of user goals in web search. In *Proceedings of the 14th international conference on World Wide Web*, pages 391–400, 2005.

35. Xiao Li, Ye-Yi Wang, and Alex Acero. Learning query intent from regularized click graphs. In *Proceedings of the 31st Annual International ACM SIGIR Conference on Research and Development in Information Retrieval*, pages 339–346, 2008.

36. Xiao Li, Ye-Yi Wang, Dou Shen, and Alex Acero. Learning with click graph for query intent classification. *ACM Trans. Inf. Syst.*, 28 (3): 12:1–12:20, 2010.

37. Yiqun Liu, Min Zhang, Liyun Ru, and Shaoping Ma. Automatic query type identification based on click through information. In *Proceedings of the Third Asia Information Retrieval Symposium*, pages 593–600, 2006.

38. Yiqun Liu, Ruihua Song, Min Zhang, Zhicheng Dou, Takehiro Yamamoto, Makoto P. Kato, Hiroaki Ohshima, and Ke Zhou. Overview of the NTCIR-11 imine task. In *Proceedings of the 11th NTCIR Conference on Evaluation of Information Access Technologies*, 2014.

39. Yuchen Liu, Xiaochuan Ni, Jian-Tao Sun, and Zheng Chen. Unsupervised transactional query classification based on webpage form understanding. In *Proceedings of the 20th ACM Conference on Information and Knowledge Management*, pages 57–66, 2011.

40. Yumao Lu, Fuchun Peng, Xin Li, and Nawaaz Ahmed. Coupling feature selection and machine learning methods for navigational query identification. In *Proceedings of the 2006 ACM CIKM International Conference on Information and Knowledge Management*, pages 682–689, 2006.

41. Marcelo Mendoza and Juan Zamora. Identifying the intent of a user query using support vector machines. In *Proceedings of the 16th International Symposium on String Processing and Information Retrieval*, pages 131–142, 2009.

42. David Nettleton, Liliana Calderón-benavides, and Ricardo Baeza-yates. Analysis of web search engine query sessions. In *Proceedings of WebKDD 2006: KDD Workshop on Web Mining and Web Usage Analysis, in conjunction with the 12th ACM SIGKDD International Conference on Knowledge Discovery and Data Mining*, 2006.

43. Filip Radlinski and Susan T. Dumais. Improving personalized web search using result diversification. In *Proceedings of the 29th Annual International ACM SIGIR Conference on Research and Development in Information Retrieval*, pages 691–692, 2006.
44. Filip Radlinski, Martin Szummer, and Nick Craswell. Inferring query intent from reformulations and clicks. In *Proceedings of the 19th International Conference on World Wide Web*, pages 1171–1172, 2010.
45. Davood Rafiei, Krishna Bharat, and Anand Shukla. Diversifying web search results. In *Proceedings of the 19th International Conference on World Wide Web*, pages 781–790, 2010.
46. Karthik Raman, Paul N. Bennett, and Kevyn Collins-Thompson. Toward whole-session relevance: exploring intrinsic diversity in web search. In *Proceedings of the 36th International ACM SIGIR conference on research and development in Information Retrieval*, pages 463–472, 2013.
47. Daniel E. Rose and Danny Levinson. Understanding user goals in web search. In *Proceedings of the 13th international conference on World Wide Web*, pages 13–19, 2004.
48. Tetsuya Sakai, Zhicheng Dou, Takehiro Yamamoto, Yiqun Liu, Min Zhang, and Ruihua Song. Overview of the NTCIR-10 INTENT-2 task. In *Proceedings of the 10th NTCIR Conference on Evaluation of Information Access Technologies*, 2013.
49. Rodrygo L. T. Santos, Jie Peng, Craig Macdonald, and Iadh Ounis. Explicit search result diversification through sub-queries. In *Proceedings of the 32nd European Conference on IR Research*, pages 87–99, 2010.
50. Dou Shen, Jian-Tao Sun, Qiang Yang, and Zheng Chen. Building bridges for web query classification. In *Proceedings of the 29th Annual International ACM SIGIR Conference on Research and Development in Information Retrieval*, pages 131–138, 2006.
51. Luo Si and James P. Callan. Relevant document distribution estimation method for resource selection. In *Proceedings of the 26th Annual International ACM SIGIR Conference on Research and Development in Information Retrieval*, pages 298–305, 2003.
52. Craig Silverstein, Monika Rauch Henzinger, Hannes Marais, and Michael Moricz. Analysis of a very large web search engine query log. *SIGIR Forum*, 33 (1): 6–12, 1999.
53. Ruihua Song, Zhenxiao Luo, Jian-Yun Nie, Yong Yu, and Hsiao-Wuen Hon. Identification of ambiguous queries in web search. *Inf. Process. Manag.*, 45 (2): 216–229, 2009.
54. Ruihua Song, Min Zhang, Tetsuya Sakai, Makoto P. Kato, Yiqun Liu, Miho Sugimoto, Qinglei Wang, and Naoki Orii. Overview of the NTCIR-9 INTENT task. In *Proceedings of the 9th NTCIR Workshop Meeting on Evaluation of Information Access Technologies: Information Retrieval, Question Answering and Cross-Lingual Information Access*, 2011.
55. Markus Strohmaier, Mark Kröll, and Christian Körner. Intentional query suggestion: making user goals more explicit during search. In *Proceedings of the 2009 workshop on Web Search Click Data*, pages 68–74, 2009.
56. Gilad Tsur, Yuval Pinter, Idan Szpektor, and David Carmel. Identifying web queries with question intent. In *Proceedings of the 25th International Conference on World Wide Web*, pages 783–793, 2016.
57. Qinglei Wang, Ya-nan Qian, Ruihua Song, Zhicheng Dou, Fan Zhang, Tetsuya Sakai, and Qinghua Zheng. Mining subtopics from text fragments for a web query. *Inf. Retr.*, 16 (4): 484–503, 2013.
58. Xiao-Jie Wang, Ji-Rong Wen, Zhicheng Dou, Tetsuya Sakai, and Rui Zhang. Search result diversity evaluation based on intent hierarchies. *IEEE Trans. Knowl. Data Eng.*, 30 (1): 156–169, 2018.
59. Xuanhui Wang and ChengXiang Zhai. Learn from web search logs to organize search results. In *Proceedings of the 30th Annual International ACM SIGIR Conference on Research and Development in Information Retrieval*, pages 87–94, 2007.
60. Yu Wang and Eugene Agichtein. Query ambiguity revisited: Clickthrough measures for distinguishing informational and ambiguous queries. In *Proceedings of the Human Language Technologies: Conference of the North American Chapter of the Association of Computational Linguistics*, pages 361–364, 2010.

61. Takehiro Yamamoto, Yiqun Liu, Min Zhang, Zhicheng Dou, Ke Zhou, Ilya Markov, Makoto P. Kato, Hiroaki Ohshima, and Sumio Fujita. Overview of the NTCIR-12 imine-2 task. In *Proceedings of the 12th NTCIR Conference on Evaluation of Information Access Technologies*, 2016.
62. Xing Yi, Hema Raghavan, and Chris Leggetter. Discovering users' specific geo intention in web search. In *Proceedings of the 18th International Conference on World Wide Web*, pages 481–490, 2009.
63. Yisong Yue and Thorsten Joachims. Predicting diverse subsets using structural SVMs. In *Proceedings of the Twenty-Fifth International Conference on Machine Learning*, pages 1224–1231, 2008.
64. Juan Zamora, Marcelo Mendoza, and Héctor Allende. Query intent detection based on query log mining. *J. Web Eng.*, 13 (1&2): 24–52, 2014.
65. Hua-Jun Zeng, Qi-Cai He, Zheng Chen, Wei-Ying Ma, and Jinwen Ma. Learning to cluster web search results. In *Proceedings of the 27th Annual International ACM SIGIR Conference on Research and Development in Information Retrieval*, pages 210–217, 2004.
66. Yue Zhao and Claudia Hauff. Temporal query intent disambiguation using time-series data. In *Proceedings of the 39th International ACM SIGIR conference on Research and Development in Information Retrieval*, pages 1017–1020, 2016.
67. Ke Zhou, Ronan Cummins, Martin Halvey, Mounia Lalmas, and Joemon M. Jose. Assessing and predicting vertical intent for web queries. In *Proceedings of the 34th European Conference on IR Research*, pages 499–502, 2012.
68. Xiaojin Zhu, Andrew B. Goldberg, Jurgen Van Gael, and David Andrzejewski. Improving diversity in ranking using absorbing random walks. In *Proceedings of the Human Language Technology Conference of the North American Chapter of the Association of Computational Linguistics*, pages 97–104, 2007.

Chapter 5
Query Spelling Correction

Yanen Li

Abstract In this chapter we will focus on the discussion of an important type of query understandings: Query spelling correction, especially on the web search queries. Queries issued by web search engine users usually contain errors and misused words/phrases. Although a user might have a clear intent in her mind, inferring the query's intent in this case becomes difficult because of the edit errors or vocabulary gap between the user's ideal query and the query issued to the search engine. Because of this, query spelling correction is a crucial component of modern search engines. The performance of the query spelling correction component will affect all other parts of the search engine. In this chapter we will first introduce early works on query spelling correction based on edit distance. Then we will discuss the noisy channel model to the problem. After that we will introduce modern approaches to more complex and realistic problem setup where it involves multiple types of spelling errors. Finally we will also summarize other components needed to support a modern large-scale query spelling correction system.

5.1 Introduction

Queries issued by web search engine users usually contain errors and misused words/phrases. Recent studies show that about 10 to 12% of all query terms entered into Web search engines are misspelled [6, 7]. Although a user might have a clear intent in her mind, inferring the query's intent in this case becomes difficult because of the edit errors or vocabulary gap between the user's ideal query and the query issued to the search engine. Query reformulation is to automatically find alternative forms of a query that eliminate or reduce such gap. Effective query reformulation has been proved to be very effective in improving the performance of information retrieval. There are several types of query reformulations, including query spelling

Y. Li (✉)
LinkedIn Inc., Mountain View, CA, USA
e-mail: yanenli2@illinois.edu

© Springer Nature Switzerland AG 2020
Y. Chang, H. Deng (eds.), *Query Understanding for Search Engines*,
The Information Retrieval Series 46, https://doi.org/10.1007/978-3-030-58334-7_5

Table 5.1 Major types of query spelling errors

Type		Example	Correction
In-word	Insertion	Essspresso	Espresso
	Deletion	Vollyball	Volleyball
	Substitution	Comtemplate	Contemplate
	Transposition	Micheal	Michael
	Misuse	Capital hill	Capitol hill
Cross-word	Concatenation	Intermilan	Inter milan
	Splitting	Power point	Powerpoint

correction, query expansion, query rewriting, etc. In this chapter we focus on an important type of query reformulation—query spelling correction, especially on the web search queries which is a major interface people seek information on the web via search engines.

The ability to automatically correct misspelled queries has become an indispensable component of modern search engines. People make errors in spelling frequently. Particularly, search engine users are more likely to commit misspellings in their queries as they are in most scenarios exploring unfamiliar contents. Automatic spelling correction for queries helps the search engine to better understand the users' intents and can therefore improve the quality of search experience. However, query spelling is not an easy task, especially under the strict efficiency constraint. More importantly, people not only make typos on single words (insertion, deletion, and substitution), but can also easily mess up with word boundaries (concatenation and splitting). Moreover, different types of misspelling could be committed in the same query, making it even harder to correct. In Table 5.1 we summarize major types of misspellings in real search engine queries.

Query spelling correction has long been an important research topic [17]. Traditional spellers focused on dealing with non-word errors caused by misspelling a known word as an invalid word form. A common strategy at that time was to utilize a trusted lexicon and certain distance measures, such as Levenshtein distance [18]. The size of lexicon in traditional spellers is usually small due to the high cost of manual construction of lexicon. Consequently, many valid word forms such as human names and neologisms are rarely included in the lexicon. Later, statistical generative models were introduced for spelling correction, in which the error model and n-gram language model are identified as two critical components. Brill and Moore demonstrated that a better statistical error model is crucial for improving a speller's accuracy [3]. But building such an error model requires a large set of manually annotated word correction pairs, which is expensive to obtain. Whitelaw et al. alleviated this problem by leveraging the Web to automatically discover the misspelled/corrected word pairs [27]. Other approaches include n-grams based methods [21, 30], rule-based spelling correction systems [28], neural network based approaches [14, 22].

With the advent of the Web, the research on spelling correction has received much more attention, particularly on the correction of search engine queries.

Many research challenges are raised, which are non-existent in traditional settings of spelling correction. More specifically, as mentioned above, there are many more types of spelling errors in search queries, such as misspelling, concatenation/splitting of query words, and misuse of legitimate yet inappropriate words. Research in this direction includes utilizing large web corpora and query log [2, 4, 6], training phrase-based error model from clickthrough data [24], and developing additional features [12]. More recently, [19] addressed multi-types of spelling errors using a generalized Hidden Markov Model. And [11] addressed a similar issue via a discriminative model trained by latent structural SVM.

In the rest of this chapter we will cover the following topics: (1) early works on query spelling correction based on edit distance and the Trie data structure; (2) query spelling correction using noisy channel model; (3) modern approaches for query spelling correction with multiple types of errors; (4) structural learning approaches for query spelling correction; (5) other components for supporting a modern query spelling correction system.

5.1.1 Problem Setup and Challenges

Formally, let Σ be the alphabet of a language and $L \subset \Sigma^+$ be a large lexicon of the language. We define the query spelling correction problem as:

Given a query $q \in \Sigma^+$, generate top-K most effective corrections $C = (c^1, c^2, \ldots, c^k)$, where $c^i \in L^+$ is a candidate correction, and C is sorted according to the probability of c^i being the correct spelling of the target query.

The problem of query spelling correction—especially on the web search queries—is significantly harder than the traditional spelling correction. Previous researches show that approximately 10–15% of search queries contain spelling errors [6]. First, it is difficult to cover all the different types of errors. The spelling errors generally fall into one of the following four categories: (1) in-word transformation, e.g., insertion, deletion, misspelling of characters. This type of error is most frequent in web queries, and it is not uncommon that up to 3 or 4 letters are misspelled; (2) misuse of valid word, e.g., "persian golf" → "persian gulf." It is also a type of in-word transformation errors; (3) concatenation of multiple words, e.g., "unitedstatesofamerica" → "united states of america"; (4) splitting a word into parts, e.g., "power point slides" → "powerpoint slides." Among all these types, the splitting and concatenation errors are especially challenging to correct. Indeed, no existing approaches in the academic literature can correct these two types of errors. Yet, it is important to correct all types of errors because users might commit different types of errors or even commit these errors at the same time.

Second, it is difficult to ensure complete search of all the candidate space because the candidate space is very large. Some existing work address this challenge by using a two-stage method, which searches for a small set of candidates with simple scoring functions and does re-ranking on top of these candidates [12]. Unfortunately, the simple scoring function used in the first stage cannot ensure that the nominated candidate corrections in the first stage always contain the best correction, thus no matter how effective the final scoring function is, we may miss the best correction simply because of the use of two separate stages. More recent works addressed this problem by employing the one-stage strategy where the candidate scoring and model parameter update are conducted together in one stage [11, 19].

5.2 Early Works on Spelling Correction

Early works on spelling correction focus on single correcting spelling errors on single words [8, 18]. Early researches found that the typing errors in very large text files contributed to the majority of the wrong spellings (80–95%). And these errors are mostly within the type of in-word spelling errors [8] (see Table 5.1 and Fig. 5.1 for example). Edit distance based methods were among the most popular ones to correct such types of errors [8, 18, 26]. Edit distance, or Levenshtein distance [18], is a simple technique. The distance between two words is the number of editing operations required to transform one into another. Thus the candidate corrections contain words that differ from the original ones in a minimum number of editing operations.

5.2.1 Edit Distance with Dynamic Programming

As mentioned above, given the pattern string p and target string s, the edit distance between them is the minimum number of edit operations required to transform t into s, for example, the edit distance between "bat" and "cat" is one because there is only one edit operation needed to transform "bat" into "cat." The allowed edit operation is among the ones illustrated in Fig. 5.1. Algorithm 1 describes the dynamic programming procedure to calculate the edit distance between pattern string p and target string s. Note that in Algorithm 1 all edit operations are equally weighted. However these edit operations can be also weighted differently, thus leading to the weighted edit distance.

The dynamic programming approach of calculating the edit distance between p and s basically is to score each cell of the dynamic programming table (DP table)

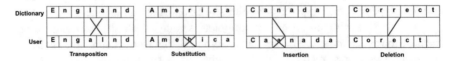

Fig. 5.1 Common types of in-word spelling errors

Algorithm 1 Edit distance between pattern string p and target string s

---

Input: Pattern string p and target string s
Output: The edit distance between p and s
1: Init Set all $m[i, j] = 0$
2: **for** $i \leftarrow 1$ **to** $|p|$ **do**
3:      $m[i, 0] = i$
4: **end for**
5: **for** $j \leftarrow 1$ **to** $|s|$ **do**
6:      $m[0, j] = j$
7: **end for**
8: **for** $i \leftarrow 1$ **to** $|p|$ **do**
9:      **for** $j \leftarrow 1$ **to** $|s|$ **do**
10:         $t = (p[i] == s[j])?0 : 1$
11:         $m[i, j] = \min\{m[i - 1, j - 1] + t, m[i - 1, j] + 1, m[i, j - 1] + 1\}$
12:     **end for**
13: **end for**
14: **return** $m[|p|, |s|]$

Fig. 5.2 Edit distance calculation example

	s	a	m	p	l	e	
	0	1	2	3	4	5	6
e	1	1	2	3	4	5	5
x	2	2	2	3	4	5	6
a	3	3	2	3	4	5	6
m	4	4	3	2	3	4	5
p	5	5	4	3	2	3	4
l	6	6	5	4	3	2	3
e	7	7	6	5	4	3	2

of the dimension of ($|p| \cdot |s|$). Figure 5.2 shows an example of a DP table so as to illustrate the scoring process. A typical cell $[i, j]$ has four entries formatted as a 2×2 cell. The lower right entry in each cell is the minimum value of the other three. The other three entries are $m[i - 1, j - 1] + 0$ or $m[i - 1, j - 1] + 1$ depending on whether $s_1[i] == s_2[j]$ (diagonal entry), $m[i - 1, j] + 1$ (left entry), and $m[i, j - 1] + 1$ (upper entry). Finally the value at the far most right corner cell determines the edit distance between two input strings.

5.2.2 Spelling Correction Search over a Trie

For the purpose of query spelling correction, given a potentially misspelled pattern string, we were to look for all possible correction candidates in the dictionary that are within k edit distance of the pattern string. However, to search all such target strings by comparing the pattern string p to each of the target string in a dictionary is too time-consuming. Researches in [23] and [25] found that it is much more efficient to look for target strings within k edit distance of p using dynamic programming over a Trie. Trie is a tree-like data structure that can represent a dictionary of target strings in a very compact way. Given a dictionary of words "enfold sample enface same example," there will be six branches in the Trie, as illustrated in Fig. 5.3.

Notice that the common prefixes of all strings in the Trie are stored only once, which gives substantial data compression, and are important when indexing a very large dictionary. Because of this characteristic of a Trie, searching all target strings that are within k edit distance of a pattern string can be done in $O(k \cdot |\Sigma|^k)$ expected worst time. The search time is independent of n, the number of words in the Trie. Before introducing the actual algorithm, let us talk about two key observations that lay the foundation of this efficient algorithm:

- Observation I (column sharing): Each Trie branch is a prefix shared by all strings in the subtrie. When evaluating the dynamic programming (DP) tables for these strings, we will have identical columns up to the prefix. Therefore, these columns need to be evaluated only once.
- Observation II (early termination): If all entries of a column in the DP table are > k, no word with the same prefix can have an edit distance $\leq k$. Therefore, we can stop searching down the subtrie. This observation is implemented in Ukkonen's algorithm as "Ukkonen's Cutoff" [25].

Fig. 5.3 Strings in a Trie. Note: sistrings are suffix strings of the original text. For instance, *example* is a subfix string of *same example*

```
Text:
    echo enfold sample enface same example

Sistrings:
    echo enfold sample enface same example
    enfold sample enface same example
    sample enface same example
    enface same example
    same example
    example
```

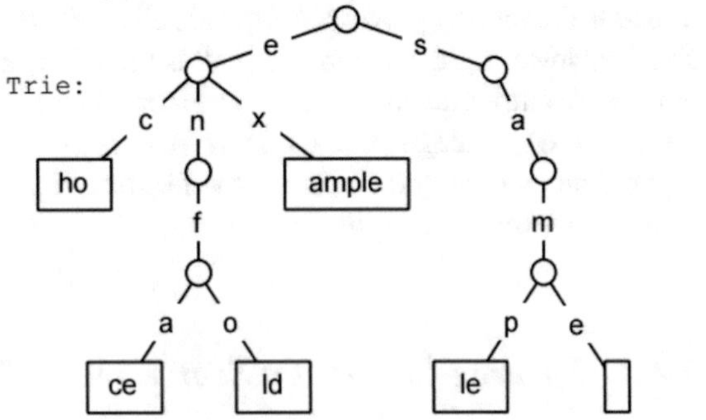

The search algorithm for searching all spelling corrections that are $\leq k$ edit distance of the misspelled pattern string p is described in Fig. 5.4. Please refer to [23] for more details.

5.3 Noisy Channel Model

Query spelling correction has become a crucial component in modern information systems. Particularly, search engine users rely heavily on the query correction mechanism to formulate effective queries. Given a user query q, which is potentially misspelled, the goal of query spelling correction is to find a correction of the query c that could lead to better search experience. A typical query spelling correction system employs a noisy channel model [16]. Figure 5.5 in [15] illustrates the idea of the noisy channel model for query spelling correction. The model assumes that the correct query c is formed in the user's mind before entering the noisy channels, e.g., typing, and gets misspelled. This channel introduces "noise" in the form of insertion/deletion/substitution or other types of changes to the original query, making it hard to recognize the original words in the query. So the motivation of the query spelling correction via noisy channel model is to build a model of the channel such that the original, un-misspelled query can be recovered correctly by the model. Usually the noisy channel model will have two major components, one is to measure the likelihood of transforming the corrected query c to the corrupted query, which is called error model. The other is the soundness of the corrected query c, which is called the prior.

Formally, the model maximizes the posterior probability $p(c|q)$:

$$\hat{c} = \arg\max_c p(c|q). \tag{5.1}$$

Applying Bayes rule, the formulation can be rewritten as:

$$\begin{aligned} \hat{c} &= \arg\max_c p(q|c)p(c) \\ &= \arg\max_c [\log p(q|c) + \log p(c)]. \end{aligned} \tag{5.2}$$

The model uses two probabilities. The prior probability $p(c)$ represents how likely it is that c is the original correct query in the user's mind. The probability is usually modeled by a language model estimated from a sizable corpus, such as unigram, bigram, or trigram model. For example, for the misspelled query "aple sotre in los angeles," one correction candidate is "apple store in los angeles." The

```
/* T :array [-1..max,-1..max] of integer; [i,0]=[0,j]=i+j,
   [-1,]=[,-1]=∞                                                    */
/* C :array [0..max] of integer; variables for Ukkonen's
   cutoff, C[0]=k                                                   */
/* P,W :array [0..max] of character; pattern and target
   string, W[0]=P[0]=ø                                             */
/* k :integer; number of allowable errors                         */
/* depth-first trie search                                        */
```

DFSearch(TrieNode : Anode, Level : integer)
if *(TrieNode in a leaf node)* **then**
> **for** *each character in the node* **do**
>> ```
>> /* retrieve characters one by one                          */
>> ```
>> W[Level] := the retrieved character;
>> **if** *(W[Level] = ' ')* **then**
>>> ```
>>> /* find a target word                                  */
>>> ```
>>> output W[1]W[2]...W[j-1]
>>> return;
>>
>> **if** *(EditDist(Level) = ∞)* **then**
>>> ```
>>> /* more than k mistakes                                */
>>> ```
>>> *return;*
>>
>> *Level := Level + 1;*

else
> **for** *each child node* **do**
>> ```
>> /* retrieve child node one by one                          */
>> ```
>> ChildNode := the retrieved node;
>> W[Level] := the retrieved character;
>> **if** *(W[Level] = ' ')* **then**
>>> ```
>>> /* find a target word                                  */
>>> ```
>>> output W[1]W[2]...W[j-1]
>>> return;
>>
>> **if** *(EditDist(Level) = ∞)* **then**
>>> ```
>>> /* cut off here! don't search subtrie down              */
>>> ```
>>> *return;*
>>
>> ```
>> /* search down the subtrie                                 */
>> ```
>> *DFSearch(ChildNode, Level+1)*
```

---

```
1 FunctionEditDist( j : integer) : integer
  /* evaluate one column of DP table                              */
  C[j] :=0;
  for i :=1 to Min(C[j-1]+1, length(p)) do
      /* evaluate one table entry                                 */
      s := if (P[i]=W[j]) then 0 else 1;
      r =: if (P[i-1]=W[j] and P[i]=W[j-1] then 1 else ∞
      T[i,j] := Min(T[i,j-1]+1, T[i-1,j]+1, T[i-1,j-1]+s, T[i-2,j-2]+r);
      C[j] := if (T[i,j]) ≤ k)thenielseC[j]
      return (if (C[j]=0) then ∞ else T[i-1,j]);
```

Fig. 5.4 Spelling correction search over a Trie
```

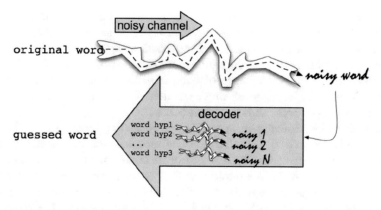

Fig. 5.5 The noisy channel model

prior probability $p(c)$ of this correction can be measured by the bigram probability as:

$$p(c) = p(apple) \cdot p(store|apple) \cdot p(in|store) \cdot p(los|in) \cdot p(angeles|los). \tag{5.3}$$

The transformation probability $p(q|c)$ measures how likely it is that q is the output given that c has been formed by the user. This probability can be either heuristic-based (edit distance) or learned from samples of well-aligned corrections. For example, $p(aple|apple)$ can be estimated by the normalized number of times that the word "apple" is misspelled as "aple" in a large corpus of paired corrected query and misspelled query.

One problem with the noisy channel model is that there is no weighting for the two kinds of probabilities, and since they are estimated from different sources, there are usually issues regarding their scale and comparability, resulting in suboptimal performance [12]. Another limitation of this generative model is that it is not able to take advantage of additional useful features.

5.4   Query Spelling Correction with Multiple Types of Errors

As mentioned in the introduction, users not only make typos on single words, but can also easily mess up with word boundaries (concatenation and splitting). Moreover, different types of misspelling could be committed in the same query, making it even harder to correct. Despite its importance, few query spelling correction approaches in the literature are able to correct all major types of errors, especially for correcting splitting and concatenation errors. The only work that can potentially address this problem is [13] in which a conditional random field (CRF) model is proposed to handle a broad set of query refinements. However, this work considers query correction and splitting/merging as different tasks, hence it is unable to correct queries with mixed types of errors, such as substitution and splitting errors in one query. In fact splitting and merging are two important error types in query spelling correction, and a major challenge of query spelling correction is to accurately correct all major types of errors simultaneously. We summarize the major types of query spelling errors as shown in Table 5.1.

Another major difficulty in automatic query spelling correction is the huge search space. Theoretically, any sequence of characters could potentially be the correction of a misspelled query. It is clearly intractable to enumerate and evaluate all possible sequences for the purpose of finding the correct query. Thus a more feasible strategy is to search in a space of all combinations of candidate words that are in a neighborhood of each query word based on edit distance. The assumption is that a user's spelling error of each single word is unlikely too dramatic, thus the correction is most likely in the neighborhood by edit distance. Unfortunately, even in this restricted space, the current approaches still cannot enumerate and evaluate all the candidates because their scoring functions involve complex features that are expensive to compute. As a result, a separate filtering step must first be used to prune the search space so that the final scoring can be done on a small working set of candidates. Take [12] as a two-stage method example, in the first stage, a Viterbi or A* search algorithm is used to generate a small set of most promising candidates, and in the second stage different types of features of the candidates are computed and a ranker is employed to score the candidates. However, this two-stage strategy has a major drawback in computing the complete working set. Since the filtering stage uses a non-optimal objective function to ensure efficiency, it is quite possible that the best candidate is filtered out in the first stage, especially because we cannot afford a large working set since the correction must be done online while a user is entering a query. The inability of searching the complete space of candidates leads to non-optimal correction accuracy.

In this chapter, we are going to introduce the work of [19] which describes a generalized Hidden Markov Model (gHMM) for query spelling correction. This approach can address the deficiencies of the approaches discussed above. The gHMM model can model all major types of spelling errors, thus enabling consideration of multiple types of errors in query spelling correction. In the gHMM model, the hidden states represent the correct forms of words, and the outcomes are the observed misspelled terms. In addition, each state is associated with a type, indicating merging, splitting, or in-word transformation operation. This Hidden Markov Model is generalized in the sense that it would allow adjustment of both emission probabilities and transition probabilities to accommodate the non-optimal parameter estimation. Unfortunately, such an extension of HMM makes it impossible to use a standard EM algorithm for parameter estimation. To solve this problem, in [19] they proposed a perceptron-based discriminative training method to train the parameters in the HMM.

We will also describe the Viterbi-like search algorithm in [19] for top-K paths to efficiently obtain a small number of highly confident correction candidates. This algorithm can handle splitting/merging of multiple words. It takes into account major types of local features such as error model, language model, and state type information. The error model is trained on a large set of query-correction pairs from the web. And web scale language model is obtained by leveraging the Microsoft Web N-gram service [1].

5.4.1   A Generalized HMM for Query Spelling Correction

Now we are going to introduce the query spelling correction model and algorithm proposed in [19]. This algorithm accepts a query as input and then generates a small list of ranked corrections as output by a generalized Hidden Markov Model (gHMM). It is trained by a discriminative method with labeled spelling examples. Given a query, it scores candidate spelling corrections in a one-stage fashion and outputs the top-K corrections, without using a re-ranking strategy. Other components of this algorithm include a large clean lexicon, the error model, and the language model. In this section we will focus on the gHMM model structure, the discriminative training of it, as well as the efficient computation of spelling corrections.

Let us start by describing the gHMM Model Structure. Let an input query be $q = q_{[1:n]}$ and a corresponding correction be $c = c_{[1:m]}$ where n, m are the length of the query and correction, which might or might not be equal. Here we introduce hidden state sequence $z = z_{[1:n]} = (s_1, s_2, \ldots, s_n)$ in which z and q have the same length. An individual state s_i is represented by a phrase corresponding to one or more terms in correction $c_{[1:m]}$. Together the phrase representing z is equal to c. Therefore, finding best-K corrections $C = (c^1, c^2, \ldots, c^k)$ is equivalent to finding best-K state sequences $Z = (z^1, z^2, \ldots, z^k)$. In addition, there is a type t associated with each state, indicating the operation such as substitution, splitting, merging, etc. Also, in order to facilitate the merging state we introduce a NULL state. The NULL state is represented by an empty string, and it does not emit any phrase. There can be multiple consecutive NULL states followed by a merging state. Table 5.2 summarizes the state types and the spelling errors they correspond to. Having the

Table 5.2 State types in gHMM

State type	Operation	Spelling errors
In-word transformation	Deletion	Insertion
	Insertion	Deletion
	Substitution	Substitution
Misuse	Transformation	Word misuse
Merging	Merge multiple words	Splitting
Splitting	Split one word to multiple words	Concatenation

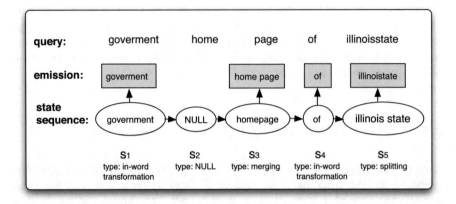

Fig. 5.6 Example of the gHMM model

hidden states defined, the hypothesized process of observing a misspelled query is as follows:

1. sample a state s_1 and state type t_1 from the state space Ω and the typeset T;
2. emit a word in q_1, or empty string if the s_1 is a NULL state according to the type specific error model;
3. transit to s_2 with type t_2 according to the state transition distribution, and emit another word, or multiple words in $q_{[1:n]}$ if s_2 is a merging state;
4. continue until the whole misspelled query q is observed.

Figure 5.6 illustrates the gHMM model with a concrete example. In this example, there are three errors with different error types, e.g., "goverment" → "government" (substitution), "home page" → "homepage" (splitting), "illinoisstate" → "illinois state" (concatenation). The state path shown in Fig. 5.6 is one of the state sequences that can generate the query. Take state s_3, for example, s_3 is represented by phrase *homepage*. Because s_3 is a merging state, it emits a phrase *home page* with probability $P(home\ page|homepage)$. And s_3 is transited from state s_2 with probability $P(s_3|s_2)$. With this model, it is able to come up with arbitrary corrections instead of limiting ourselves to an incomprehensive set of queries from query log. By simultaneously modeling the misspellings on word boundaries, it is able to correct the query in a more integrated manner.

5.4.2 Generalization of HMM Scoring Function

For a standard HMM [20], let $\theta = \{A, B, \pi\}$ be the model parameters of the HMM, representing the transition probability, emission probabilities, and initial state probabilities, respectively. Given a list of query words $q_{[1:n]}$ (obtained by splitting empty spaces), the state sequence $z^* = (s_1^*, s_2^*, \ldots, s_n^*)$ that best explains

$q_{[1:n]}$ can be calculated by

$$z^* = \arg\max_z P(z|q_{[1:n]}, A, B, \pi). \qquad (5.4)$$

However, theoretically the phrase in a state can be chosen arbitrarily, so estimating $\{A, B, \pi\}$ in such a large space is almost impossible in the standard HMM framework. In order to overcome this difficulty, the gHMM model generalizes the standard HMM as follows: (1) gHMM introduces state type for each state, which indicates the correction operations and can reduce the search space effectively; (2) it adopts feature functions to parameterize the measurement of probability of a state sequence given a query. Such treatment can not only map the transition and emission probabilities to feature functions with a small set of parameters, but can also add additional feature functions such as the ones incorporating state type information. Another important benefit of the feature function representation is that we can use discriminative training on the model with labeled spelling corrections, which will lead to a more accurate estimation of the parameters.

Formally, in gHMM model, there is a one-to-one relationship between states in a state sequence and words in the original query. For a given query $q = q_{[1:n]}$ and the sequence of states $z = (s_1, s_2, \ldots, s_n)$, we define a context h_i for every state in which an individual correction decision is made. The context is defined as $h_i = < s_{i-1}, t_{i-1}, s_i, t_i, q_{[1:n]} >$, where $s_{i-1}, t_{i-1}, s_i, t_i$ are the previous and current state and type decisions and $q_{[1:n]}$ are all query words.

The gHMM model measures the probability of a state sequence by defining feature vectors on the context-state pairs. A feature vector is a function that maps a context-state pair to a d-dimensional vector. Each component of the feature vector is an arbitrary function operated on (h, z). Particularly, [19] defines 2 kinds of feature vectors, one is $\phi_j(s_{i-1}, t_{i-1}, s_i, t_i)$, $j = 1 \ldots d$, which measures the interdependency of adjacent states. We can treat such function as a kind of transition probability measurement. The other kind of feature function, $f_k(s_i, t_i, q_{[1:n]})$, $k = 1 \ldots d'$ measures the dependency of the state and its observation. We can consider it as a kind of emission probability in the standard HMM point of view. Such feature vector representation of HMM had been introduced by Collins [5] and successfully applied to the POS tagging problem.

Here are some examples of the feature functions. We can define a function of $\phi(s_{i-1}, t_{i-1}, s_i, t_i)$ as

$$\phi_1(s_{i-1}, t_{i-1}, s_i, t_i) = \log P_{LM}(s_i|s_{i-1}, t_{i-1}, t_i) \qquad (5.5)$$

to measure the language model probabilities of two consecutive states. Where $P_{LM}(s_i|s_{i-1})$ is the bigram probability calculated by using Microsoft Web N-gram Service [1]. The computation of $P_{LM}(s_i|s_{i-1})$ may depend on the state types, such as in a merging state.

We can also define a set of functions in the form of $f_k(s_i, t_i, q_{[1:n]})$, which depend on the query words and state type. They measure the emission probability of a state.

For example, we define

$$f_1(s_i, t_i, q_{[1:n]}) = \begin{cases} log\, P_{err}(s_i, q_i) & \text{if } q_i \text{ is in-word transformed to } s_i \\ & \textbf{and } q_i \notin \text{Lexicon } L \\ 0 & \text{otherwise} \end{cases} \qquad (5.6)$$

as a function measuring the emission probability given the state type is in-word transformation and q_i is out of dictionary, e.g., "goverment" $\rightarrow$ "government." $P_{err}(s_i, q_i)$ is the emission probability computed by an error model which measures the probability of mistyping "government" to "goverment." We define

$$f_2(s_i, t_i, q_{[1:n]}) = \begin{cases} log\, P_{err}(s_i, q_i) & \text{if } t_i \text{ is splitting } \textbf{and } q_i \in \text{Lexicon } L \\ 0 & \text{otherwise} \end{cases} \qquad (5.7)$$

to capture the emission probability if the state is of splitting type and q_i is in dictionary, e.g., "homepage" $\rightarrow$ "home page." And define

$$f_3(s_i, t_i, q_{[1:n]}) = \begin{cases} log\, P_{err}(s, q_i) & \text{if } t_i \text{ is Misuse } \textbf{and } q_i \in \text{Lexicon } L \\ 0 & \text{otherwise} \end{cases} \qquad (5.8)$$

to get the emission probability if a valid word is transformed to another valid word.

Note that in the above equations we use the same error model $P_{err}(s_i, q_i)$ to model the emission probabilities from merging, splitting errors, etc. in the same way as in-word transformation errors. However we assign different weights to the transformation probabilities resulted from different error types via discriminative training on a set of labeled query-correction pairs.

Overall, we have introduced a set of feature functions that are all relied on local dependencies, ensuring that the top-K state sequences can be computed efficiently by dynamic programming. With this feature vector representation, the log-probability of a state sequence and its corresponding types $log\, P(z, t|q_{[1:n]})$ is proportional to:

$$Score(z, t) = \sum_{i=1}^{n} \sum_{j=1}^{d} \lambda_j \phi_j (s_{i-1}, t_{i-1}, s_i, t_i) \qquad (5.9)$$

$$+ \sum_{i=1}^{n} \sum_{k=1}^{d'} \mu_k f_k (s_i, t_i, q_{[1:n]}),$$

where λ_j, μ_k are the coefficients needed to be estimated. And the best state sequence can be found by

$$z^* t^* = \arg\max_{z,t} Score(z, t). \qquad (5.10)$$

5.4.3 Discriminative Training

Now let us introduce the perceptron algorithm (Algorithm 2) used to train the gHMM model in [19], which is similar to [5]. We will first describe how to estimate the parameters λ_j, μ_k from a set of <query, spelling correction> pairs. The estimation procedure follows the perceptron learning framework. Take the λ_j for example. We first set all the λ_j at random. For each query q, we search for the most likely state sequence with types $z^i_{[1:n_i]}, t^i_{[1:n_i]}$ using the current parameter settings. Such search process is described in Algorithm 3 by setting $K = 1$. After that, if the best decoded sequence is not correct, we update λ_j by simple addition: we promote the amount of λ_j by adding up ϕ_j values computed between the query and labeled correction c', and demote the amount of λ_j by the sum of all ϕ_j values computed between the query and the top-ranked predictions. We repeat this process for several iterations until converge. Finally in steps 17 and 18, we average all $\lambda_j^{o,i}$ in each iteration to get the final estimate of λ_j, where $\lambda_j^{o,i}$ is the stored value for the parameter λ_j after i's training example is processed in iteration o. Similar procedures can apply to μ_k. The detailed steps are listed in Algorithm 2. Note that in steps 9 and 10 the feature functions $\phi_j(q^i, c'^i, t'^i)$ and $f_k(q^i, c'^i, t'^i)$ depend on unknown types t'^i that are inferred by computing the best word-level alignment between q^i and c'^i. This discriminative training algorithm will converge after several iterations.

5.4.4 Query Correction Computation

Once the optimal parameters are obtained by the discriminative training procedure introduced above, the final top-K corrections can be directly computed. Because the feature functions are only relied on local dependencies, it enables the efficient search of top-K corrections via dynamic programming. This procedure involves three major steps: (1) candidate states generation; (2) score function evaluation; (3) filtering.

At the first step, for each word in query q, we generate a set of state candidates with types. The phrase representations in such states are in Lexicon L and within edit distance δ from the query word. Then a set of state sequences are created by combining these states. In addition, for each state sequence we have created, we also create another state sequence by adding a NULL state at the end, facilitating a (potential) following merging state. It is important to note that if the δ is too small, it will compromise the final results due to the premature pruning of state sequences.

At the score function evaluation step, we update the scores for each state sequence according to Eq. (5.9). The evaluation is different for sequence with different ending state types. Firstly, for a sequence ending with a NULL state, we do not evaluate the scoring function. Instead, we only need to keep track of the state representation of its previous state. Secondly, for a sequence ending with a merging

---

Algorithm 2 Discriminative training of gHMM

Input: A set of <query, spelling correction> pairs $q^i_{[1:n_i]}, c'^i_{[1:m_i]}$ for $i = 1...n$

Output: Optimal estimate of $\hat{\lambda}_j, \hat{\mu}_k$, where $j \in \{1, ..., d\}, k \in \{1, ..., d'\}$

1: Init Set $\hat{\lambda}_j, \hat{\mu}_k$ to random numbers;
2: **for** $o \leftarrow 1$ **to** O **do**
3:    **for** $i \leftarrow 1$ **to** n **do**
4:       `/* identify the best state sequence and the associated`
      `types of the i'th query with the current parameters via`
      `Algorithm 3: */`
5:       $z^i_{[1:n_i]}, t^i_{[1:n_i]} = \arg\max_{u_{[1:n_i]}, t_{[1:n_i]}} Score(u, t)$
6:       `/* where ` $u_{[1:n_i]} \in \mathbb{S}^{n_i}, \mathbb{S}^{n_i}$ ` is all possible state sequences given`
      $q^i_{[1:n_i]}$ `*/`
7:       **if** $z^i_{[1:n_i]} \neq c'^i_{[1:m_i]}$ **then**
8:          update and store every λ_j, μ_k according to:
9:          $\lambda_j = \lambda_j + \sum_{i=1}^{n_i} \phi_j(q^i, c'^i, t'^i) - \sum_{i=1}^{n_i} \phi_j(q^i, z^i, t^i)$
10:         $\mu_k = \mu_k + \sum_{i=1}^{n_i} f_k(q^i, c'^i, t'^i) - \sum_{i=1}^{n_i} f_k(q^i, z^i, t^i)$
11:       **else**
12:          Do nothing
13:       **end if**
14:    **end for**
15: **end for**
16: `/* Average the final parameters by: */`
17: $\hat{\lambda}_j = \sum_{o=1}^{O} \sum_{i=1}^{n} \lambda_j^{o,i}/nO$, where $j \in \{1, ..., d\}$
18: $\hat{\mu}_k = \sum_{o=1}^{O} \sum_{i=1}^{n} \mu_k^{o,i}/nO$, where $k \in \{1, ..., d'\}$
19: **return** parameters $\hat{\lambda}_j, \hat{\mu}_k$;

---

state, it merges the previous one or more consecutive NULL states. And the scoring function takes into account the information stored in the previous NULL states. For instance, to $\phi_1(s_{i-1}, t_{i-1} = NULL, s_i, t_i = merging)$, we have

$$\phi_1(s_{i-1}, \text{NULL}, s_i, \text{merging}) = log\, P_{LM}(s_{i-2}|s_i) \qquad (5.11)$$

i.e., skipping the NULL state and pass the previous state representation to the merging state. In this way, we can evaluate the scoring function in multiple consecutive NULL states followed by a merging state, which enables the correction by merging multiple query words. Thirdly, for a sequence ending with a splitting state, the score is accumulated by all bigrams within the splitting state. For example,

$$\phi_1(s_{i-1}, t_{i-1}, s_i, t_i = splitting) = log\, P_{LM}(w_1|s_{i-1}) + \sum_{j=1}^{k-1} log\, P_{LM}(w_{i+1}|w_i), \qquad (5.12)$$

where $s_i = w_1 w_2 \ldots w_k$. Conversely, the evaluation of $f_k(s_i, t_i, q_{[1:n]})$ is easier because it is not related to previous states. The error model from the state representation to the query word is used to calculate these functions.

Algorithm 3 Decoding top-K corrections

Input: A query $q_{[1:n]}$, parameters λ, μ

Output: top K state sequences with highest likelihood

```
/* Z[i,si]: top-K state sequences for sub-query q[1:i] that ending
with
```
state s_i. For each $z \in Z[i, s_i]$, *phrase* denotes the representation and *score* denotes the likelihood of z given $q_{[1:i]}$. */

```
/* Z[i]: top state sequences for all Z[i,si]. */
```

1: Init $Z[0] = \{\}$
2: **for** $i \leftarrow 1$ **to** n **do**
3:     /* for term q_i, get all candidate states */
4:     $S \leftarrow s_i, \forall s_i : edit\_dist(s_i, q_i) \leq \delta, s_i$ has type $s_i.type$
5:     **for** $s_i \in S$ **do**
6:         **for** $z \in Z[i-1]$ **do**
7:             $a \leftarrow$ new state sequence
8:             $a.phrase \leftarrow z.phrase \cup \{s_i\}$
9:             update $a.score$ according to $s_i.type$ and Eq. (5.9), Eq. (5.11) and Eq. (5.12)
10:            $Z[i, s_i] \leftarrow a$
11:        **end for**
12:        /* delay truncation for *NULL* states */
13:        **if** $s_i.type \neq NULL$ and $i \neq n$ **then**
14:            sort $Z[i, s_i]$ by *score*
15:            truncate $Z[i, s_i]$ to size K
16:        **end if**
17:    **end for**
18: **end for**
19: sort $Z[n]$ by *score*
20: truncate $Z[n]$ to size K
21: **return** $Z[n]$;

At the final step, we filter most of the state sequences and only keep top-K best state sequences in each position corresponding to each query word. Algorithm 3 summarizes the core steps for efficiently computing top-K state sequences (corrections). If there are n words in a query, and the maximum number of candidate states for each query word is M, the computational complexity for finding top-K corrections is $O(n \cdot K \cdot M^2)$.

5.5 Structural Learning Approaches for Query Spelling Correction

In the previous chapter, we introduce the work of [19] that can correct all major types of query spelling errors. In order to infer the best correction, a discriminative approach using Perceptron is used for training the model coefficients. The query spelling correction problem is a typical structural learning problem with latent variables. There are more advanced techniques for discriminative training of such learning problems, such as latent structural SVM [29]. Here we introduce another work that first applies the latent structural SVM to the problem of query spelling correction. With this discriminative model, we can directly optimize the search phase of query spelling correction without loss of efficiency.

5.5.1 The Discriminative Form of Query Spelling Correction

In query spelling correction, given a user entered query q, which is potentially misspelled, the goal is to find a correction c, such that it could be a more effective query which improves the quality of search results. A general discriminative formulation of the problem is of the following form:

$$f(q) = \arg max_{c \in \mathcal{V}_*}[w \cdot \Psi(q, c)], \tag{5.13}$$

where $\Psi(q, c)$ is a vector of features and w is the model parameter. This discriminative formulation is more general compared to the noisy channel model. It has the flexibility of using features and applying weights. The noisy channel model is a special case of the discriminative form where only two features, the source probability and the transformation probability, are used and uniform weightings are applied. However, this problem formulation does not give us much insight on how to proceed to design the model. Especially, it is unclear how $\Psi(q, c)$ can be computed.

To enhance the formulation, we explore the fact that spelling correction follows a word-by-word procedure. Let us first consider a scenario where word boundary error does not exist. In this scenario, each query term matches and only matches to a single term in the correction. Formally, let us denote $q = q_1, \ldots, q_n$ and $c = c_1, \ldots, c_m$ as structured objects from the space of $\mathcal{V}^*$, where $\mathcal{V}$ is our vocabulary of words and $\mathcal{V}^*$ is all possible phrases formed by words in $\mathcal{V}$. Both q and c have an intrinsic sequential structure. When no word boundary error exists, $|c| = |q|$ holds for any candidate correction c. q_i and c_i establish a one-to-one mapping. In this case, we have a more detailed discriminative form:

$$f(q) = \arg max_{c \in \mathcal{V}^{|q|}}[w \cdot (\Psi_0 + \sum_{i=1}^{|q|} \Psi_1(q_i, c_i))], \tag{5.14}$$

where Ψ_0 is a vector of normalizing factors, $\Psi_1(q_i, c_i)$ is the decomposed computation of $\Psi(q, c)$ for each query term q_i and c_i, for $i = 1$ to $|q|$.

However, merging and splitting errors are quite common in misspelling. So the assumption of one-to-one mapping does not hold in practice. In order to address these word boundary errors, we introduce a latent variable a to model the unobserved structural information. More specifically, $a = a_1, a_2, \ldots a_{|a|}$ is the alignment between q and c. Each alignment node a_t is represented by a quadruple $(q_{start}, q_{end}, c_{start}, c_{end})$. Figure 5.7 shows a common merge error and its best

Fig. 5.7 Example of merge
error and alignment

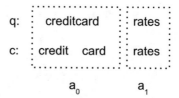

alignment. The phrase "credit card," in this case, is incorrectly merged into one
word "creditcard" by the user.

Taking into consideration the latent variable, the discriminative form of query
spelling correction becomes

$$
\begin{aligned}
f(q) &= \arg max_{(c,a) \in \mathcal{V}^n \times \mathcal{A}} [w \cdot \Psi(q, c, a)] \\
&= \arg max_{(c,a) \in \mathcal{V}^* \times \mathcal{A}} [w \cdot (\Psi_0 + \sum_{t=0}^{|a|} \Psi_1(q_{a_t}, c_{a_t}, a_t))].
\end{aligned}
\tag{5.15}
$$

The challenges of successfully applying a discriminative model to this problem
formulation are (1) how can we design a learning algorithm to learn the model
parameter w to directly optimize the maximization problem; (2) how can we solve
the maximization efficiently without having to enumerate all candidates; (3) how
can we design features to guarantee the correctness of the search algorithm.

5.5.2   Latent Structural SVM

Here we describe how [11] applies the latent structural SVM (LS-SVM) model for
learning the discriminative model of query spelling correction. LS-SVM is a large
margin method that deals with structured prediction problems with latent structural
information [29]. LS-SVM has the merit of allowing task specific, customizable
solutions for the inference problem. This makes it easy to adapt to learning the
model parameters for different problems. Let us first give a brief introduction of
LS-SVM.

Without loss of generality, let us aim at learning a prediction function $f : \mathcal{X} \to \mathcal{Y}$
that maps input $x \in \mathcal{X}$ to an output $y \in \mathcal{Y}$ with latent structural information $h \in \mathcal{H}$.
The decision function is of the following form:

$$
f(x) = \arg max_{(y,h) \in \mathcal{Y} \times \mathcal{H}} [w \cdot \Psi(x, y, h)],
\tag{5.16}
$$

where $\Psi(x, y, h)$ is the set of feature functions defined jointly over the input x, the
output y, and the latent variable h. w is the parameter of the model. Given a set
of training examples that consist of input and output pairs $\{(x_1, y_1), \ldots (x_n, y_n)\} \in$

$(\mathcal{X} \times \mathcal{Y})^n$, the LS-SVM method solves the following optimization problem:

$$
\begin{aligned}
min_w & \frac{1}{2}\|w\|^2 \\
&+C \sum_{i=1}^{n} \max_{(\hat{y},\hat{h})\in\mathcal{Y}\times\mathcal{H}} [w \cdot \Psi(x_i, \hat{y}, \hat{h}) + \Delta(y_i, \hat{y})] \\
&-C \sum_{i=1}^{n} \max_{h\in\mathcal{H}}[w \cdot \Psi(x_i, y_i, h)],
\end{aligned}
\tag{5.17}
$$

where $\Delta(y_i, \hat{y})$ is the loss function for the i-th example. The details of the derivation are omitted in this paper. Readers who are interested can read more from [29].

There are two maximization problems that are essential in Eq. (5.17). The first one is the loss augmented decision function:

$$
\max_{(\hat{y},\hat{h})\in\mathcal{Y}\times\mathcal{H}} [w \cdot \Psi(x_i, \hat{y}, \hat{h}) + \Delta(y_i, \hat{y})],
\tag{5.18}
$$

and the second is the inference of latent variable given the label of the training data:

$$
\max_{h\in\mathcal{H}}[w \cdot \Psi(x_i, y_i, h)].
\tag{5.19}
$$

The latent structural SVM framework does not specify how the maximization problems in Eqs. (5.18) and (5.19) are solved, as well as the inference problem in 5.16. Being able to efficiently solve maximization problems is the key to successfully applying the latent structural SVM method.

For training the LS-SVM model, a concave–convex procedure (CCCP) was proposed to solve this optimization problem [29]. The method resembles the expectation–maximization (EM) training method as it updates the model by iteratively recomputing the latent variable. However, rather than performing "sum-product" training as in EM where a distribution over the hidden variable is maintained, the CCCP method used for LS-SVM is more similar to the "max-product" paradigm where we "guess" the best hidden variable in each iteration, except here we "guess" by minimizing a regularized loss function instead of maximizing the likelihood.

5.5.3 Query Spelling Correct Inference by LS-SVM

The inference problem in query spelling correction is to find the correction that maximizes the scoring function according to the model (i.e., the decision function in Eq. (5.16)). For this purpose we design a best first search algorithm similar to the standard search algorithm in the noisy channel model. The essence of the search

---

Algorithm 4 Best first search algorithm

Input: Vocabulary Trie V, query q, output size k, max order m, candidate pool size n
Output: List l of top k corrections for q

1: Initialize List l;
2: Initialize PriorityQueue pq;
3: Enqueue to pq a start path with position set to 0, string set to empty string, score set to $w \cdot \Psi_0$, and path alignment set to empty set;
4: **while** pq is not Empty **do**
5:    Path $\pi \leftarrow pq$.Dequeue();
6:    **if** π.pos $<$ q.terms.length **then**
7:       **for** $i \leftarrow 0$ **to** m **do**
8:          $ph \leftarrow q.terms[\pi.pos + 1...\pi.pos + i]$;
9:          $sug \leftarrow$ GetSuggestions(ph, V, n);
10:         **for** each s in sug **do**
11:            $pos' \leftarrow \pi.pos + i$;
12:            $str' \leftarrow concat(\pi.str, s.str)$;
13:            $a' \leftarrow \pi.a \cup s.a$;
14:            $sc' \leftarrow \pi.sc + w \cdot \Psi_1(q_{s.a}, c_{s.a}, s.a)$;
15:            Enqueue pq with the new path (pos', str', sc', a');
16:         **end for**
17:      **end for**
18:   **else**
19:      Add suggestion string $\pi.str$ to l;
20:      **if** l.Count $> $ k **then**
21:         **return** l;
22:      **end if**
23:   **end if**
24: **end while**
25: **return** l;

---

algorithm is to bound the score of each candidate so that we could evaluate the most promising candidates first. The algorithm is given in Algorithm 4.

Specifically, the algorithm maintains a priority queue of all search paths. Each time the best path is de-queued, it is expanded with up to $m - 1$ words in q by searching over a vocabulary trie of up to m-gram. Each path is represented as a quadruple (pos, str, sc, a), representing the current term position in query, the string of the path, the path's score, and the alignment so far. The priority queue is sorted according to the score of each path in descending order. The *GetSuggestions*() function retrieves the top n similar words to the given word with a vocabulary trie according to an error model.

Splitting errors are dealt with in Algorithm 4 by "looking forward" m words in the query when generating candidate words. Merging errors are accounted for by including up to m-gram in the vocabulary trie.

The solution to the loss augmented inference in the LS-SVM model depends on the loss function we use. In spelling correction, usually only one correction is valid for an input query. Therefore, we apply the 0–1 loss to our model:

$$\Delta(c, \hat{c}) = \begin{cases} 0 \ c = \hat{c} \\ 1 \ c \neq \hat{c} \\ . \end{cases} \tag{5.20}$$

Given this loss function, the loss augmented inference problem can be solved easily with an algorithm similar to Algorithm 4. This is done by initializing the loss to be 1 at the beginning of each search path. During the search procedure, we check if the loss decreases to 0 given the correction string so far. If this is the case, we decrease the score by 1 and add the path back to the priority queue. More advanced functions may also be used [9], which may lead to better training performance.

The inference of the latent alignment variable can be solved with dynamic programming, as the number of possible alignments is limited given the query and the correction.

5.5.4 Features

In this section, we will describe some interesting features used in [11]. Let us start with the source probability and transformation probability which empirically are the two most important features in query spelling correction. [11] includes them in a normalized form. Taking the source probability, for example, we define the following feature:

$$\psi(q, c, a) = \frac{\mu + \sum_1^{|a|} \log p(c)}{\mu} \\ = 1 + \sum_1^{|a|} \frac{\log p(c)}{\mu}, \tag{5.21}$$

where μ is a normalizing factor computed as:

$$\mu = -|q| \log p_{min}, \tag{5.22}$$

where p_{min} is the smallest probability we use in practice.

The formula fits the general form we define in 5.15 in that $\psi_0 = 1$ and $\psi_1(q_{a_t}, c_{a_t}, a_t) = \frac{\log p(c)}{\mu}$ for any $t = 1$ to $|a|$.

Similarly, we have the following feature for the transformation probability:

$$\psi'(q, c, a) = \frac{\mu + \sum_1^{|a|} \log p(q|c)}{\mu} \\ = 1 + \sum_1^{|a|} \frac{\log p(q|c)}{\mu}. \tag{5.23}$$

Microsoft n-gram model [1] is used to compute source model $p(c)$. And transformation model for the transformation probability $p(q|c)$ is trained according to [10].

Despite the goal of query spelling correction is to deal with misspellings, in real world most queries are correctly spelled. A good query spelling correction system shall prevent as much as possible from misjudging a correctly spelled query as misspelled. With this idea in mind, [11] includes some local and global heuristic functions to avoid misjudging. Please refer to [11] for details.

5.6 Other Components for Query Spelling Correction

In order to build a modern large-scale query speller, other than the advanced models and algorithm, we also need other components for supporting the computation in the training or prediction process. Here we introduce some of these components, namely the large-scale trusted lexicon, the error model, and the N-gram language model.

- **Large-Scale Trusted Lexicon** We find that with a clean vocabulary, it will significantly improve the performance of spelling correction. However, to obtain such a clean vocabulary is usually difficult in practice. Traditional dictionaries are used in some query spelling correct works. However, only using these dictionaries cannot keep up with the vocabulary used on the web. Recent works make use of the Wikipedia data [11, 19]. For example, [19] obtains 1.2 million highly reliable words in the vocabulary, which is much larger than a traditional dictionary.
- **Error Model** The error model intends to model the probability that one word is misspelled into another (either valid or invalid). Previous studies have shown that a weighted edit distance model trained with sufficiently large set of correction pairs could achieve a comparable performance with a sophisticated n-gram model [10]. Meanwhile, a higher order model has more tendency to overfit if the training data is not large enough. For example, in [10], the joint probability of character transformations is modeled as the weighted edit distance. In this model, the basic edit operation is defined as a pair of characters from source and destination of the correction, respectively. Null character is included in the vocabulary to model the insertion and deletion operation. The misspelled word and its correction are viewed as generated from a sequence of edit operations. The parameters in this model are trained with an EM algorithm which iteratively maximizes the likelihood of the training set of correction pairs.
- **N-gram Language Model** Another important factor in selecting and ranking the correction candidates is the prior probability of a correction phrase. It represents our prior belief about how likely a query will be chosen by the user without seeing any input from the user. Recent works [19] make use of the Web n-grams provided by Microsoft [1] or Google N-gram. Web n-gram model intends to

model the n-gram probability of English phrases with the parameters estimated from the entire Web data. It also differentiates the sources of the data to build different language models from the title, anchor text and body of Web pages, as well as the queries from query log. Despite trained with the Web data, Web n-gram model may also suffer from data sparseness in higher order models. To avoid this issue, **bigram** model is more popular in building the query spelling systems.

5.7 Summary

In this chapter we have introduced the problem of query spelling correction, which is an important problem for query understanding. We first introduced edit distance based approaches for query spelling correction [23, 25]. We also introduced the noisy-channel model to the problem [16]. Then we covered modern approaches [11, 19], for addressing multiple types of spelling errors, for example, the generalized HMM model and latent structural SVM model. Finally we described other components for supporting a large-scale query spelling correction system.

References

1. https://www.microsoft.com/cognitive-services/en-us/web-language-model-api.
2. Farooq Ahmad and Grzegorz Kondrak. Learning a spelling error model from search query logs. In *Proceedings of the Human Language Technology Conference and Conference on Empirical Methods in Natural Language Processing*, pages 955–962, 2005.
3. Eric Brill and Robert C. Moore. An improved error model for noisy channel spelling correction. In *Proceedings of the 38th Annual Meeting of the Association for Computational Linguistics*, pages 286–293, 2000.
4. Qing Chen, Mu Li, and Ming Zhou. Improving query spelling correction using web search results. In *Proceedings of the 2007 Joint Conference on Empirical Methods in Natural Language Processing and Computational Natural Language Learning*, pages 181–189, 2007.
5. Michael Collins. Discriminative training methods for hidden Markov models: Theory and experiments with perceptron algorithms. In *Proceedings of the 2002 Conference on Empirical Methods in Natural Language Processing*, pages 1–8, 2002.
6. Silviu Cucerzan and Eric Brill. Spelling correction as an iterative process that exploits the collective knowledge of web users. In *Proceedings of the 2004 Conference on Empirical Methods in Natural Language Processing*, pages 293–300, 2004.
7. Hercules Dalianis. Evaluating a spelling support in a search engine. In *Proceedings of the 6th International Conference on Applications of Natural Language to Information Systems*, pages 183–190, 2002.
8. Fred Damerau. A technique for computer detection and correction of spelling errors. *Commun. ACM*, 7 (3): 171–176, 1964.
9. Markus Dreyer, David A. Smith, and Noah A. Smith. Vine parsing and minimum risk reranking for speed and precision. In *Proceedings of the Tenth Conference on Computational Natural Language Learning*, pages 201–205, 2006.

10. Huizhong Duan and Bo-June Paul Hsu. Online spelling correction for query completion. In *Proceedings of the 20th International Conference on World Wide Web*, pages 117–126, 2011.
11. Huizhong Duan, Yanen Li, ChengXiang Zhai, and Dan Roth. A discriminative model for query spelling correction with latent structural SVM. In *Proceedings of the 2012 Joint Conference on Empirical Methods in Natural Language Processing and Computational Natural Language Learning*, pages 1511–1521, 2012.
12. Jianfeng Gao, Xiaolong Li, Daniel Micol, Chris Quirk, and Xu Sun. A large scale ranker-based system for search query spelling correction. In *Proceedings of the 23rd International Conference on Computational Linguistics*, pages 358–366, 2010.
13. Jiafeng Guo, Gu Xu, Hang Li, and Xueqi Cheng. A unified and discriminative model for query refinement. In *Proceedings of the 31st Annual International ACM SIGIR Conference on Research and Development in Information Retrieval*, pages 379–386, 2008.
14. Victoria J. Hodge and Jim Austin. A novel binary spell checker. In *Proceedings of the 2001 International Conference on Artificial Neural Networks*, pages 1199–1204, 2001.
15. Daniel Jurafsky and James H. Martin. *Speech and language processing - an introduction to natural language processing, computational linguistics, and speech recognition*. Prentice Hall, 2000. ISBN 978-0-13-095069-7.
16. Mark D. Kernighan, Kenneth Ward Church, and William A. Gale. A spelling correction program based on a noisy channel model. In *Proceedings of the 13th International Conference on Computational Linguistics*, pages 205–210, 1990.
17. Karen Kukich. Techniques for automatically correcting words in text. *ACM Comput. Surv.*, 24 (4): 377–439, 1992.
18. V. I. Levenshtein. Binary codes capable of correcting deletions, insertions and reversals. *Soviet Physics Doklady.*, 10 (8): 707–710, February 1966.
19. Yanen Li, Huizhong Duan, and ChengXiang Zhai. A generalized hidden Markov model with discriminative training for query spelling correction. In *Proceedings of the 35th International ACM SIGIR conference on research and development in Information Retrieval*, pages 611–620, 2012.
20. Lawrence R. Rabiner. A tutorial on hidden Markov models and selected applications in speech recognition. In *Proceedings of the IEEE*, pages 257–286, 1989.
21. Edward M. Riseman and Allen R. Hanson. A contextual postprocessing system for error correction using binary n-grams. *IEEE Trans. Computers*, 23 (5): 480–493, 1974.
22. Terrence J. Sejnowski and Charles R. Rosenberg. Parallel networks that learn to pronounce English text. *Complex Systems*, 1 (1), 1987.
23. Heping Shang and T. H. Merrett. Tries for approximate string matching. *IEEE Trans. Knowl. Data Eng.*, 8 (4): 540–547, 1996.
24. Xu Sun, Jianfeng Gao, Daniel Micol, and Chris Quirk. Learning phrase-based spelling error models from clickthrough data. In *Proceedings of the 48th Annual Meeting of the Association for Computational Linguistics*, pages 266–274, 2010.
25. Esko Ukkonen. Finding approximate patterns in strings. *J. Algorithms*, 6 (1): 132–137, 1985.
26. Robert A. Wagner and Michael J. Fischer. The string-to-string correction problem. *J. ACM*, 21 (1): 168–173, 1974.
27. Casey Whitelaw, Ben Hutchinson, Grace Chung, and Ged Ellis. Using the web for language independent spellchecking and autocorrection. In *Proceedings of the 2009 Conference on Empirical Methods in Natural Language Processing*, pages 890–899, 2009.
28. E. J. Yannakoudakis. Expert spelling error analysis and correction. In *Proceedings of a Conference held by the Aslib Informatics Group and the Information Retrieval Group of the British Computer Society*, pages 39–52, 1983.
29. Chun-Nam John Yu and Thorsten Joachims. Learning structural svms with latent variables. In *Proceedings of the 26th Annual International Conference on Machine Learning*, volume 382 of *ACM International Conference Proceeding Series*, pages 1169–1176, 2009.
30. E. M. Zamora, Joseph J. Pollock, and Antonio Zamora. The use of trigram analysis for spelling error detection. *Inf. Process. Manag.*, 17 (6): 305–316, 1981.

Chapter 6
Query Rewriting

Hui Liu, Dawei Yin, and Jiliang Tang

Abstract It is well known that there is a lexical chasm between web documents and user queries. As a result, even when the queries can fully capture users' information needs, the search engines could not retrieve relevant web documents to match these queries. Query rewriting aims to bridge this gap by rewriting a given query to alternative queries such that the mismatches can be reduced and the relevance performance can be improved. Query rewriting has been extensively studied and recent advances from deep learning have further fostered this research field. In this chapter, we give an overview about the achievements that have been made on query rewriting. In particular, we review representative algorithms with both shallow and deep architectures.

6.1 Introduction

With the advance of technologies, information in the web has been increased exponentially. It had become increasingly hard for online users to find information they are interested in. Modern search engines have been proven to successfully mitigate this information overload problem by retrieving relevant information from massive web documents according to users' information needs (or queries) [3]. However, it is well known that there exists a "lexical chasm" [26] between web documents and user queries. The major reason is that web documents and user queries are created by different sets of users and they may use different vocabularies and distinct language styles. Consequently, even when the queries can perfectly match users' information needs, the search engines may be still unable to locate relevant web documents. For example, users want to find price information about

H. Liu · J. Tang (✉)
Michigan State University, East Lansing, MI, USA
e-mail: liuhui7@msu.edu; tangjili@msu.edu

D. Yin
Baidu Inc., Beijing, China
e-mail: yindawei@outlook.com

Tesla using a query "price tesla," while such information is expressed as "how much tesla" in web documents indexed by the search engines. Thus, it is demanding that search engines should intelligently match information needs of their users by understanding the intrinsic intent in queries.

Query rewriting (QRW), which targets to alter a given query to alternative queries that can improve relevance performance by reducing the mismatches, is a critical task in modern search engines and has attracted increasing attention in the last decade [11, 20, 26]. Thus, we have witnessed a rapid development of the query rewriting techniques. At the early stage, methods have been developed to find terms related to these in a given query and then substitute terms in the original queries with these related ones (or substitution-based methods). Then if we treat queries as the source language and web documents as the target language, the query rewriting problem can be naturally considered as a machine translation problem; thus, machine translation techniques have been applied for QRW (or translation-based methods) [26]. Recently, deep learning techniques have been widely applied in information retrieval [21] and natural language processing [33]. There are very recent works applying deep learning in query rewriting that achieve the state-of-the-art performance [17]. Thus, in this survey, we will follow the used techniques to review representative query rewriting methods and the structure of the survey is as follows:

- In Sect. 6.2, we will review representative methods with traditional shallow models including substitution-based methods and translation-based methods.
- In Sect. 6.3, we will review algorithms based on deep learning techniques such as word embedding, seq2seq models, deep learning to rewrite frameworks, and deep reinforcement learning.
- In Sect. 6.4, we will conclude the survey and discuss some promising directions in query rewriting.

6.2   QRW with Shallow Models

In the section, we will review shallow query rewriting algorithms including substitute-based and translation-based methods.

6.2.1   Substitution-Based Methods

Given the original query, substitution-based methods aim to generate rewritten queries by replacing the query as a whole or by substituting constituent phrases [20]. There are two key steps for substitution-based methods: substitution generation and candidate selection. The substitution generation step is to find substitutions in the levels of queries, phrases, or terms for the original query. The substitution generation step can suggest many rewritten candidates for the original query. Thus the candidate selection step is to select good candidates. Many possible resources can be used to generate query or term substitutions. One type resource is static such as WordNet [12] and Wikipedia [32]. However, these static resources generally do not allow us to generate substitutions for new concepts. It is also challenging to consider contextual information. Thus, resources based on users' search feedback have been widely adapted and we will introduce several representative methods in the following.

In [20], user sessions from search query logs have been used for query rewriting. These sessions have been reported to include 50% reformulations [19]. Query reformulation is that a user reformulates a query to other related queries in a query session by inserting, deleting, substituting, or rephrasing words of the original query [2]. Query reformulation is very similar to the query rewriting task; thus, it is natural to use user session reformulation data.

A pair of successive queries issued by a single user on a single day is referred as a candidate reformulation or a query pair. Then, they aggregate query pairs over users. For phrase substitutions, the authors segment the whole query into phrases using point-wise mutual information and find query pairs that differ by only one segment. This pair of phrases is selected as a candidate phrase pair.

To identify highly related query pairs and phrase pairs, the work makes two hypotheses to evaluate that the probability of term q_2 is the same whether term q_1 is present or not.

$$H_1 : P(q_2|q_1) = p = P(q_2|\neg q_1) \tag{6.1}$$

$$H_2 : P(q_2|q_1) = p_1 \neq p_2 = P(q_2|\neg q_1) \tag{6.2}$$

The log-likelihood ratio score based on the probabilities of the two hypotheses is used to measure the dependence between two terms q_1 and q_2.

$$\text{LLR} = -2 \log \frac{L(H_1)}{L(H_2)} \tag{6.3}$$

The query pairs and phrase pairs with a high LLR score are identified as substitutable pairs because of the statistically significant relevance.

The work extracts a list of features from the queries and uses human judgments and machine learning to train a classifier for high quality query suggestions. Since this method could precompute offline the whole-query substitutions and their scores and the edit distance for phrase similarity evaluation, it only requires look-up substitutions at run-time.

In [30], the authors work on mining search engine log data at the level of terms rather than the level of queries. The user session information is leveraged for query refinement. This method is based on an observation that terms with similar meaning tend to co-occur with the same or similar terms in the queries. The associated terms are discovered from search engine logs to substitute the previous terms or add new terms to the original query. The term associations are extracted based on the context distribution. A contextual model was proposed by investigating the context similarity of terms in historical queries from log data. Two terms in a pair with similar contexts are used to substitute each other in new query generation. The contextual model is defined based on the maximum likelihood estimation

$$P_C(a|\omega) = \frac{c(a, C(\omega))}{\sum_i c(i, C(\omega))} \qquad (6.4)$$

where $C(\omega)$ is the context of a word ω. This model evaluates the likelihood of a word a to appear in the context of a given word ω. The Kullback–Leibler (KL) divergence $D(\cdot||\cdot)$ has been used in the language modeling approach to measure the similarity between two contexts. In [30], the metric of the similarity between the original word ω and the candidate word s is given based on the KL-divergence as follows:

$$t_C(s|\omega) = \frac{\exp(-D[P_C(\cdot|s)||\tilde{P}_C(\cdot|\omega)])}{\sum_s \exp(-D[P_C(\cdot|s)||\tilde{P}_C(\cdot|\omega)])} \qquad (6.5)$$

where $\tilde{P}_C(\cdot|\omega)$ is the smoothed contextual model of ω using Dirichlet prior smoothing approach. The position information is introduced in the contextual models.

$$\prod_{j=1,i-j>0}^{k} \tilde{P}_{L_{i-j}}(\omega_{i-j}|s) \times \prod_{j=1,i+j\leq n}^{k} \tilde{P}_{L_{i+j}}(\omega_{i+j}|s) \qquad (6.6)$$

where k is the number of adjacent terms to be considered. The impact of a word far away from the word in consideration is insignificant. Mutual information is used to capture the relation between two terms over user sessions inside queries.

$$I(s, \omega) = \sum_{X_s, X_\omega \in \{0,1\}} P(X_s, X_\omega) \log \frac{P(X_s, X_\omega)}{P(X_s)P(X_\omega)} \qquad (6.7)$$

where X_s and X_ω are binary variables indicating the presence/absence of term s and term ω in each user session. A normalized version of mutual information is generalized to make the mutual information of different pairs of words comparable. Then, all the candidate queries are sorted according to the probability given by Eq. 6.6. The top ranked candidate queries are recommended.

In [1], queries are rewritten based on a historical click graph in sponsored search. Given a query q, it first tries SimRank [18] to find similar queries to q. However, the authors found the cases where SimRank could fail in weighted click graph. For example, when two queries lead to clicks on two same ads rather than one ads, their similarity value would be even lower as measured by SimRank. Based on these observations, the authors develop two extended models based on SimRank to measure query similarities for query rewriting. SimRank++ makes similarity scores to include evidence factor between nodes as well as weights of edges in the click graph and finds high proximity nodes using the historical click data. The evidence factor is defined as:

$$\text{evidence}(a, b) = \sum_{i=1}^{|E(a) \cap E(b)|} \frac{1}{2^i} \tag{6.8}$$

where $E(a)$ and $E(b)$ are the neighbors of node a and node b, respectively. The range of the evidence factor is [0.5, 1]. As the common neighbors increase, the evidence scores get closer to one. Let $s(a, b)$ denote the similarity metric from SimRank,

$$s(a, b) = \frac{C}{|E(a)| \cdot |E(b)|} \sum_{i \in E(a)} \sum_{j \in E(b)} s(i, j) \tag{6.9}$$

where the x and y are the two ads. The enhanced similarity scores including the evidence are designed as follows:

$$s_{evidence}(a, b) = evidence(a, b) \cdot s(a, b) \tag{6.10}$$

To support the weighted click graph, the authors make the extension to include the impact of weights as

$$s_{weighted}(a, b) = evidence(a, b) \cdot C \sum_{i \in E(a)} \sum_{j \in E(b)} W(a, i) W(b, j) s_{weighted}(i, j) \tag{6.11}$$

where $W(a, i)$ and $W(b, j)$ are functions of the weight set and its variance. The basic concept for SimRank and SimRank++ is that two objects are similar if they reference the same objects. The authors' work in [1] makes SimRank similarity scores more intuitive for the area of sponsored search and the two enhanced versions yield better query rewriting results.

In [15], a unified and discriminative model is proposed based on conditional random field (CRF) for query refinements on the morphological level. The proposed CRF-QR model involves different refinement tasks simultaneously, including spelling error correction, word merging, word splitting, and phrase segmentation. The authors designed two variants of the CRF-QR model, a basic model for single refinement task and an extended model for multiple refinement tasks. Let $\mathbf{x} = x_1 x_2 \ldots x_n$ and $\mathbf{y} = y_1 y_2 \ldots y_n$ denote a sequence of query words and sequence of refined query words, respectively. Let $\mathbf{o}$ denote a sequence of refinement operations.

Here n is the length of the sequence. The basic CRF-QR model is obtained as follows:

$$Pr(\mathbf{y}, \mathbf{o}|\mathbf{x}) = \frac{1}{Z(\mathbf{x})} \prod_{i=1}^{n} \phi(y_{i-1}, yi)\phi(y_i, o_i, \mathbf{x}) \tag{6.12}$$

where $\phi(y_{i-1}, y_i)$ is the potential function showing the adjacent y's mutual dependence, and $\phi(y_i, o_i, \mathbf{x})$ is the potential function showing the dependence of y_i on the operation o_i and the input query $\mathbf{x}$. Z is the normalizing factor. The individual o's are independent from each other to simplify the model, because the dependency existing between o's has been captured by the dependency between y's. The space of the refined query y is as extremely large as the space of the original query x before introducing o into the model. An operation o can be insertion, deletion, and substitution of letters in a word or transposition. Because the space of operation o is very limited, the mapping from x's to y's under operation o is not completely free. o works as a constraint in the CRF-QR model to reduce the space of y for given x. When multiple refinement tasks are needed, the extended CRF-QR model uses multiple sequences of operations $\overrightarrow{o_i} = o_{i,1}o_{i,2}, \ldots, o_{i,m_i}$ and the corresponding sequences of intermediate results in $\overrightarrow{z_i} = z_{i,1}z_{i,2}, \ldots, z_{i,m_i}$.

$$Pr(\mathbf{y}, \overrightarrow{\mathbf{o}}, \overrightarrow{\mathbf{z}}|\mathbf{x}) = \frac{1}{Z(\mathbf{x})} \prod_{i=1}^{n} (\phi(y_{i-1}, y_i) \prod_{j_i=1}^{m_i} \phi(z_{i,j_i}, o_{i,j_i}, z_{i,j_i-1})) \tag{6.13}$$

The prediction of the most likely refined query $\mathbf{y}^*$ satisfies

$$\mathbf{y}^*\mathbf{o}^* = \arg\max_{\mathbf{y},\mathbf{o}} Pr(\mathbf{y}, \mathbf{o}|\mathbf{x}) \tag{6.14}$$

The extended CRF-QF model can perform different query refinement tasks or operations simultaneously. Because the tasks are interdependent sometimes, the accuracy of tasks can be enhanced.

In [4], to solve the query rewriting problem, the authors leverage the query log data and follow the common procedure to generate some candidate queries first before using a scoring method to rank the quality of the candidate queries. Query term substitution is applied as the major approach for candidate query generation. Social tagging data is utilized as a helpful resource for extracting candidate substitution term. A graphical model taking into account the semantic consistency is designed for query scoring. The authors exploit the latent topic space of a graph model to assess the candidate query quality.

In addition to query reformulation and click graph data, anchor texts are used for the query rewriting problem in [8] that are often associated with links to documents. Since they are selected manually to describe the associated web documents, they provide very relevant information to these documents. It is demonstrated that anchor texts usually offer more accurate description of their associated documents than the web documents themselves [6].

6.2.2 Translation-Based Methods

If we consider user queries as the source language and web documents as the target language, one natural way for query rewriting is to translate a source language of user queries into a target language of web documents [26, 27].

In [27], statistical machine translation (SMT) models have been adopted for query rewriting. The alignment template approach in [25] is adopted as SMT for query rewriting. It contains a translation model and a language model. It aims to seek the English string $\hat{e}$ as a translation of a foreign string f:

$$\hat{e} = arg \max_e p(e|f) = arg \max_e p(f|e)p(e) \tag{6.15}$$

where $p(f|e)$ is the translation model and $P(e)$ is the language model. $\hat{e}$ is further formulated as a combination of a set of feature functions $h_m(e, f)$ with the corresponding weight λ_m as:

$$\hat{e} = arg \max_e \sum_{m=1}^{M} \lambda_m h_m(e, f) \tag{6.16}$$

The translation model used in query rewriting is according to the sequence of alignment models [24]. A hidden variable is introduced to capture the relation between translation and alignment models for source string $f = f_1^J$ and target string $e = e_1^I$. The hidden variable is used to denote an alignment mapping from source position j to target position a_j:

$$P(f_1^J|e_1^I) = \sum_{a_1^J} P(f_1^J, a_1^J|e_1^I) \tag{6.17}$$

To align source words to the empty word, a_1^J includes null-word alignments $a_j = 0$. In the query rewriting, we adopt an n-gram language model which gives a string w_1^L of words with the following probability:

$$P(w_1^L) = \prod_{i=1}^{L} P(w_i|w_1^{i-1}) \approx \prod_{i=1}^{L} P(w_i|w_{i-n+1}^{i-1}) \tag{6.18}$$

A corpus of user queries is utilized to estimate the n-gram probabilities. A variety of smoothing techniques are used to mitigate the data sparse problems [5].

Once the SMT system is trained, to translate unseen queries, a standard dynamic-programming beam-search decoder is used [25].

In detail, pairs of user queries and snippets of clicked results are used as the parallel corpus and then a machine translation model is trained on the corpus. Once the model is trained, query rewriting is similar to the decoding process in machine translation. During decoding, a large n-gram language model is trained on queries. It is shown that the proposed method achieves improved query rewriting performance compared to methods based on term correlations.

The SMT system in [27] is used as a black box and it is hard to verify the contributions of its components. Thus, lexicon models have been utilized in [11]. There are two phases for the proposed framework: candidate generation and candidate ranking. In the phase of candidate generation, the original query is tokenized as a term sequence. For each non-stop word, a lexicon model is used to generate its translated words according to the word translation probabilities. In the candidate ranking phase, a ranking algorithm based on Markov random field (MRF) is used to rank all candidates. In this work, three lexicon models have been studied. The first lexicon model is the word model from IBM model 1 [7] which learns the translation probability between single words. The word model does not incorporate contextual information. Thus, the second lexicon model is a triplet model that uses triplets to incorporate word dependencies [16]. The third model is a bilingual topic model (BLTM) [10]. The intuition behind BLTM is through a query and its relevant documents can use different language styles or vocabularies, they should share similar topic distributions. The lexicon models are trained on pairs of queries and titles of clicked web documents. It is shown that the word model can generate rich candidates, and the triplet and topic models can select good expansion words effectively.

In [10], this paper provides a quantitative analysis of the language discrepancy issue and explores the use of clickthrough data to bridge documents and queries. We assume that a query is parallel to the titles of documents clicked on for that query. Two translation models are trained and integrated into retrieval models: A word-based translation model that learns the translation probability between single words and a phrase-based translation model that learns the translation probability between multi-term phrases. Experiments are carried out on a real-world dataset. The results show that the retrieval systems that use the translation models outperform significantly the systems that do not.

In [9], the authors follow [27] to consider the query rewriting problem as a machine translation problem and use pairs of queries and titles of clicked documents to train a machine translation model with the word model. Similar to [27], it shows that SMT based system outperforms systems based on term correlation. However, the word model considers isolated words while ignoring completely the context. It is observed that (1) consecutive words often form a phrase and (2) neighboring words can offer helpful contextual information. Thus, they introduce the constrained groups of term as concepts and propose concept-based translation models for query rewriting.

6.3   QRW with Deep Models

Deep learning techniques have powered a number of applications from various domains such as computer vision, speech recognition, and natural language processing. Recently, deep learning techniques have been adopted in the query rewriting task and in this section, we will review representative deep learning based query rewriting algorithms.

6.3.1   Word Embedding for QRW

In [14], the authors propose three models for query rewriting of sponsored search based on context and content-aware word embedding. The first model, context2vec, considers a query as a single word in a sentence and each query session as a sentence. Similar queries of similar context are supposed to have similar embeddings. The skip-gram model is used in this model for query representation learning by maximizing the objective function,

$$\mathcal{L} = \sum_{s \in S} \sum_{q_m \in s} \sum_{-b \leq i \leq b, i \neq 0} \log \mathbb{P}(q_{m+i} | q_m) \tag{6.19}$$

where S is the set of all search sessions, b is the window size of neighboring queries for the context, and $\mathbb{P}$ is the probability of observing a neighboring query q_{m+i} given the query q_m. The second model, content2vec, considers a query as a paragraph for word prediction without the session information. The word vectors are used to train the model for context words prediction within the query only by maximizing the objective function

$$\mathcal{L} = \sum_{s \in S} (\sum_{q_m \in s} \log \mathbb{P}(q_m | \omega_{m1} : \omega_{mT_m})$$

$$+ \sum_{w_{mt} \in q_m} \log \mathbb{P}(\omega_{mt} | \omega_{m,t-c} : \omega_{m,t+c}, q_m)) \tag{6.20}$$

where c is the length of the context for words in the query. The vector representation for query q_m is $q_m = (\omega_{m1}, \omega_{m2}, \ldots \omega_{mT_m})$. A query's context should include both the content of the query and queries of the same session. The third model, context-content2vec, is a two-layer model combining the first two models and considering both the search session context and the query context.

$$\mathcal{L} = \sum_{s \in S} \sum_{q_m \in s} \left(\sum_{-b \leq i \leq b, i \neq 0} \log \mathbb{P}(q_{m+i}|q_m) + \alpha_m \log \mathbb{P}(q_m|\omega_{m1} : \omega_{mT_m}) \right.$$

$$\left. + \sum_{\omega_{mt} \in q_m} \log \mathbb{P}(\omega_{mt}|\omega_{m,t-c} : \omega_{m,t+c}, q_m) \right) \tag{6.21}$$

The models are trained on Yahoo search data including 12 billion search sessions.

6.3.2 Seq2Seq for QRW

As a neural sequence model, recurrent neural network (RNN) obtains the best performance on numerous important sequential learning tasks. The long short-term memory (LSTM), one of the most popular RNN variants, can capture long range temporal dependencies and mitigate the vanishing gradient problem. In the work [17], the authors adopt the sequence-to-sequence LSTM model to build a two-stage query rewriting frameworks [29].

In the first stage, the model training stage, the input sequence $x_1^J = x_1, \cdots, x_J$ is the original query and the target output sequence $y_1^J = y_1, \cdots, y_J$ is the rewritten queries. For the LSTM variant in the Seq2Seq model, the gates and cells are implemented by the following composite functions [13]:

$$\begin{cases} i_j = \sigma(W_{xi}x_j + W_{hi}h_{j-1} + b_i) \\ f_j = \sigma(W_{xf}x_j + W_{hf}h_{j-1} + W_{cf}c_{j-1} + b_f) \\ c_j = f_j c_{j-1} + i_j tanh(W_{xc}x_j + W_{hc}h_{j-1} + b_c) \\ o_j = \sigma(W_{xo}x_j + W_{ho}h_{j-1} + W_{co}c_j + b_o) \\ h_j = o_j tanh(c_j) \end{cases} \tag{6.22}$$

where $h_1^J = h_1, \cdots, h_J$ is the hidden vector sequence, $W_{.,.}$ terms are the weight matrices, and $b_.$ terms are the bias vectors.

The sequence-to-sequence LSTM aims to estimate the conditional probability $p(y_1, \cdots, y_I|x_1, \cdots, x_J)$, where $x_1, \cdots, x_J$ is an input sequence and $y_1, \cdots, y_I$ is its corresponding output sequence. The LSTM computes this conditional probability by first obtaining the fixed dimensional representation v of the input sequence $x_1, \cdots, x_J$ given by the last hidden state of the LSTM and then computing the probability of $y_1, \cdots, y_I$ with a standard LSTM–LM formulation whose initial hidden state is set as the representation v of $x_1, \cdots, x_J$:

$$p(y_1, \cdots, y_I|x_1, \cdots, x_J) = \prod_{i=1}^{I} p(y_i|v, y_1, \cdots, y_{i-1}) \tag{6.23}$$

where $p(y_i|v, y_1, \cdots, y_{i-1})$ is represented with a softmax over all the words in the vocabulary. It learns a large deep LSTM on large-scale query and rewrites query pairs. It is trained by maximizing the log probability of a correct rewrite query $r = rt_1, rt_2, \cdots, rt_n, < EOQ >$ given the query $q = qt_1, qt_2, \cdots, qt_m, < EOQ >$, where "$< EOQ >$" is a special end-of-query symbol. Thus the training objective is

$$\frac{1}{|D|} \sum (q, r) \in D \log p(r|q) \qquad (6.24)$$

where D is the training dataset and $p(r|q)$ is calculated according to Eq. (6.23). Once training is complete, original queries are fed to the model and rewrite candidates are produced by finding the most likely rewrites according to the LSTM.

In the second stage, the prediction stage, a beam-search method is used to output the most probable sequences. It searches for the most likely query rewrites using a simple left-to-right beam-search decoder instead of an exact decoder. It maintains a small number B of partial rewrites, where partial rewrites are prefixes of some query rewrite candidates. At each time-step, it extends each partial rewrite in the beam with every possible word in the vocabulary. It discards all but the B most likely rewrites according to the model's log probability.

In [28], a novel method is proposed to translate a natural language query into a keyword query relevant to the natural language query, which can be applicable to legacy web search engines for retrieving better search results. Since legacy search engines are optimized for short keyword queries, a natural language query submitted directly to legacy search engines will highly likely lead to search results of low relevance. The proposed method introduces a RNN encoder–decoder architecture. To translate the input natural language query $\mathbf{x} = \{x_1, \cdots, x_n\}$ into a keyword query $\mathbf{y} = \{y_1, \cdots, y_m\}$, the RNN encoder–decoder models the conditional probability $p(\mathbf{y}|\mathbf{x})$ to complete the translation process. The encoder reads $\mathbf{x}$ sequentially to generate the hidden state. The decoder generates one keyword at a time by decomposing the probability of the keyword query $\mathbf{y}$ into conditional probabilities,

$$p(\mathbf{y}) = \prod_{i=1}^{m} p(y_i|y_1, \cdots, y_{i-1}, \mathbf{x}) \qquad (6.25)$$

The prediction of the current keyword is based on the input $\mathbf{x}$ and the previously generated keywords. An attention mechanism is adopted to avoid biased representation caused by weakly relevant words in long natural language queries. The attention-based RNN encoder–decoder model is trained by maximizing the conditional log-likelihood as

$$\mathcal{L}(\theta) = \frac{1}{N} \sum_{j=1}^{N} \sum_{i=1}^{m} \log p(y_i = y_i^{(j)}|y_1^{(j)}, \cdots, y_{i-1}^{(j)}, \mathbf{x}^{(j)}) \qquad (6.26)$$

where $y_i^{(j)}$ is the i-th keyword of the j-th training instance in the training set. Since the training only needs pairs of a natural language query and its keyword query, the training is independent on the choice of the search engine and the proposed model can adapt legacy web search engines to natural language queries.

6.3.3   Learning to Rewrite Methods

In [17], a learning to rewrite framework is proposed that contains candidate generation and candidate ranking. The query rewriting problem aims to find the query rewrites of a given query for the purpose of improving the relevance of the information retrieval system. The proposed framework formulates the query rewriting problem as an optimization problem of finding a scoring function $F(q, r)$ which assigns a score for any pair of query q and its rewrite candidate r. The framework assumes that $\mathcal{G} = \{g_1, g_2, \ldots, g_M\}$ is a set of M candidate generators. Candidate generators could be any existing query rewriting techniques. In the candidate generating phase, we use candidate generators in $\mathcal{G}$ to generate a set of rewrite candidates for a given query q as $\mathcal{R} = \{r_1, \cdots, r_n\}$, where n is the number of generated rewrite candidates. Each pair of query q and its rewrite candidate r_i, i.e., (q, r_i), is scored by the function $F(q, r_i)$. The rewrite candidates from $\mathcal{R}$ are then ranked based on the scores $\{F(q, r_1), F(q, r_2), \ldots, F(q, r_n)\}$ in the candidate ranking phase. A key step of the learning to rewrite problem is how to obtain the scoring function F.

Let $\mathcal{F} = \{f : (q, r) \mapsto f(q, r) \in \mathcal{R}\}$ be the functional space of the scoring functions for any pair of query and rewrite candidate and $\mathcal{Q} = \{q_1, \cdots, q_m\}$ be a set of m queries. We use $\mathcal{R}_i = \{r_{i,1}, \cdots, r_{i,n_i}\}$ to denote the set of rewrite candidates of query q_i generated by $\mathcal{G}$, where n_i is the number of rewrite candidates for q_i. For each query q_i, we further assume that $\mathcal{I}_i$ is the learning target that encodes the observed information about the quality of rewrite candidates in $\mathcal{R}_i$. Note that the forms of I_i are problem-dependent that could be the label for each pair (q, r_i) or the preferences among $\mathcal{R}_i$ for q_i. With the aforementioned notations and definitions, the problem of searching in $\mathcal{F}$ for a scoring function $F(q, r)$ is formally stated as the following minimization problem:

$$F = \arg\min_{f \in \mathcal{F}} \sum_{i=1}^{m} L(f, q_i, \mathcal{R}_i, \mathcal{I}_i) \tag{6.27}$$

The exact forms of the loss function $L(f, q_i, \mathcal{R}_i, \mathcal{I}_i)$ depend on the learning target $\mathcal{I}_i$ and three types of loss functions are introduced including point-wise, pair-wise, and list-wise loss. Generating the learning target $\mathcal{I}_i$ is challenging especially for a large set of queries and their corresponding rewrite candidates. One straightforward way is to use human labeling. However, it is not practical, if not impossible, to achieve this for a web-scale query rewriting the application. First, it is very time and effort consuming to label millions of query rewriting pairs. Second, the relevance performance depends on many components of a search engine such as relevance ranking algorithms, thus it is extremely difficult for human editors to compare the quality of rewrite candidates. Third, for a commercial search engine, its components are typically evolved rapidly and in order to adapt to these changes, human labels are consistently and continuously needed. Therefore it is desirable for an automatic approach to generate the learning target. In this work, we specifically focus on boosting the relevance performance via query rewriting, thus the learning target should indicate the quality of the rewrite candidates from the perspective of search relevance. Intuitively a better rewrite candidate could attract more clicks to its retrieved documents. In other words, the number of clicks on the returned document from a rewrite candidate could be a good indicator about its quality in terms of relevance. These intuitions pave us a way to develop an automatic approach to generate learning target based on the query-document click graph that is extracted from search logs.

In [31], a co-training framework is proposed for query rewriting and semantic matching based on the learning to rewrite framework in [17]. It first builds a huge unlabeled dataset from search logs, on which the two tasks can be considered as two different views of the relevance problem. Then it iteratively co-trains them via labeled data generated from this unlabeled set to boost their performance simultaneously. A series of offline and online experiments have been conducted on a real-world e-commerce search engine, and the results demonstrate that the proposed method improves relevance significantly.

6.3.4 Deep Reinforcement Learning for QRW

In [22], the authors propose a query rewriting system by maximizing the number of relevant documents returned based on a neural network trained with reinforcement learning. The original query and each candidate term t_i from either the original query q_0 or from documents retrieved using q_0 are converted to a vector representation by using a CNN or a RNN. Then the probability of selecting each candidate term is computed. The search engine is treated as a black box that an agent learns to use to retrieve terms to maximize the retrieval performance. Thus, an agent can be trained to use a search engine for a specific task. An extended model is introduced to sequentially generate reformulated queries to produce more concise queries based on RNN or LSTM. Rather than being queried for each newly added term, the search engine is queried with multiple new terms at each retrieval step for faster query reformulation.

In [23], methods are investigated to efficiently learn diverse strategies in reinforcement learning for query rewriting. In the proposed framework an agent consists of multiple specialized sub-agents and a meta-agent that learns to aggregate the answers from sub-agents to produce a final answer. Sub-agents are trained on disjoint partitions of the training data, while the meta-agent is trained on the full training set. The proposed method makes learning faster, because it is highly parallelizable and has better generalization performance than strong baselines, such as an ensemble of agents trained on the full data.

6.4   Conclusion

Query rewriting is a key task in modern search engines and has attracted increasing attention in the last decade. The recent achievements of deep learning have further advanced this research topic. In this chapter, we roughly divided existing query rewriting algorithms according to the architectures they adopted to shallow and deep query writing. For shallow query rewriting, we discuss representative algorithms for substitution-based and translation-based methods. For deep query rewriting, we detail key algorithms for methods based on word embedding, Seq2Seq, learning to rewrite and deep reinforcement learning.

References

1. Ioannis Antonellis, Hector Garcia-Molina, and Chi-Chao Chang. Simrank++: query rewriting through link analysis of the click graph. *Proceedings of the VLDB Endowment*, 1 (1): 408–421, 2008.
2. Yigal Arens, Craig A. Knoblock, and Wei-Min Shen. Query reformulation for dynamic information integration. *Journal of Intelligent Information Systems*, 6 (2–3): 99–130, 1996.
3. Ricardo A. Baeza-Yates and Berthier A. Ribeiro-Neto. *Modern information retrieval*, volume 463. ACM Press New York, 1999.
4. Lidong Bing, Wai Lam, and Tak-Lam Wong. Using query log and social tagging to refine queries based on latent topics. In *Proceedings of the 20th ACM Conference on Information and Knowledge Management*, pages 583–592, 2011.
5. Thorsten Brants, Ashok C Popat, Peng Xu, Franz J Och, and Jeffrey Dean. Large language models in machine translation. In *Proceedings of the 2007 Joint Conference on Empirical Methods in Natural Language Processing and Computational Natural Language Learning*, pages 858–867, 2007.
6. Sergey Brin and Lawrence Page. The anatomy of a large-scale hypertextual web search engine. *Computer networks and ISDN systems*, 30 (1–7): 107–117, 1998.
7. Peter F. Brown, Stephen Della Pietra, Vincent J. Della Pietra, and Robert L. Mercer. The mathematics of statistical machine translation: Parameter estimation. *Computational linguistics*, 19 (2): 263–311, 1993.
8. Van Dang and W. Bruce Croft. Query reformulation using anchor text. In *Proceedings of the Third International Conference on Web Search and Data Mining*, pages 41–50, 2010.
9. Jianfeng Gao and Jian-Yun Nie. Towards concept-based translation models using search logs for query expansion. In *Proceedings of the 21st ACM international conference on Information and knowledge management*, pages 1–10, 2012.
10. Jianfeng Gao, Xiaodong He, and Jian-Yun Nie. Clickthrough-based translation models for web search: from word models to phrase models. In *Proceedings of the 19th ACM Conference on Information and Knowledge Management*, pages 1139–1148, 2010.

11. Jianfeng Gao, Shasha Xie, Xiaodong He, and Alnur Ali. Learning lexicon models from search logs for query expansion. In *Proceedings of the 2012 Joint Conference on Empirical Methods in Natural Language Processing and Computational Natural Language Learning*, pages 666–676, 2012.

12. Zhiguo Gong, Chan Wa Cheang, and Leong Hou U. Web query expansion by wordnet. In *International Conference on Database and Expert Systems Applications*, volume 3588, pages 166–175, 2005.

13. Alex Graves. Supervised sequence labelling. In *Supervised sequence labelling with recurrent neural networks*, pages 5–13. 2012.

14. Mihajlo Grbovic, Nemanja Djuric, Vladan Radosavljevic, Fabrizio Silvestri, and Narayan Bhamidipati. Context- and content-aware embeddings for query rewriting in sponsored search. In *Proceedings of the 38th International ACM SIGIR Conference on Research and Development in Information Retrieval*, pages 383–392, 2015.

15. Jiafeng Guo, Gu Xu, Hang Li, and Xueqi Cheng. A unified and discriminative model for query refinement. In *Proceedings of the 31st Annual International ACM SIGIR Conference on Research and Development in Information Retrieval*, pages 379–386, 2008.

16. Sasa Hasan, Juri Ganitkevitch, Hermann Ney, and Jesús Andrés-Ferrer. Triplet lexicon models for statistical machine translation. In *Proceedings of the Conference on Empirical Methods in Natural Language Processing*, pages 372–381, 2008.

17. Yunlong He, Jiliang Tang, Hua Ouyang, Changsung Kang, Dawei Yin, and Yi Chang. Learning to rewrite queries. In *Proceedings of the 25th ACM International on Conference on Information and Knowledge Management*, pages 1443–1452, 2016.

18. Glen Jeh and Jennifer Widom. Simrank: a measure of structural-context similarity. In *Proceedings of the Eighth ACM SIGKDD International Conference on Knowledge Discovery and Data Mining*, pages 538–543, 2002.

19. Rosie Jones and Daniel C. Fain. Query word deletion prediction. In *Proceedings of the 26th Annual International ACM SIGIR Conference on Research and Development in Information Retrieval*, pages 435–436, 2003.

20. Rosie Jones, Benjamin Rey, Omid Madani, and Wiley Greiner. Generating query substitutions. In *Proceedings of the 15th international conference on World Wide Web*, pages 387–396, 2006.

21. Hang Li and Zhengdong Lu. Deep learning for information retrieval. In *Proceedings of the 39th International ACM SIGIR conference on Research and Development in Information Retrieval*, pages 1203–1206, 2016.

22. Rodrigo Nogueira and Kyunghyun Cho. Task-oriented query reformulation with reinforcement learning. In *Proceedings of the 2017 Conference on Empirical Methods in Natural Language Processing*, pages 574–583, 2017.

23. Rodrigo Nogueira, Jannis Bulian, and Massimiliano Ciaramita. Multi-agent query reformulation: Challenges and the role of diversity. In *Deep Reinforcement Learning Meets Structured Prediction, ICLR 2019 Workshop*, 2019.

24. Franz Josef Och and Hermann Ney. A systematic comparison of various statistical alignment models. *Computational linguistics*, 29 (1): 19–51, 2003.

25. Franz Josef Och and Hermann Ney. The alignment template approach to statistical machine translation. *Computational linguistics*, 30 (4): 417–449, 2004.

26. Stefan Riezler and Yi Liu. Query rewriting using monolingual statistical machine translation. *Computational Linguistics*, 36 (3): 569–582, 2010.

27. Stefan Riezler, Yi Liu, and Alexander Vasserman. Translating queries into snippets for improved query expansion. In *Proceedings of the 22nd International Conference on Computational Linguistics*, pages 737–744, 2008.

28. Hyun-Je Song, A.-Yeong Kim, and Seong-Bae Park. Translation of natural language query into keyword query using a RNN encoder-decoder. In *Proceedings of the 40th International ACM SIGIR Conference on Research and Development in Information Retrieval*, pages 965–968, 2017.

29. Ilya Sutskever, Oriol Vinyals, and Quoc V. Le. Sequence to sequence learning with neural networks. In *Advances in Neural Information Processing Systems*, pages 3104–3112, 2014.

30. Xuanhui Wang and ChengXiang Zhai. Mining term association patterns from search logs for effective query reformulation. In *Proceedings of the 17th ACM Conference on Information and Knowledge Management*, pages 479–488, 2008.
31. Rong Xiao, Jianhui Ji, Baoliang Cui, Haihong Tang, Wenwu Ou, Yanghua Xiao, Jiwei Tan, and Xuan Ju. Weakly supervised co-training of query rewriting and semantic matching for e-commerce. In *Proceedings of the Twelfth ACM International Conference on Web Search and Data Mining*, pages 402–410, 2019.
32. Yang Xu, Gareth J. F. Jones, and Bin Wang. Query dependent pseudo-relevance feedback based on Wikipedia. In *Proceedings of the 32nd Annual International ACM SIGIR Conference on Research and Development in Information Retrieval*, pages 59–66, 2009.
33. Tom Young, Devamanyu Hazarika, Soujanya Poria, and Erik Cambria. Recent trends in deep learning based natural language processing. *IEEE Computational intelligence magazine*, 13 (3): 55–75, 2018.

Chapter 7
Query Auto-Completion

Liangda Li, Hongbo Deng, and Yi Chang

Abstract Search assist plays an important role in modern search engines to reduce users' search efforts and satisfy their information needs. Query auto-completion (QAC) is among one of the key search assist services, which help users type less while submitting a query. The QAC engine generally offers a list of suggested queries that start with a user's input as a prefix, and the list of suggestions is changed to match the updated input after the user types each keystroke. In this chapter, we formally introduce the definition of the QAC problem and present state-of-the-art QAC methods. More specifically, how the user's search intent can be predicted by exploring rich information, including temporal, contextual, personal, and underlying various search behaviors. We also describe the popular datasets and metrics that are utilized in evaluating the performance of QAC methods.

7.1 Problem Definition

Query auto-completion (QAC) has been widely used in modern search engines to reduce users' efforts to submit a query by predicting the users' intended queries. The QAC engine generally offers a list of suggested queries that start with a user's input as a prefix, and the list of suggestions is changed to match the updated input after the user types each character. Suppose that a user is going to submit a query q to the search engine, and the user types the prefix of the query q of length i as $q[1..i]$ sequentially. The QAC engine will return the corresponding suggestion list

L. Li (✉)
Yahoo Research, Sunnyvale, CA, USA
e-mail: liangda@yahoo-inc.com

H. Deng
Alibaba Group, Zhejiang, China
e-mail: hbdeng@acm.org

Y. Chang
Jilin University, Jilin, China
e-mail: yichang@jlu.edu.cn

© Springer Nature Switzerland AG 2020
Y. Chang, H. Deng (eds.), *Query Understanding for Search Engines*,
The Information Retrieval Series 46, https://doi.org/10.1007/978-3-030-58334-7_7

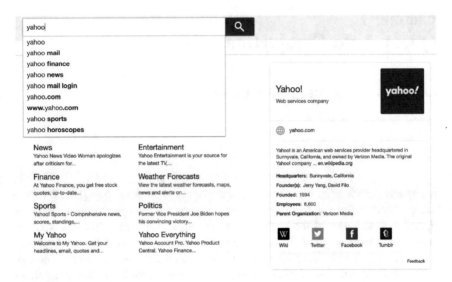

Fig. 7.1 Example of query auto-completion

after the user types each character until user clicks the suggestion q from the list or presses return, ending the interaction with the QAC engine. Figure 7.1 shows an example of the QAC service from the Yahoo search engine.

In the following, we give a formal introduction of the query auto-completion (QAC) problem. Let p denote the prefix entered by a user u, and $C(p)$ denote the set of query completions that start with the prefix p, the output of a QAC method is $R(p)$, a ranking of a subset of queries from $C(p)$. Provided that the actual search intent of user u is query q, and a loss function $L(q, R(p))$ to measure how likely user u will click query q from the selected order query set $R(p)$. (Obviously, if $q \notin R(p)$, there is no click chance.) The target of a QAC method is to optimize the loss function $L(q, R(p))$ as:

$$\hat{R}(p) = \min_{R(p) \subset C(p)} L(q, R(p)) \tag{7.1}$$

Notice that $R(p)$ is an ordered set, different $R(p)$ can have the exact same set of queries with different rankings.

Typical loss functions prefer the q to be ranked as top position as possible in the ranking list $R(p)$, since normally a user prefers his/her intent query to be ranked as higher position as possible.

7.2   Evaluation Metrics for QAC

To evaluate the effectiveness of QAC methods, two main categories of metrics have been developed and explored: (1) metrics that focus on the quality of ranking and (2) metrics that focus on how user's effort in using QAC is saved.

7.2.1   Ranking Metrics

Since the output of a QAC method is a ranking of limited number of selected query candidates given the current prefix to best satisfy user's search intent, a good QAC method is supposed to rank the query that better satisfies user's intent in higher positions. As for the search intent judgment, different strategies were used in the literature:

- Using user's final submitted query in a QAC session. For instance, if a user clicks "facebook" among the queries in the suggestion list, "facebook" is regarded as the query that satisfies the user's real search intent. This is the most popular evidence used for the relevance judgment.
- Using user's submitted query's frequency within the most recent time slot. Such relevance judgment prefers query ranking suggestions that represent the search trend of general users instead of the unique search intent of individual users.
- Using manual judgments for each suggestion [3]. The major drawbacks of this strategy are that: (1) it requires a large amount of human resources for conducting the judgment, while the size of the data is usually limited to thousands of examples only; (2) the correctness of the judgment is usually not guaranteed, which can result in strong noise to the model training considering the limited data size of the editorial data.
- Using the quality of the search results retrieved by each suggested query [21]. Such relevance judgments benefit a search engine user who does not have a clear search intent before starting a QAC session, by suggesting him/her the most promising queries (with the best quality search results). However, the quality of search results is out of the control of a QAC engine, and a suggestion with better search results does not necessarily meet user's real search intent. Such a measurement tends to recommend user popular queries, thus fails to satisfy users who are searching tail queries which have a limited number of high quality search results, or the search engine itself performs poorly in indexing the high quality search results for them.

With the search intent judgment, traditional ranking metrics in information retrieval(IR) have been widely employed to measure the performance of QAC methods. Below, we list some popularly used measures.

- Mean reciprocal rank (MRR): This is a statistical measure that evaluates processes predicting a list of possible responses to a sample of queries. MRR is the most popular evaluation metric in measuring QAC performance [1, 19, 26],

$$MRR = \frac{1}{|Q|} \sum_{q \in Q} \frac{1}{\text{rank}_q},$$
(7.2)

where Q is the set of correct corresponds which, in our case, the query q a user finally submitted, and rank_q denotes the rank of the query q in the suggested query list. This evaluation setup assumes that items placed towards the top of a ranked list receive more attention and are therefore more useful to a search engine user.

Since most existing QAC works conducted experiments on normal QAC logs, which contained the query suggestion list under the last prefix of a QAC session only, MRR is calculated as the average reciprocal rank (RR) score of the last keystroke of each QAC session. Variations of MRR include:

- MRR@All: As introduced above, the normal MRR score only pays attention to the ranking of query suggestions under the last keystroke of a QAC session. However, in a real QAC scenario, a user is very likely to make the click at a shorter keystroke if his/her intended query is already shown at a reasonable position under that keystroke. Thus QAC methods that target to optimize the normal MRR score may fail to improve the query suggestion ranking at shorter keystrokes as well, while such an improvement can significantly save user's QAC action effort.

  Recently, the availability of high-resolution QAC data enabled the measurement of the quality of query suggestions at shorter keystrokes. A variation of the normal MRR score is proposed, named MRR@All, to calculate the average reciprocal rank (RR) score of all keystrokes, instead of the last keystroke only. Compared with the normal MRR score, such a variation prefers QAC methods that are able to infer user's real search intent as early as possible in a QAC session. To differentiate this variation from the normal MRR score, the normal score is named MRR@Last in those QAC works.

- Weighted mean reciprocal rank (wMRR): The normal MRR score assigns an equal weight to the last keystroke of each QAC session. However, one thing that is worth attention is that the effort of typing a specific prefix can also be different. For instance, if the user input is the letter "z," since there is only limited number of words that start with "z," the number of candidates to suggesting and ranking is also limited, which makes it a relatively easier task for a QAC model than the letter with larger number of candidates, such as "d." Thus, a weighted version of MRR, named weighted mean reciprocal rank (wMRR) [1] is proposed to each prefix based on the number of query suggestions available.

- Success Rate at top K (SR@K): This metric calculates the average ratio of the query that satisfied user's search intent can be found within the top K positions of the predicted query suggestion list. It is widely used for tasks that have only one ground truth among all candidates[10].

The major difference between ranking metrics in web document ranking and QAC problems is that, the judgment of the query that satisfies user's real search intent is relatively easier than the relevance judgment of web documents given the search query. A user's search intent in one QAC session is most likely the query that he/she finally submitted, while the relevance of web documents can hardly be determined by a user's click or dwell time on them. In learning to ranking tasks, editorial judgments of query-document relevance are very critical in measuring the performance, while QAC metrics rarely rely on the editorial effort. Such an advantage enables the collection of a large-scale golden evaluation dataset for the QAC tasks.

7.2.2   User Assist Metrics

Since the intuition of QAC is to assist search engine users' query formulation and save their interaction efforts, a good QAC method is supposed to reduce the cost of users' interaction with the search engine. Below we list some popularly used measures.

- Minimum Keystroke Length (MKS) [9]: It measures the number of actions a user has to take to submit a target query. This metric can be understood as a simulation of a search engine user's behavior during a QAC session. The user action taken into consideration includes both the letter typing and Down Arrow key pressing to reach the position of the target query. For instance, for the target query of a user that is located at the i-th position at the j-th keystroke, the number of actions will be calculated as $i + j$. Among all the potential positions in which the target query appears, the minimal number of actions needed will be counted as the value of MKS.

  A variation of the MKS metric is penalized Minimum Keystroke Length (PMKS), which considers an additional action, user's view of each suggestion for correctness. A penalty value of 0.1 is added for showing each suggestion, i.e., the latter keystroke a target query locates at, the larger penalty value is added. Such a variation can be view as an encouragement of users to make selections at shorter keystrokes.
- e-Saved and p-Saved [15]: p-Saved is proposed to compute the expected QAC usage as:

$$\text{pSaved}(q) = \sum_{i=1}^{|q|} \sum_{j} I(S_{ij}) P(S_{ij} = 1) = \sum_{i=1}^{|q|} \sum_{j} P(S_{ij} = 1) \qquad (7.3)$$

where $P(S_{ij} = 1)$ measures the probability that a user ends the current QAC session at the j-th position under the i-th keystroke. And $I(S_{ij}) = 1$ when user actually used the corresponding query suggestion (at the j-th position under the i-th keystroke). This metric can be understood as the probability that a user actually uses the QAC engine rather than typing the target query on his/her own.

Conversely, e-Saved is proposed to measure the amount of effort saved in terms of keystrokes as:

$$\text{eSaved}(q) = \sum_{i=1}^{|q|} (1 - \frac{i}{|q|}) \sum_j P(S_{ij} = 1) \qquad (7.4)$$

This metric is actually calculating the expected ratio of characters a user can skip inputting until his/her query is submitted. It prefers the improvements in the query suggestions for longer queries in particular, since a user usually prefers the effort saving benefit from a QAC engine when submitting long queries than the benefit when submitting short queries.

7.3 QAC Logs

Most of the research works on QAC built models based on the normal search query log. Traditionally, the search query log only includes the user ID, the timestamp, the submitted query and its associated search results. While the content of submitted queries in the log lays the foundation of search intent prediction for in general during the QAC process, other information like the timestamp, the submitted query and its associated search results provid more precise evidence for the search intent prediction given a certain user under a certain scenario. Typical public query log that is widely used in existing QAC works includes: the AOL dataset [24], the MSN dataset [8], and the SogouQ dataset.[1]

Those normal search query logs do not contain the sequential keystrokes (prefixes) users typed in the search box, as well as their corresponding QAC suggestions. In order to better analyze and understand real users' behaviors, a high-resolution QAC log is introduced and analyzed in [19], which records users' interactions with a QAC engine at each keystroke and associated system respond in an entire QAC process. For each submitted query, there is only one record in a traditional search query log. However, in the high-resolution QAC log, each submitted query is associated with a **QAC session**, which is defined to begin with the first keystroke a user typed in the search box towards the final submitted query. The recorded information in each QAC session includes each keystroke a user has

---

[1] http://www.sogou.com/labs/dl/q.html.

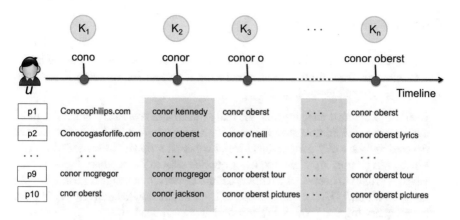

Fig. 7.2 High-resolution QAC log

entered, the timestamp of a keystroke, the corresponding top 10 suggested queries to a prefix, the anonymous user ID, and the final clicked query.

Formally, a **QAC session** contains S keystrokes and each keystroke has a suggested query list of length D as shown in Fig. 7.2.[2] A QAC session ends at the keystroke where the user clicks a query in the suggested query list, or when the prefix at that keystroke is exactly the query the user enters into the search engine. Among the $S \times D$ *slots* in each QAC session, where each slot q_{ij} is indexed by the i-th position at the j-th keystroke, a user clicks at most one of them, although the user's intended query may appear in many slots.

7.4   QAC Methods

The basic idea to solve the QAC problem is taking the general interest and all users in a search engine and recommend users the most popular queries in search history. A normal query auto-completion engine usually makes an assumption that what a user searched in history is most likely to imply his/her current search intent and maintain a list of all candidate queries with their frequencies. However, such prediction only works under very limited scenario and fails to consider the variations across different users, time slots, etc. In the following, we discuss how different types of information are utilized by existing QAC works. Those information can be generally categorized into: temporal information, contextual information, personal information, user's interaction in QAC, and user's interaction besides QAC.

---

[2]In real-world search engines, $D = 4\,4$ for Baidu and Google, $D = 8$ for Bing, $D = 10$ for Yahoo.

7.4.1 Time-Sensitive QAC

Temporal information plays an important role in QAC, since search engine user's interest changes from time to time. Significant temporal factors that can result in user's search intent change include:

- User's own interest change along the daily time. Both "star wars" and "star trek" are famous movie/drama series started from many years ago. A user can be very devoted to "star trek" last year and divert his/her attention to "star wars" this year. Since both queries are high-frequency queries existed in the query log for many years, it is hard to decide which query should be ranked in a higher position under the prefix "star." QAC methods need to learn such knowledge from user's most recent query log and provide the appropriate recommendation.
- Periodic events that users participate in regularly. Search engine users can have some periodic interest in certain types of queries (like travel, shopping) that are closely related to seasonal events, such as weekend, yearend, holiday, anniversary, etc. Those queries are usually very different from user's submitted queries in regular days and unable to be predicted from user's recent history. Under this scenario, QAC methods need to utilize user's history at the same/similar seasonal events occurred previously to make the prediction.
- Breaking news that catch up users' attention. User's search intent may also follow the breaking news that happen from time to time. Queries related to those breaking news are likely never recorded in the query log before. QAC methods need to detect the trending queries in the most recent time period and promote those queries in query suggestion lists.

Most popular completion (MPC) is proposed by [1] to rank candidate queries based on their frequencies in the historical query log. This method is a quite straightforward utilization of some basic temporal features and can be regarded as an approximate maximum likelihood estimator as:

$$\text{MPC} = \text{argmax}_{q \in C(p)} \omega(q), \quad \text{where} \quad \omega(q) = \frac{f(q)}{\sum_{q_i \in Q} f(q_i)} \tag{7.5}$$

where $C(p)$ denotes the set of query completions that start with the prefix p, and $f(q)$ denotes the frequency of query q in the query log Q.

The main drawback of MPC is that it assumed user's interest is stable within the range of the collected historical query logs. However, as pointed out in previous paragraphs, user's interest changes from time to time and can be influenced by various types of temporal signals. Thus it makes us difficult to find a certain time window which can be used to predict user's current search intent.

Based on MPC, Shokouhi and Radinsky [27] proposed a time-sensitive QAC ranking model (TS), which replaced the real frequency of candidate queries utilized in MPC with forecasted scores computed by time-series modeling of historical query logs. The score of each candidate at time t is calculated based on its predicted frequency through time-series models that designed to detect the trending queries. This time-sensitive QAC ranking model is formalized as:

$$TS(p, t) = \text{argmax}_{q \in C(p)} \omega(q|t), \quad \text{where} \quad \omega(q|t) = \frac{\hat{f}_t(q)}{\sum_{q_i \in Q} \hat{f}_t(q_i)} \tag{7.6}$$

where p is the input prefix, $C(p)$ denotes the set of query completions that start with the prefix p, and $\hat{f}_t(q)$ denotes the estimated frequency of query q at time t in the query log Q.

In practice, TS utilized the single exponential smoothing method [11] to predict the frequency of query q at time t based on the real frequency at the last time slot $t - 1$, and a smoothed frequency at the time slot $t - 2$.

$$\hat{f}_t = \bar{f}_{t-1} = \lambda * f_t + (1 - \lambda) * \bar{y}_{t-2} \tag{7.7}$$

where f_{t-1} and $\bar{f}_{t-1}$ denote the real observed and smoothed values for the query frequency at time slot $t - 1$, $\hat{f}_t$ is the estimated frequency of the query at the current time slot t, and λ is a trade-off parameter in the range of [0, 1]. Notice that the smoothed value $\bar{f}_{t-1}$ at the last time slot $t - 1$ is used as the predicted value $\hat{f}_t$ at the current time slot t.

Although this single exponential smoothing can produce reasonable forecasts for stationary time-series, it is proved to perform poorly in capturing the trending queries. Double exponential smoothing methods [11] are proposed to address this issue by extending the previous model with a trend variable involved.

$$\hat{f}_t = \bar{f}_{t-1} + F_{t-1} \tag{7.8}$$

$$\bar{f}_{t-1} = \lambda_1 * f_{t-1} + (1 - \lambda_1) * (\bar{f}_{t-2} + F_{t-2}) \tag{7.9}$$

$$F_{t-1} = \lambda_2 * (\bar{f}_{t-1} - \bar{f}_{t-2}) + (1 - \lambda_2) * F_{t-2} \tag{7.10}$$

Here, parameter F_{t-1} models the linear trend of time-series at time $t - 1$, f_t and $\bar{f}_t$ represent the real and smoothed frequency at time t. λ_1 and λ_2 are smoothing parameters.

In addition to the double exponential smoothing, triple exponential smoothing (or HoltWinters smoothing) [11] goes one step further to model the periodical queries as:

$$\hat{f}_t = (\bar{f}_{t-1} + F_{t-1}) * S_{t-T} \tag{7.11}$$

$$\bar{y}_{t-1} = \lambda_1 * (f_{t-1} - S_{t-1-T}) + (1 - \lambda_1) * (\bar{f}_{t-2} + F_{t-2}) \tag{7.12}$$

$$F_{t-1} = \lambda_2 * (\bar{f}_{t-1} - \bar{f}_{t-2}) + (1 - \lambda_2) * F_{t-2} \tag{7.13}$$

$$S_{t-1} = \lambda_3 * (f_{t-1} - \bar{f}_{t-1}) + (1 - \lambda_3) * S_{t-1-T} \tag{7.14}$$

$$\lambda_1 + \lambda_2 + \lambda_3 = 1 \tag{7.15}$$

where λ_1, λ_2, and λ_3 are free smoothing parameters in [0, 1], S_{t-1} captures the periodicity of query at time $t - 1$, and T denotes the length of periodic cycle.

Another solution based on time-series analysis is a time-sensitive QAC method proposed by Cai et al. [7], which attempted to detect both cyclically and instantly frequent queries. This method estimated the current query frequency as a linear combination of its periodicity score and trending score. It not only inherited the merits of time-series analysis for long-term observations of query popularity, but also considered recent variations in query frequency. In specific, it predicted the frequency of a query q at time slot t through:

$$\hat{f}_t(q, \lambda) = \lambda * \hat{f}_t(q)_{trend} + (1 - \lambda) * \hat{f}_t(q)_{peri} \qquad (7.16)$$

where $\hat{f}_t(q)_{trend}$ tries to capture the trending of query q, and $\hat{f}_t(q)_{peri}$ tries to capture the periodicity of query q. This method sets $\lambda = 1$ for aperiodic queries and $0 \leq \lambda < 1$ for periodic queries.

The term $\hat{f}_t(q)_{trend}$ is formulated as a linear combination of the trending queries during the most recent N days:

$$\hat{f}_t(q)_{trend} = \sum_{i=1}^{N} \omega_i * \hat{f}_t(q, i)_{trend} \qquad (7.17)$$

Here ω_i is a time decay weight while constrained by the condition that $\sum_i \omega_i = 1$.

The trending prediction for each day i is calculated based on the first order derivative of the frequency of query q within time slot t:

$$\hat{f}_t(q, i)_{trend} = f_{t-1-TD(i)}(q) + \int_{t-1-TD(i)}^{t} \frac{\partial C(q, t)}{\partial t} dt \qquad (7.18)$$

Here $f_{t-TD(i)}(q)$ is actual the frequency of query q at day i, while $C(q, t)$ denotes the frequency of query q within time slot t.

The term $\hat{f}_t(q)_{peri}$ is formulated as the smoothing term that averages the query frequency of the most recent M preceding time slots $t_p = t - 1 * T_q, \ldots, t - M * T_q$ in the query log as:

$$\hat{f}_t(q)_{peri} = \frac{1}{M} \sum_{m=1}^{M} f_{t-m*T_q}(q) \qquad (7.19)$$

Here T_q is the length of periodic cycle of query q.

The temporal information recorded in the QAC log is not limited to be utilized in the query frequency estimation. Recent works [17] also made use of this information to reveal the relationship between user's click behaviors in QAC logs, such as the click position. Different search engine users can have different preferences in the positions to click during the QAC process. For instance, some users prefer to make clicks at lower positions under shorter prefixes, while others prefer higher positions under longer prefixes. For the same user, such kind of preference may also change with respect to time. Thus in learning a user's preference of click position, it is reasonable to assign higher weights to the recent historical click positions. To quantify the degree of the influence between click events from the temporal aspect, this method employed the following formula:

$$\kappa(t_l - t) \tag{7.20}$$

where t is the timestamp when a user makes the current click, t_l is the timestamp when the l-th historical click event occurs, and $\kappa(t_l - t)$ represents a time decay effect.

7.4.2 Context-Sensitive QAC

Context-sensitive QAC methods take the context which a search engine user has input into consideration in user search intent prediction. Different from the normal query frequency based QAC methods, which predict the probability that whether a candidate queries will be issued by a user based on the exact same query recorded in historical query logs, context-aware QAC methods make the prediction based on the submission of other queries that share a certain relationship with the predicted candidate query. Such relationship can be:

- With similar content. Queries that shared similar content are very likely to reflect the same or similar user search intent. Thus besides the original query, other queries with similar content can provide additional evidence in the search intent prediction. For instance, "star wars" and "star wars the old republic" can both tell a user's interest in the movie/drama "star wars," and the frequency of both queries can be very high. Such kind of information is especially useful in predicting user's search intent under short keystrokes, such as "st" in this case, since the frequency of the single query "star wars" is not able to represent user's real relative degree of interest in this movie/drama, when compared with other queries which also started with "st" but do not have so many high-frequency queries with similar content.
- Belong to the same category. Such information can be helpful in revealing a user's interest when little information is given, for instance, only one keystroke is entered. One typical example is that, if most queries submitted by a user are shopping queries, it is very likely that he/she will click "amazon" rather than "aol" under the keystroke 'a'.
- Co-occurred frequently in the query log. If two consecutive queries "hollywood" and "beverly hills" are issued by the same user, then the previous query "hollywood" can also be viewed as the context of query "beverly hills." Generally, two consecutive queries issued many times by different users are more likely

to have a strong correlation between each other. It makes more sense to take into account the explicit temporal information of query sequences exhibited by many different users in the whole-query logs. The basic intuition is that if two consecutive or temporally close queries are issued many times by the same user or many other users, it is more likely that these two queries are semantically related to each other. Those queries are very likely to form a search task, which target to accomplish a single search intent goal (travel in western los angeles in the previous example). Thus the co-occurrence of those queries can happen frequently in the future across different users that conduct the same search task.

The NearestCompletion method [1] utilized users' recent queries as the context of the user input. This method did a good job in predicting user's search intent when matching the context of the user.

NearestCompletion described a context-sensitive extension of the Maximum Likelihood Estimator, which tried to predict the candidate query q that started with prefix x whose presentation vector v_q has the highest cosine similarity to the search context representation v_C:

$$\text{NearestCompletion}(p, C) = \text{argmax}_{q \in C(p)} \frac{< v_q, v_C >}{\|v_q\| \cdot \|v_C\|}. \tag{7.21}$$

Here $C(p)$ is the set of candidate queries starting with prefix p.

The context representations in NearestCompletion are based on the query representations. Given $v_{q_1}, \ldots, v_{q_t}$ as the corresponding vectors of context $C = q_1, \ldots, q_t$. The context vector v_C is formulated as a linear combination of the query vectors $v_C = \sum_{i=1}^{t} \omega_i v_{q_i}$, with weights $\omega_1, \ldots, \omega_t \geq 0$. Those weights described the degree of the influence from the historical query as context to the current search intent of a user. They are required to be time decayed, since the more recent submitted queries are more likely to be relevant to the current query. Popular weight functions that satisfy this condition include: recent-query-only ($w_t = 1$ and $w_i = 0$ for all $i < t$), linear decay ($w_i = 1/(t - i + 1)$), logarithmic decay ($w_i = 1/(1 + \log(t - i + 1))$), and exponential decay ($w_i = 1/e_{t-i}$).

Notice that using the output of NearestCompletion alone for a QAC task is not working well for when a new user joins or a user's current search intent is not relevant to the context collected for the user. In practice, this work used a linear combination of the score from the NearestCompletion function and the MPC function introduced above as the final score for the query candidates ranking in QAC.

Cai et al. [7] utilized two different types of context for search intent prediction. One is the set of queries in the current search session, denoted as Q_s, the other is the set of historical queries issued by user u, denoted as Q_u. This method calculated the scores of the candidates $q_c \in S(p)$ through a linear combination of similarity scores $\text{Score}(Q_s, q_c)$ and $\text{Score}(Q_u, q_c)$ as follows:

$$\text{Pscore}(q_c) = \omega * \text{Score}(Q_s, q_c) + (1 - \omega) * \text{Score}(Q_u, q_c) \tag{7.22}$$

here ω weights the above two components.

To compute the similarity scores, this method used n-gram to represent each query, thus enabling the proposed similarity score to capture syntactic reformulations. Moreover, to overcome the problem that the query vocabulary is too sparse to capture semantic relationships, it treated a user's preceding queries Q_s in the current session and Q_u in the historical log as context to personalize QAC where the similarity is measured at the character level.

Jiang et al. [13] studied user's reformulation behaviors in QAC based on the context information. Three types of context based features are designed to describe the reformulation behaviors of search engine users by capturing how users modify their preceding queries in a query session, including:

- Term-level features: for instance, term keeping—$|S(q_{t-1}) \cap S(q_t)|$, which describes the number of shared terms by the query issued at time slot t and the previous query at time slot $t - 1$.
- Query-level features: for instance, average cosine similarity—$\frac{1}{t-1} \sum_{i=1}^{t-1} \mathrm{sim_{cos}}(q_i, q_t)$, which calculates the content similarity between the queries issued at time slot t and all previous historical queries issued within the same query session.
- Session-level features: for instance, ratio of effective terms $|C_{\mathrm{eff}}(q_t)|/|S(q_t)|$, which is the ratio of the number of clicks on the search results of query q_t divided by the number of terms in query q_t.

Such contextual features that capture user's reformulation behaviors are proved to be an effective additional signal to the regular context features introduced above.

Li et al. [17] designed a set of contextual features that describe the relationship between the content of a historical query q' and the current suggested query q, to quantify the degree of the influence between click events from the context aspect. These features count the number of appearances of a certain pattern involving both the historical query q' and the current suggestion q in a certain time range formulated as:

$$x(p)(t, \Delta t) = \#\{p \in [t - \Delta t, t)\} \tag{7.23}$$

where p represents a certain defined pattern, $[t - \Delta t, t)$ is the time interval from some ancient timestamp to the current timestamp. Table 7.1 shows several patterns adopted in this work, which is inspired by the features proposed in [25].

As shown in Table 7.1, those contextual features generally originate from the co-occurrence of two queries in the query sequence submitted by search engine users and reflect pairwise relationship. A feature vector $\mathbf{x}_{q',q}(t)$ is formed for each query-pair (q', q) at any given timestamp t as

$$\mathbf{x}_{q',q}(t) = \{x(p)(t, \Delta t) | p \in \mathcal{P}_{q',q}, \Delta t > 0\} \tag{7.24}$$

where $\mathcal{P}_{q',q}$ refers to the set of patterns involving the pair of queries $\{q', q\}$. Thus for each timestamp t, a unique set of feature vectors $\{\mathbf{x}_{q',q}(t)\}$ imply how a historical

Table 7.1 Patterns in constructing contextual features

Pattern p	Description
$q' \rightarrow q$	Query q is submitted just after the submission of query q'
$q \longleftrightarrow q'$	Query q and q' are submitted in adjacent
$q' \xrightarrow{(v)} q$	Query q is submitted after the submission of query q', and v queries have been submitted in between
$q \xleftrightarrow{(v)} q'$	v queries are submitted between the submission of query q and q'

click event (on query q') influences the current click event (on query q) from the contextual aspect.

7.4.3 Personalized QAC

Another type of useful signal in QAC is the user's personal information. Unlike the context information that can vary with respect to time, personal information described user's inherit characteristics that are mainly to differentiate one user from other users, or a group of users from other groups. Such personal information generally includes:

- bcookie. In query logs, bcookie is unusually used as the identifier of a single search engine user, although in real-world scenario one actual user can have multiple bcookies (such as owning multiple computers), and a bcookie can be shared by multiple users (family members shared computers or public computers). Learning distinct models based on the query log under different bcookies can increase the accuracy in user's search intent prediction, since the interest and search habit of users can be very different from each other. The major drawback of bcookie based model is that the number of QAC sessions completed by a single user is very limited. Obviously, it will fail when facing new bcookies. Moreover, for most normal search engine users who regularly submit tens of queries per day, the available QAC sessions for model learning are very limited. Thus, more general categorical personal information is also important, which can jointly utilize the query logs of users within the same category to benefit the model learning.
- gender. The gender of a search engine user can be a strong signal in predicting his/her interest. A male user is more likely to submit sports queries than shopping queries, and vice versa for a female user.
- age. The age of a search engine user is another strong signal. Teenagers usually prefer gaming, while older individuals care more about health.
- location. The location information is very useful in query suggestion, since a large percentage of queries submitted by search engine users are with local intent. For instance, under the prefix "amc," a user lived in sunnyvale is more likely to search for "amc cupertino" instead of "amc san Francisco." Notice that location

is not a typical type of personal information, since a user can move across cites, states, or even countries, especially for users who spend a great amount of time in traveling. However, for regular search engine users, their locations are usually stable.

In the Personalized QAC model proposed in [26], a number of demographic features are utilized, including users' age, gender, and zip-code information from their Microsoft Live profiles. This method divides users into five groups based on age: $\{<20, 21-30, 31-40, 41-50, >50\}$. For each user, the model made use of the frequency of query candidates that submitted by all other users fall into the same age groups as a feature. Similar features are also generated based on gender and zip-code information. Notice that the zip-codes are also collapsed into 10 regions according to the corresponding first digits, so as to reduce sparsity. Those demographic features are incorporated into a supervised learning framework for personalized ranking of query auto-completion.

Cai et al. [6] also conducted experiments to test the effectiveness of the demographic features in learning to rank algorithms such as Burges et al. [5], results showed that demographic features such as location are more effective than others in the QAC task. The SQA algorithm proposed in [20] studied how to utilize location information to solve the QAC task based on a native index structure combined with a spatial index. This method utilized the longitude/latitude information to describe a certain location and ranked candidate suggestions q given a certain prefix p based on the ranking score function as:

$$\text{RankScore}(q, p) = \alpha * \frac{\text{Dis}(q_{loc}, p_{loc})}{\text{DisMax}} + (1 - \alpha) * \text{RelScore}(q, p) \qquad (7.25)$$

where $\alpha \in (0, 1)$ is a parameter that balances the spatial proximity and the normal relevancy between the candidate suggestion q and prefix p. $\text{Dis}(q_{loc}, p_{loc})$ is the Euclidean distance between q_{loc}, the location descriptor of query q, and p_{loc}, the location when user typing the prefix p. DisMax is the potential max distance value used for normalization. $\text{RelScore}(q, p)$ is the normal relevance score for the query-prefix pair (q, p) calculated based on regular QAC features.

7.4.4 User Interactions in QAC

Rich user interactions can be observed along with each keystroke until a user clicks a suggestion or types the entire query manually. It becomes increasingly important to analyze and understand users' interactions with the QAC engine, so as to improve its performance. Figure 7.3 presents the general process that a search engine user interacts with the QAC engine in a QAC session.

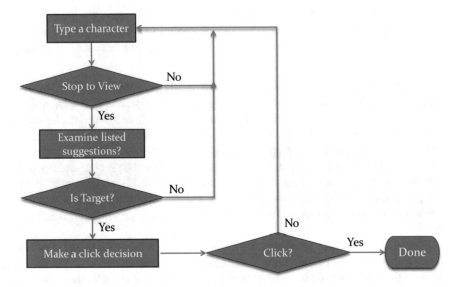

Fig. 7.3 How a search engine user interacts with the QAC engine in a QAC session

In the following, we list several typical user behaviors that can facilitate the understanding of the QAC process:

- **Click behavior.** User's click behavior is one of the key signals in understanding user's search intent, since the target of a QAC method is to increase user's click chance during a QAC session (as early as possible). There are mainly two types of information in user's click behaviors:

  - **Position bias.** One important type of click information is the click bias on vertical positions in QAC. Using the same set of QAC sessions, we have computed the distribution of clicks according to their positions in the final suggestion list and the final prefix length. Similar to the findings in the traditional click models, most of the clicks concentrate on top positions. Such vertical positional bias suggests that the relevance estimation of queries should be boosted if they are clicked on lower ranks. Compared to user's QAC behavior on PC, their clicks on mobile distribute more evenly within positions from 1 to 3. In addition, most of the clicks are located in long prefix, the click probability at short prefix length (1 and 2) is very low, suggesting that users tend to skip the suggested queries at the beginning.
  - **Click choice.** The click choice of a user can provide rich information in predicting user's search intent. The query candidates that have been suggested by the QAC engine but not clicked by a user during a QAC session have a small chance to meet user's search intent. A user is unlikely to look for the query "facebook" if he/she does not select it under prefix "f," since "facebook" is the top query suggestion.

- **Skipping and viewing behavior.** Search engine users frequently skip several intermediate lists of candidates even though these lists contain their final submitted queries. A plausible explanation for the skipping behavior is that the user did not examine it due to some reasons, such as fast typing speed, too deep to look up the query, etc. The inference of whether a user has skipped to view a certain keystroke or a certain suggested query under that keystroke can be very helpful in predicting user's real search intent, since a query that a user does not click may also satisfy his/her intent if he/she skips that query or the corresponding keystroke due to the reasons mentioned as above.
- **Typing behavior.** Typing speed is an important signal that characterizes a search engine user. A user with fast typing speed is probably an expert user who has rich experience in using search engines, usually has a clear search intent, and is aware of what exact query to enter before starting a QAC session. Thus an expert user is less likely to use the assist from the QAC engine than a new search engine user.

Jiang et al. [13] employed user's click behaviors to model user's reformulation habit. This work designed session-level features based on both the timestamps of user's clicks in QAC. It calculated the average time duration between clicks as $\frac{1}{T-1} \sum_{i=1}^{T-1} (t_{i+1} - t_i)$, and the trends of time duration as $(t_T - t_{T-1}) / \frac{1}{T-2} \sum_{i=1}^{T-2} (t_{i+1} - t_i)$, where t_i is the timestamp of the click that occurs in the i-th QAC session.

Li et al. [17] explored to learn the position bias in a user's click preference based on the positional information of historical QAC sessions from the same user. This work quantified the degree of the influence between the click events from the special slot aspect using the following formula:

$$\kappa(|\mathbf{p}_l - \mathbf{p}|) \tag{7.26}$$

where $\mathbf{p}$ is the slot where a user makes the current click, and $\mathbf{p}_l$ is the slot where the user makes the l-th historical click event, i.e., the click occurs at the l-th QAC session, and $\kappa(|\mathbf{p}_l - \mathbf{p}|)$ represents a decay effect from the slot discrepancy. Notice that $\mathbf{p} = (i, j)$ is a vector of length 2, its entries i and j denote the position and the keystroke, respectively.

TDCM [19] tried to utilize user's skipping behaviors and clicking position bias information to understand user's click choice during the QAC process. It defined a basic assumption for each type of user behaviors separately as below:

- SKIPPING BIAS ASSUMPTION: A query will not receive a click if the user did not stop and examine the suggested list of queries, regardless of the relevance of the query. This assumption explains why there are no clicks to intermediate prefix even though a relevant query is ranked at the top of the list, and all of the clicks are concentrated on the final prefix.
- VERTICAL POSITION BIAS ASSUMPTION: A query on higher rank tends to attract more clicks regardless of its relevance to the prefix.

Based on the above assumptions, TDCM proposed a Two-Dimensional Click Model to explain the observed clicks. This click model consists of a horizontal model (H Model) that explains the skipping behavior, a vertical model (D Model) that depicts the vertical examination behavior, and a relevance model (R Model) that measures the intrinsic relevance between the prefix and a suggested query.

In specific, TDCM formulated the probability of observing a click C in a session as:

$$P(C) = \sum_{H,D} P(C, H, D) \tag{7.27}$$

where $H = \{H_1, \ldots, H_n\}$, $D = \{D_1, \ldots, D_n\}$ is a set of hidden variables, respectively. Here, H_i denotes whether the user stops to examine the column i, and D_i denotes the depth of examination at column i. $C = \{C_1, \ldots, C_n\}$ is the click observation matrix in which only one click is observed: $C_{n,J} = 1$, n is the number of columns in the QAC session. This model followed the Cascade Model assumption as:

$$P(C_{n,J} = 1) = P(C_1 = 0, \ldots, C_{n1} = 0, C_{n,J} = 1, C_{n,j} = 0, j \neq J) \tag{7.28}$$

as well as the set of conditional probabilities as:

$$P(C_{ij} = 1 | H_i = 0) = 0 \tag{7.29}$$

$$P(C_{ij} = 1 | H_i = 1, D_i < j) = 0 \tag{7.30}$$

$$P(C_{ij} = 0 | H_i, D_i) = 1 - P(C_{ij} = 1 | H_i, D_i) \tag{7.31}$$

$$P(D_i > d | q_d : C_{n,d} = 1) = 0 \tag{7.32}$$

Among the above conditional probabilities, Eqs. (7.30) and (7.32) modeled the SKIPPING BIAS ASSUMPTION, and Eqs. (7.31) and (7.32) modeled the VERTICAL POSITION BIAS ASSUMPTION. Equation (7.32) stated that if a relevant query is ranked in depth d, the examination depth at the i-th column must not exceed d.

In the H model, TDCM attempted to capture user's skipping behavior via the following features: TypingSpeed: an expert user is less likely to use QAC than a slow user. CurrPosition: a user tends to examine the queries at the end of typing. IsWordBoundary: a user is more likely to look up queries at word boundaries. NbSuggQueries: it is more likely to be examined if the list of queries is short. ContentSim: a user may be more likely to examine the list if all queries are coherent in content. QueryIntent: a user tends to skip the list more when searching for navigational queries. Also, in the D model, TDCM utilized the positions a query candidate is ranked to measure the pure vertical position bias.

Zhang et al. [32] studied how user's click behavior can be utilized as the implicit negative feedback during user-QAC interactions. The key challenge is that this kind of implicit negative feedback can be strong or weak, and its strength cannot be directly observed. It utilized additional information such as dwell time and position to capture the confidence in using an unclicked suggestion as implicit negative feedback in search intent prediction.

If a user dwells on a suggestion list for a longer time, the user may have more time to carefully examine the suggested queries. Conversely, if a user dwells for a shorter time, the suggested queries will more likely be ignored; thus, even if these queries are unselected, whether the user favors them or not is unknown. Since different users may have different typing speeds, the inference of implicit negative feedback strength by dwell time should be personalized. This method represented implicit negative feedback from the user u to the query q at the k-th keystroke during the c-th QAC session in the QAC log by a feature vector $\mathbf{x}^{(k)}(u, q, c)$. The features utilized include: DwellT-M, the maximum dwell time when query q is suggested; DwellT, total dwell time where query q is suggested; WordBound, the number of the keystrokes at word boundaries when query q is suggested; SpaceChar, the number of the keystrokes at space characters when query q is suggested; OtherChar, the number of the keystrokes at non-alphanum char when query q is suggested; IsPrevQuery, 1 if query q is the immediately previous query; 0 otherwise; and Pos@i, the number of the keystrokes when query q is at position i ($i = 1, 2, \ldots, 10$) of a suggestion list.

Then a generalized additive model, named AdaQAC, is proposed to predict the preference $p^{(k)}(u, q, c)$ for a query q of a user u at a keystroke k in the c-th QAC session:

$$p^{(k)}(u, q, c) = r^{(k)}(u, q, c) + \phi^{\top}(u)\mathbf{x}^{(k)}(u, q, c) \tag{7.33}$$

Here, the preference model $p^{(k)}(u, q, c)$ is able to reflect a user u's preference for a query q after the implicit negative feedback $\mathbf{x}^{(k)}(u, q, c)$ is expressed to q before the k-th keystroke in the c-th QAC session. With the associated feature weights $\phi(u)$ personalized for u, $\phi^{\top}(u)\mathbf{x}^{(k)}(u, q, c)$ encodes the strength of implicit negative feedback to q from u with personalization.

In addition to the above introduced QAC methods which modeled user's interaction at each keystroke independently, RBCM [16] made a further step to study the relationship between users' behaviors at different keystrokes, which includes:

1. **State transitions between skipping and viewing.** The study on high-resolution query log data revealed that a user may choose to either view or skip the suggestion list at each keystroke in a QAC session. Besides the above introduced factors that influence users' decisions on skipping or viewing, such as typing speed and whether the end of current prefix is at word boundary. This work believed that such decisions should also be influenced by their decisions on skipping or viewing at the previous keystroke. For instance, imagining a user u has 5 sequential skipping moves in one QAC session and 2 sequential skipping moves in another QAC session, the chance becomes higher for the same user to stop and view the suggestion list at the current keystroke after 5 sequential

skipping moves. Conversely, if the same user has already viewed too many keystrokes continuously but found no intended query, it becomes more likely that he/she may skip the next one;

2. **Users' real preference of suggestions**. This work claimed that, for each keystroke, the associated users' real preference is hard to be detected from the current suggested query list alone. The rankings of suggested query lists of latter keystrokes together with users' final click choices should also be utilized to re-rank the suggested queries in the list of the current keystroke. Intuitively, a clicked query, i.e., the user's intended query, should get a higher rank not only at the keystroke he/she makes the click, but also at previous keystrokes where this query appears, despite that it is not clicked at that time;

3. **User-specific cost between position clicking and typing**. Some users prefer typing than viewing and clicking, while others do not. Consequently, users' click choices are not only affected by their intent, but also by the position where the intended query is shown and their preference of clicking that position over typing the remaining keystrokes. For instance, a user that prefers clicking will probably click an intended query the first time it is shown to him/her, despite that it may be shown in a low position; while another user focuses on typing his/her intended query despite that the query already appears in the suggestion list, until it is ranked at the top position, or even worse, he/she will type the entire query manually without any intent to click the suggestions.

7.4.5 User Interactions Besides QAC

Besides the information recorded in the QAC log, user's behavior on other types of search logs can also be very useful in predicting user's search intent. One typical example is user's click log, which recorded user's click behavior on the returned web results after submitting a query.

Figure 7.4 shows a toy example of QAC and click logs that align in the timeline. We can observe that the QAC session of a query is followed by the click session of that query, and that click session is followed by another QAC session of the next query. Such sequential behaviors indicate the promising opportunity of exploring appropriate relationship between QAC and click logs. Although the user's behaviors on QAC and click logs are of different types, they imply the same underlying relationship between the user and his/her issued query, such as whether the issued query satisfies the user's intent, and how familiar the user is with the issued query or the domain that query belongs to. For instance, if a user is familiar with the issued query in QAC log, he/she may type the query very fast. Then in click log, if the SERP page provides many relevant results, the user may take a long time to click and check some relevant results in more details; however, if the SERP page does not provide relevant results, the user may reformulate a new query shortly which will start a new QAC session similar to previous query.

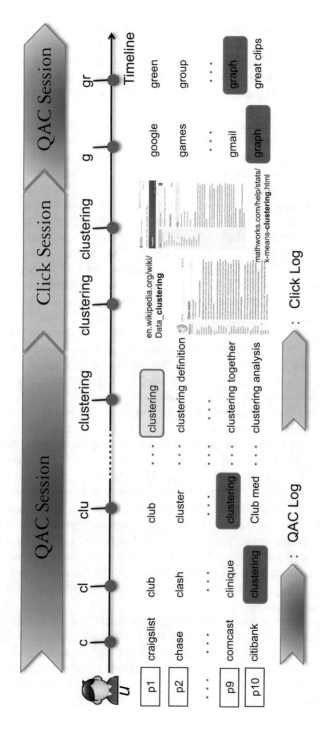

Fig. 7.4 A toy example of how QAC and click logs align in the timeline. Yellow tag highlights the query a user finally clicks, red tag highlights the user's intended query he/she does not click

Moreover, user's search behaviors on one type of log can be used as the contextual data for the other type of log across different query sessions, since users generally behave consistently in adjacent time slots. For instance, according to the click log, if a user's behaviors indicate he is very familiar with the current query, then similar behaviors will be likely observed in the QAC session of the next query; if the issued query is under the same topic, the user will probably type the following query fast as well.

Li et al. [18] studied and designed various QAC and click features in quantitatively capturing user behaviors on QAC and click logs, Among features of QAC behaviors, "Type Speed Standard Deviation" is designed to reflect the stability of a user's typing speed. A user who examines his/her intended queries from the suggestion list from time to time may hardly maintain a stable typing speed, even if the user has good typing skills. On the contrary, a user who plans to type the entire query without clicking a suggestion may illustrate a stable typing speed. "Typing Completion" is designed to show whether a user prefers typing than clicking suggestions. Among the features of click behaviors, "Search Time" is defined to be how fast a user can find his/her intended web documents after submitting a query. Notice that users' behaviors on different types of logs are not independent. On the QAC log, an experienced user usually spends less time to complete a QAC session than an unexperienced user, i.e., has a small "Time Duration." While on the click log, he/she is very likely to make his/her first click after only a short while, i.e., a small feature value for "Search Time." A user who tends to trust the results of search engines may miss the QAC behavior feature "Typing Completion" and own a higher value of the click behavior feature "Click Number." Thus the above designed QAC and click behavior features are somehow related.

To detect user behavior patterns from logs, this work proposed a graphical model based on latent Dirichlet allocation (LDA) [4], which has been proven to be effective in topic discovery by clustering words that co-occur in the same document into topics. It treats each user's query sequence as a document, and clustered user behaviors that co-occur frequently in the same query sequence into topics, since each user maintains certain behavior patterns in query submission, and different groups of users prefer different behavior patterns. The model assumed K behavior patterns lie in the given query sequences, and each user m is associated with a randomly drawn vector π_m, where $\pi_{m,k}$ denotes the probability that the user behavior in a query session of user m belongs to behavior pattern k. For the n-th query in the query sequence of user m, a K-dimensional binary vector $Y_{m,n} = [y_{m,n,1}, \ldots, y_{m,n,K}]^T$ is used to denote the pattern membership of the user behavior in that query session.

To model the influence of the context on user's choice of the behavior pattern in the current query session, the proposed model assumed user's preference of behavior patterns depends on the context, rather than the user alone. That is to say, a "document" in the LDA model does not contain the user behaviors in all query sessions of a user, but only the behaviors in those query sessions that the user conducts under the same status, for instance, in the same mood, or sharing the same topic.

7.5   Historical Notes

Query auto-completion (QAC) has been attracting people's attention for quite a long time. The main objective of QAC is to predict users' intended queries and assist them to formulate a query while typing. The most popular QAC algorithm is to suggest completions according to their past popularity. Generally, a popularity score is assigned to each query based on the frequency of the query in the query log from where the query database was built. This simple QAC algorithm is called Most Popular Completion (MPC), which can be regarded as an approximate maximum likelihood estimator [1].

Several QAC methods [1, 26, 27, 31] were proposed to extend MPC from various aspects. Bar-Yossef and Kraus [1] introduced the context-sensitive QAC method by treating users' recent queries as context and taking into account the similarity of QAC candidates with this context for ranking. But there is no consensus of how to optimally train the relevance model. Shokouhi [26] employed a learning-based strategy to incorporate several global and personal features into the QAC model. However, these methods only exploit the final submitted query or simulate the prefixes of the clicked query, which do not investigate the users' interactions with the QAC engine.

In addition to the above models, there are several studies addressing different aspects of QAC. For example, [27, 31] focused on the time-sensitive aspect of QAC. Other methods studied the space efficiency of index for QAC [2, 12]. Duan and Hsu [9] addressed the problem of suggesting query completions when the prefix is misspelled. Kharitonov et al. [15] proposed two new metrics for offline QAC evaluation and [14] investigated user reformation behavior for QAC.

The QAC is a complex process where a user goes through a series of interactions with the QAC engine before clicking on a suggestion. Smith et al. [28] presented an exploratory study of QAC usage during complete search sessions based on the lab study of tens of search engine users, the result implicated the effectiveness of the knowledge from prior queries within the same search session in improving the suggestions over successive queries in query auto-completion. As can be seen from the related work, little attention has been paid to understand the interactions with the QAC engine. Until recently, Li et al. [19] created a two-dimensional click model to combine users' behaviors with the existing learning-based QAC models. This study assumed users' behaviors at different keystrokes, even for the consecutive two keystrokes, are independent in order to simplify the model estimation, which results in information loss. In advance, Li et al. [16] attempted to directly model and leverage the relationship between users' behaviors, so as to improve the performance of QAC. Furthermore, users' behaviors besides the QAC process, such as the behaviors in click logs, have also be explored in benefiting the QAC task in [18].

In recent years, more and more special scenarios under the QAC problem have been explored. Wang et al. [30] formulated the QAC task as a ranked Multi-Armed Bandits (MAB) problem to timely and adaptively suggest queries and expected to reflect time-sensitive changes in an online fashion. Vargas et al. [29] claimed that the traditional whole-query completion mechanism is not the optimal solution for mobile search scenarios. Inspired by predictive keyboards that suggests to the user one term at a time, they proposed the idea of term-by-term QAC. Liu et al. [22] investigated into the promotion campaign issue in QAC engines, where some malicious users provided a new malicious advertising service by attacking the search engines through using manipulated contents to replace legitimate auto-completion candidate suggestions, so as to promote their customers' products in QAC. Modern techniques have also been utilized in solving the QAC problem. Recurrent neural network (RNN) models have been employed to address the QAC task in [23], in order to improve the quality of suggested queries when facing previously unseen text.

7.6 Summary

Last, we briefly summarize the main content introduced in this chapter and discuss potential future research directions.

In this chapter, we have presented the main contributions in the field of query auto-completion in information retrieval. In specific, in Sect. 7.1, we gave a general introduction of query auto-completion and provided a formal definition of the QAC problem. In Sect. 7.2, we introduced existing metrics utilized in measuring the QAC performance, including both ranking quality and assist efficiency. In Sect. 7.3, different types of QAC logs utilized in existing QAC works are studied. In Sect. 7.4, we have introduced the most prominent QAC approaches in the literature, and how the usage of different types of information can benefit the prediction of user intent. Those information includes temporal, contextual, personal information, and user's interaction inside and outside the QAC process.

References

1. Ziv Bar-Yossef and Naama Kraus. Context-sensitive query auto-completion. In *Proceedings of the 20th International Conference on World Wide Web*, pages 107–116, 2011.
2. H. Bast and Ingmar Weber. Type less, find more: fast autocompletion search with a succinct index. In *Proceedings of the 29th Annual International ACM SIGIR Conference on Research and Development in Information Retrieval*, pages 364–371, 2006.
3. Sumit Bhatia, Debapriyo Majumdar, and Prasenjit Mitra. Query suggestions in the absence of query logs. In *Proceeding of the 34th International ACM SIGIR Conference on Research and Development in Information Retrieval*, pages 795–804, 2011.
4. David M. Blei, Andrew Y. Ng, and Michael I. Jordan. Latent Dirichlet allocation. *J. Mach. Learn. Res.*, 3: 993–1022, 2003.
5. Christopher J. C. Burges, Krysta M. Svore, Paul N. Bennett, Andrzej Pastusiak, and Qiang Wu. Learning to rank using an ensemble of lambda-gradient models. In *Proceedings of the Yahoo! Learning to Rank Challenge, held at ICML 2010*, volume 14 of *JMLR Proceedings*, pages 25–35, 2011.

6. Fei Cai and Maarten de Rijke. A survey of query auto completion in information retrieval. *Found. Trends Inf. Retr.*, 10 (4): 273–363, 2016.

7. Fei Cai, Shangsong Liang, and Maarten de Rijke. Time-sensitive personalized query auto-completion. In *Proceedings of the 23rd ACM International Conference on Conference on Information and Knowledge Management*, pages 1599–1608, 2014.

8. Nick Craswell, Rosie Jones, Georges Dupret, and Evelyne Viegas. WSCD '09: Proceedings of the 2009 workshop on web search click data. 2009.

9. Huizhong Duan and Bo-June Paul Hsu. Online spelling correction for query completion. In *Proceedings of the 20th International Conference on World Wide Web*, pages 117–126, 2011.

10. Katja Hofmann, Bhaskar Mitra, Filip Radlinski, and Milad Shokouhi. An eye-tracking study of user interactions with query auto completion. In *Proceedings of the 23rd ACM International Conference on Conference on Information and Knowledge Management*, pages 549–558, 2014.

11. Charles C. Holt. Forecasting seasonals and trends by exponentially weighted moving averages. In *International Journal of Forecasting*, volume 20, pages 5–10, 2004.

12. Bo-June Paul Hsu and Giuseppe Ottaviano. Space-efficient data structures for top-k completion. In *Proceedings of the 22nd International World Wide Web Conference*, pages 583–594, 2013.

13. Jyun-Yu Jiang, Yen-Yu Ke, Pao-Yu Chien, and Pu-Jen Cheng. Learning user reformulation behavior for query auto-completion. In *Proceedings of the 37th International ACM SIGIR Conference on Research and Development in Information Retrieval*, pages 445–454, 2014a.

14. Jyun-Yu Jiang, Yen-Yu Ke, Pao-Yu Chien, and Pu-Jen Cheng. Learning user reformulation behavior for query auto-completion. In *Proceedings of the 37th International ACM SIGIR Conference on Research and Development in Information Retrieval*, pages 445–454, 2014b.

15. Eugene Kharitonov, Craig Macdonald, Pavel Serdyukov, and Iadh Ounis. User model-based metrics for offline query suggestion evaluation. In *Proceedings of the 36th International ACM SIGIR conference on research and development in Information Retrieval*, pages 633–642, 2013.

16. Liangda Li, Hongbo Deng, Anlei Dong, Yi Chang, Hongyuan Zha, and Ricardo Baeza-Yates. Analyzing user's sequential behavior in query auto-completion via Markov processes. In *Proceedings of the 38th International ACM SIGIR Conference on Research and Development in Information Retrieval*, pages 123–132, 2015.

17. Liangda Li, Hongbo Deng, Jianhui Chen, and Yi Chang. Learning parametric models for context-aware query auto-completion via Hawkes processes. In *Proceedings of the Tenth ACM International Conference on Web Search and Data Mining*, pages 131–139, 2017a.

18. Liangda Li, Hongbo Deng, Anlei Dong, Yi Chang, Ricardo Baeza-Yates, and Hongyuan Zha. Exploring query auto-completion and click logs for contextual-aware web search and query suggestion. In *Proceedings of the 26th International Conference on World Wide Web*, pages 539–548, 2017b.

19. Yanen Li, Anlei Dong, Hongning Wang, Hongbo Deng, Yi Chang, and ChengXiang Zhai. A two-dimensional click model for query auto-completion. In *Proceedings of the 37th International ACM SIGIR Conference on Research and Development in Information Retrieval*, pages 455–464, 2014.

20. Chunbin Lin, Jianguo Wang, and Jiaheng Lu. Location-sensitive query auto-completion. In *Proceedings of the 26th International Conference on World Wide Web*, pages 819–820, 2017.

21. Yang Liu, Ruihua Song, Yu Chen, Jian-Yun Nie, and Ji-Rong Wen. Adaptive query suggestion for difficult queries. In *Proceedings of the 35th International ACM SIGIR conference on research and development in Information Retrieval*, pages 15–24, 2012.

22. Yuli Liu, Yiqun Liu, Ke Zhou, Min Zhang, Shaoping Ma, Yue Yin, and Hengliang Luo. Detecting promotion campaigns in query auto completion. In *Proceedings of the 25th ACM International Conference on Information and Knowledge Management*, pages 125–134, 2016.

23. Dae Hoon Park and Rikio Chiba. A neural language model for query auto-completion. In *Proceedings of the 40th International ACM SIGIR Conference on Research and Development in Information Retrieval*, pages 1189–1192, 2017.

24. Greg Pass, Abdur Chowdhury, and Cayley Torgeson. A picture of search. In *Proceedings of the 1st International Conference on Scalable Information Systems*, volume 152, page 1, 2006.

25. Patrick O. Perry and Patrick J. Wolfe. Point process modeling for directed interaction networks. *CoRR*, abs/1011.1703, 2010.

26. Milad Shokouhi. Learning to personalize query auto-completion. In *Proceedings of the 36th International ACM SIGIR conference on research and development in Information Retrieval*, pages 103–112, 2013.

27. Milad Shokouhi and Kira Radinsky. Time-sensitive query auto-completion. In *Proceedings of the 35th International ACM SIGIR conference on research and development in Information Retrieval*, pages 601–610, 2012.

28. Catherine L. Smith, Jacek Gwizdka, and Henry Feild. The use of query auto-completion over the course of search sessions with multifaceted information needs. *Inf. Process. Manag.*, 53 (5): 1139–1155, 2017.

29. Saúl Vargas, Roi Blanco, and Peter Mika. Term-by-term query auto-completion for mobile search. In *Proceedings of the Ninth ACM International Conference on Web Search and Data Mining*, pages 143–152, 2016.

30. Suhang Wang, Yilin Wang, Jiliang Tang, Charu C. Aggarwal, Suhas Ranganath, and Huan Liu. Exploiting hierarchical structures for unsupervised feature selection. In *Proceedings of the 2017 SIAM International Conference on Data Mining*, pages 507–515, 2017.

31. Stewart Whiting and Joemon M. Jose. Recent and robust query auto-completion. In *Proceedings of the 23rd International World Wide Web Conference*, pages 971–982, 2014.

32. Aston Zhang, Amit Goyal, Weize Kong, Hongbo Deng, Anlei Dong, Yi Chang, Carl A. Gunter, and Jiawei Han. adaQAC: Adaptive query auto-completion via implicit negative feedback. In *Proceedings of the 38th International ACM SIGIR Conference on Research and Development in Information Retrieval*, pages 143–152, 2015.

Chapter 8
Query Suggestion

Zhen Liao, Yang Song, and Dengyong Zhou

Abstract Query suggestion is one of the few fundamental problems in Web search. It assists users to refine queries in order to satisfy their information needs. Many query suggestion techniques have been proposed in the past decades. The mainstream idea is to leverage query logs which contain the search behaviors of users to generate useful query suggestions. In this chapter, we introduce several log-based query suggestion techniques. These methods fall into four categories: (1) query co-occurrence; (2) query-URL bipartite graph; (3) query transition graph; and (4) short-term search context. We also briefly discuss other related work in this field and point out several future directions.

8.1 Introduction

8.1.1 An Overview of Query Suggestion Approaches

How effectively users are able to retrieve information from the Web largely depends on whether they can formulate input queries properly to express their information needs. However, formulating effective queries is never meant to be an easy task. On the one hand, given the same query, different search engines may return different results. This means that it is unlikely to define a single standard to guide query formulation across different search engines. On the other hand, queries are typically expressed in just a few words [11, 20, 22], which potentially increases the difficulty for search engines to understand query intents.

Z. Liao
Facebook Inc., Menlo Park, CA, USA
e-mail: zhangzliao@fb.com

Y. Song (✉) · D. Zhou
Google Research, Seattle, WA, USA
e-mail: ys@sonyis.me; dennyzhou@google.com

© Springer Nature Switzerland AG 2020
Y. Chang, H. Deng (eds.), *Query Understanding for Search Engines*,
The Information Retrieval Series 46, https://doi.org/10.1007/978-3-030-58334-7_8

Most commercial search engines, including Google,[1] Yahoo![2], and Bing[3] provide query suggestions on their search result pages to help user formulating queries. A recent study [28] shows that query suggestions are particularly useful in the following scenarios: (1) the original query is a rare query; (2) the original query consists of only one word; (3) the suggested queries are unambiguous; and (4) the suggested queries are generalizations or error corrections of the original query. Based on the study in [15], around 30% of searches in commercial search engines are generated from query suggestions.

Studies on query suggestions can be traced back to the early years of this century [4, 20, 46]. Since then, many techniques [2, 3, 8, 10, 18, 21, 23, 26, 29–32, 36, 40–42, 47] have been proposed to improve the quality of query suggestions. Roughly speaking, query suggestions have the following major objectives [35]: (1) when a user's information need is not satisfied, the search results from the suggestions should provide more relevant results or (2) when a user's information need is satisfied but the user wants to explore more, the suggestions can provide useful guideline to obtain related information.

Search engine logs contain information on how users refine their queries as well as how users click on suggested queries, which can help address both of the aforementioned objectives. As a result, most query suggestion techniques leverage search logs as a useful source of information.

Formally, given a query q, query suggestion aims at optimizing a scoring function $f(q, q') \in \mathbb{R}$ that can be used to rank suggestion candidates q'. To include short-term search context in query suggestion, the relevance function $f(q, q')$ can also be extended as $f(q_{1,...,i}, q')$, where $q_{1,...,i} = \{q_1, \ldots, q_i\}$ $(i \geq 1)$ represents the previous search sequence.

8.1.2 Examples of Query Suggestion Approaches

As we mentioned above, one of the most important and effective query suggestion techniques leverages query logs [3, 8, 10, 18, 21, 29–32, 36, 40–42, 46]. Query logs record user interactions with search engines. A typical query log entry contains *timestamp*, *query*, *clicked URL* as well as other information (e.g., anonymous user ID, search platform, etc.). In contrast, suggestion methods that do not use query logs [5] often generate candidates from external data sources. Those approaches do not consider the fact that the text used in formulating search queries is usually quite different from text in external sources (e.g., typos, acronym, no grammar, etc.). Thus, they are less effective in practice.

---

[1]http://www.google.com.

[2]http://www.yahoo.com.

[3]http://www.bing.com.

From the perspective of modeling and organizing search logs, query suggestion techniques can be categorized into four classes: (1) query co-occurrence; (2) query-URL bipartite graph; (3) query transition graph; and (4) short-term search context methods.

Query co-occurrence methods utilize the query co-occurrence information to provide suggestions. Co-occurrence is often computed from search sessions [20] or tasks [30], where the relevance functions range from simple raw counts to statistical methods like log likelihood ratio (LLR) [25].

Query-URL bipartite graph methods leverage clicks on URLs. These methods often represent queries and URLs into bipartite graphs with the edges indicating the click information. Graph traversal methods like random walks are often employed to estimate the similarities between queries. Examples include random walk with restart [40, 44], forward and backward random walks [4, 10], hitting time [36], etc.

Query transition graph methods model the query refinement process in the search sequence by constructing query transition graphs where edges on the graph indicate the reformulation relationships between queries. Examples in this category include query flow graph (QFG) [7], term transition graph (TTG) [42], etc.

Short-term search context methods focus on leveraging immediate previous queries as contextual information to model and disambiguate the current input query. Typical methods in this category are based on decay factors [7, 20], query clustering [8, 29], Markov models [9, 18, 31], etc.

Besides the classical query suggestion methods which mainly rely on a single data source, other studies proposed to combine different data sources for generating suggestion candidates through various strategies (e.g., machine learning for query suggestion candidates ranking [38, 42], query suggestion diversification [34, 41], query suggestions personalization [24], etc.). There are also approaches to build better visualization [48] or user interface [27] for query suggestions.

8.1.3 Evaluation Metrics for Query Suggestion

The evaluation metrics for query suggestions can be categorized into offline (e.g., precision, recall) and online (e.g., click-through rate) approaches.

For offline evaluation, previous work often leverage a small number of case studies [4, 46], while recent methods focus more on leveraging human assessors [8, 29, 40, 42]. Examples of metrics in this category include Precision [8], Mean Average Precision (MAP) [40], Normalized Discounted Cumulative Gain (NDCG) [42], and Mean Reciprocal Rank (MRR) [1].

Formally, given a binary label $r(i) \in \{0, 1\}$ indicating whether a suggestion ranked at position-i is relevant (1) or not (0), precision at position K is defined as:

$$Precision@K = \frac{\sum_{i=1}^{K} r(i)}{K}. \tag{8.1}$$

Similarly, we can also define the recall at position K as:

$$Recall@K = \frac{\sum_{i=1}^{K} r(i)}{M},$$ (8.2)

where M is the total number of relevant suggestions. Comparing to precision, recall is rarely used since it is nearly impossible to get all relevant suggestions for a query.

Instead of computing recall, coverage is often used as an alternative [29]:

$$Coverage = \frac{\# \text{ of testing queries with suggestions}}{\# \text{ of testing queries}}.$$ (8.3)

MAP is defined as the mean of the average precision (AP) of all suggested queries:

$$AP = \frac{1}{M} \cdot \sum_{i=1} \frac{Precision@i \cdot r(i)}{i}.$$ (8.4)

NDCG at position K is defined based on $DCG@K = \sum_{i=1}^{K} \frac{2^{r(i)}-1}{log_2(i+1)}$:

$$NDCG@K = \frac{1}{Z_K} \sum_{i=1}^{K} DCG@K,$$ (8.5)

where Z_K is the normalized factor of $DCG@K$ which corresponds to the ideal ranking results.

MRR is defined as:

$$MRR = \frac{1}{Q} \sum_{q=1}^{Q} \frac{1}{rank_q},$$ (8.6)

where Q is the number of testing queries in the evaluation dataset and $rank_q$ is the rank of first relevant query in the suggestion list for a testing query q.

For online evaluation, click-through rate (CTR) is widely used, which is defined as [38]:

$$CTR@K = \frac{\# \text{ of clicks at top-}K \text{ suggestions}}{\# \text{ of impression with at least } K \text{ suggestions}}.$$ (8.7)

Due to the difficulty of reproducing all methods on a standard evaluation dataset for comparable results, in this chapter we do not emphasize on the evaluation metrics comparison among different methods. In addition, it is hard to compare different query suggestion techniques while they are proposed in different scenarios (e.g., for Web documents search, image search, or sponsored search) or optimizing different metrics (e.g., coverage, diversity, etc.). Therefore, we focus on the motivation and mathematical formulation of these methods. For effectiveness comparison, we provide illustrative examples to show the differences. Readers can refer to the original publications if they are interested in the detailed comparison of metrics.

8.1.4 Notation Used in This Chapter

Table 8.1 lists notations with detailed meanings in this chapter.

8.1.5 Structure of This Chapter

In the rest of this chapter, we introduce several query suggestion techniques in Sects. 8.2–8.5 which correspond to co-occurrence, query-URL bipartite graph,

Table 8.1 Notations used in this chapter

Meaning	Notation
Query	q, q_i, q_j
Search sequence with last query as q_i	$q_{1,\dots,i}$
Query suggestion candidate	q'
URL	u, u_j, u_x
Set of queries, URLs	Q, U
Number of queries, URLs	$|Q|$ or N_q, $|U|$ or N_u,
Count/frequency	$Cnt(\cdot)$
Frequency of query in sessions	f_i, f_j
Query co-occurrence matrix	$\mathbf{C}$
Co-occurrence between q_i and q_j	$\mathbf{C}_{ij}$
Query-URL click matrix	$\mathbf{B}$
Click frequency of q_i on u_j	$\mathbf{B}_{ij}$
Query transition probability matrix	$\mathbf{A}$
Transition probability from q_i to q_j	$\mathbf{A}_{ij}$
One-hot vector of query q_i	$\mathbf{v}_i^0$
Final optimized suggestion results	$\mathbf{v}^*, \mathbf{v}_i^*, h_i^*$ (with *)
Number of iterations	t
Re-start probability for forward random walk	α
Self-transition probability for backward random walk	s
Terms in query	w, w_i
Search topic of a query	T
Decay factor for short-term search context	β
Hidden search state for a search sequence	z, z_{i+1}

query transition graph, and short-term search context methods, respectively. After that, we summarize other related suggestion techniques as well as evaluation studies in Sect. 8.6. In Sect. 8.7 we conclude this chapter with discussions and future directions.

8.2 Query Co-occurrence Methods

In this section, we introduce several widely used methods that compute the similarity between queries by leveraging their co-occurrence information from search logs. Given a sequence of queries $\{q_1, \ldots, q_n\}$, traditional approaches [8, 18, 29, 39] defined search sessions to segment search logs. Specifically, consecutive events are segmented into different sessions if the time interval between them exceeds a certain threshold (e.g., 30 min). Within each session, different similarity functions can be defined to find similar queries [25, 30, 33].

8.2.1 Similarity Functions

Let $\mathbf{C}$ denote a co-occurrence matrix where $\mathbf{C}_{ij}$ indicates the co-occurrence count between query q_i and q_j. Let $f_i = \sum_j \mathbf{C}_{ij}$ denote the total number of sessions that contain query q_i. Depending on the scenarios, $\mathbf{C}$ can be either symmetric [30] or asymmetric [16, 18], where the symmetric way ignores the issuing order of queries, while the asymmetric way considers the issuing order of queries. Specifically, asymmetric $\mathbf{C}$ defines $\mathbf{C}_{ij} = Cnt(q_i \rightarrow q_j)$ and $q_i \rightarrow q_j$ denotes q_j occurring after q_i.

Below are some examples of co-occurrence methods proposed in [20]:

$$Jaccard(q_i, q_j) = \frac{\mathbf{C}_{ij}}{f_i + f_j - \mathbf{C}_{ij}} \tag{8.8}$$

$$Dependence(q_i, q_j) = \frac{\mathbf{C}_{ij}}{\min(f_i, f_j)} \tag{8.9}$$

$$Cosine(q_i, q_j) = \frac{\sum_k \mathbf{C}_{ik} \cdot \mathbf{C}_{jk}}{\sqrt{\sum_k \mathbf{C}_{ik}^2} \cdot \sqrt{\sum_k \mathbf{C}_{jk}^2}}. \tag{8.10}$$

Both Jaccard and Dependence functions define the relative co-occurrence between q_i and q_j, which tends to favor popular queries. The Cosine function tries to address this bias by adding an L_2 normalization on query frequencies.

From probabilistic perspective, we can define the probability of issuing q_j after q_i as:

$$P(q_j|q_i) = \frac{C_{ij}}{f_i} \propto C_{ij}. \tag{8.11}$$

Since the denominator f_i is independent of q_j, $P(q_j|q_i)$ is in favor of popular queries. To address this issue, we can leverage the pointwise mutual information (PMI) and mutual information (MI) [23, 38]:

$$PMI(q_i, q_j) = \log \frac{P(q_i, q_j)}{P(q_i) \cdot P(q_j)} \propto \frac{C_{ij}}{f_i \cdot f_j}, \tag{8.12}$$

$$
\begin{aligned}
MI(q_i, q_j) = {} & P(q_i, q_j) \cdot PMI(q_i, q_j) + P(q_i, \overline{q_j}) \cdot PMI(q_i, \overline{q_j}) \\
& + P(\overline{q_i}, q_j) \cdot PMI(\overline{q_i}, q_j) + P(\overline{q_i}, \overline{q_j}) \cdot PMI(\overline{q_i}, \overline{q_j}). \tag{8.13}
\end{aligned}
$$

Here $\overline{q_i}$ denotes all queries in the search logs except q_i, and $P(q_i, q_j) = \frac{C_{ij}}{\sum_{ij} C_{ij}}$.

Jones et al. [26] leveraged LLR [13] to measure the degree of correlation between queries q_i and q_j. Their method makes the null hypothesis that $H_1 : P(q_j|q_i) = P(q_j|\overline{q_i})$ and the alternative hypothesis that $H_2 : P(q_j|q_i) \neq P(q_j|\overline{q_i})$. The LLR function is defined as the log ratio of the likelihood between H_1 and H_2:

$$LLR(q_i, q_j) = -2 \cdot \log \lambda = -2 \cdot \log \frac{L(H_1)}{L(H_2)}, \tag{8.14}$$

where a higher LLR score indicates a stronger correlation between q_i and q_j. Using the notation above, $LLR(q_i, q_j)$ is defined as:

$$LLR(q_i, q_j) = -2 \cdot \{L_{h1}(k_1, n_1) + L_{h1}(k_2, n_2) - L_{h2}(k_1, n_1) - L_{h2}(k_2, n_2)\}, \tag{8.15}$$

where $L_{h1}(k, n) = \log\{k \cdot \log \frac{k_1 + k_2}{n_1 + n_2} + (n - k) \cdot \log(1 - \frac{k_1 + k_2}{n_1 + n_2})\}$, $L_{h2}(k, n) = \log\{k \cdot \log \frac{k}{n} + (n - k) \cdot \log(1 - \frac{k}{n})\}$, and $k_1 = C_{ij}, k_2 = C_{\overline{i}, j}, n_1 = \sum_j C_{ij}, n_2 = \sum_j C_{\overline{i}j}$.

In [38], the authors have shown that MI and LLR are mathematically similar in evaluating query correlations.

8.2.2 Extracting Tasks from Sessions

Using the co-occurrence information to define the query similarity function highly relies on the segmentation of query sequences. As we described before, *session* has been widely used to extract co-occurrence in existing work. However, time-based segmentation can possibly lose the inner correlation among queries that span longer period of time than a single session. Therefore, a concept of *task* is proposed [25, 30, 33, 45] to address this issue. Below we introduce the approach in [30] to extract tasks from sessions. In the common definition, task is defined as an atomic user information need [25, 30, 33].

The motivation of task extraction can be illustrated from the example shown in Table 8.2, which is a real user search session from search engine Bing. The user began this session with query "facebook" and finished the session with several attempts to search for lyrics of a song. From the table, we can see that one session may contain multiple or interleaved tasks. The reasons behind that are: (1) web search logs are ordered chronologically; (2) users often perform multiple tasks at the same time. On the one hand, treating the entire session as an atomic unit may not accurately capture the multi-tasking behavior. As shown in Table 8.2, query "gmail log in" seems to have no correlation with its adjacent queries. Besides, failing in searching for lyrics of a song does not mean that the user did not find useful information for query "facebook." On the other hand, dividing sessions at query level may lose information of reformulation by users. For example, in Table 8.2, even if the user had no click on query "amazon", he still managed to find relevant information by reformulating "amazon" into "amazon kindle books" and made a click. From the study of [30], about 30% of sessions contain multiple tasks and about 5% of sessions contain interleaved tasks.

To extract tasks from sessions, Liao et al. [30] proposed the following approach. First, the similarity between queries is learnt from a binary classifier; Second, queries within a session are grouped into tasks using a clustering algorithm. This approach is motivated by [25, 33], where Jones and Klinkner [25] proposed to classify queries into tasks using a binary classification approach, and Lucchese et

Table 8.2 An example of session in web search logs from [30]

Time	Event type	Detailed entry information	User ID	Session ID	Task ID
09:03:26 AM	Query	Facebook	U1	S1	T1
09:03:39 AM	Click	www.facebook.com	U1	S1	T1
09:06:34 AM	Query	Amazon	U1	S1	T2
09:07:48 AM	Query	faecbook.com	U1	S1	T1
09:08:02 AM	Click	facebook.com/login.php	U1	S1	T1
09:10:23 AM	Query	Amazon kindle	U1	S1	T2
09:10:31 AM	Click	kindle.amazon.com	U1	S1	T2
09:13:13 AM	Query	Gmail log in	U1	S1	T3
09:13:19 AM	Click	mail.google.com/mail	U1	S1	T3
09:15:39 AM	Query	Amazon kindle books	U1	S1	T2
09:15:47 AM	Click	amazon.com/Kindle-eBooks?b=......	U1	S1	T2
09:17:51 AM	Query	i'm picking up stones	U1	S1	T4
09:18:54 AM	Query	i'm picking up stones lyrics	U1	S1	T4
09:19:28 AM	Query	pickin' up stones lyrics	U1	S1	T4

Table 8.3 Basic statistics of browse and search logs reported in [30]

Statistics	Browse logs	Search logs
Avg. # of queries in sessions	5.81	2.54
Avg. # of queries in tasks	2.06	1.60
Avg. # of tasks in sessions	2.82	1.58
% of single-task sessions	53.29	70.72
% of multi-task sessions	46.71	29.28
% of interleaved task sessions	15.25	4.78
% of single-query tasks	48.75	71.86
% of multi-query tasks	51.24	28.13

Table 8.4 Query refinement pattern within tasks from browse and search logs in [30]

Reformulation patterns	Browse logs	Search logs
% of identical	66.37	50.45
% of shorter	12.48	16.77
% of longer	21.45	32.76

al. [33] proposed to cluster queries into tasks based on empirically designed distance functions.

Specifically, a similarity function between queries $sim(q, q')$ can be learnt through features from submitting time, textual similarity (e.g., edit distance, word similarity), result set (e.g., similarity between search engine result pages (SERPs) of q and q'), etc. Next, a graph can be constructed with queries as nodes and $sim(q, q')$ as the weight of an edge. With the constructed graph, graph cutting methods can be used to group queries into tasks. In [30], the authors applied an SVM classifier to learn $sim(q, q')$ and proposed a heuristic based query task clustering (QTC) algorithm to group queries into tasks.

Table 8.3 shows the statistics regarding query distribution as in tasks and sessions reported in [30]. From the table we can observe that multi-tasking behavior is quite common in users' searches. For consecutive queries within a task, Table 8.4 presents their length distribution from the previous query to its next query. More than half adjacent query pairs are identical, where about 90% of identical pairs are from refreshing search result pages or clicking the back button, and about 10% of identical patterns are from pagination. Besides, we can see that longer reformulation pattern occurs twice more often than shorter reformulation pattern. These statistics indicate that it is more effective to recommend longer and more specific queries than queries that are more general and have fewer words.

8.2.3 Method Analysis and Comparison

To better understand the difference between co-occurrence and LLR methods, a few examples are shown in Table 8.5. As we can see, using purely frequency-based method (e.g., Jaccard in Eq. (8.8) and $P(q_j|q_i)$ in Eq. (8.11)), those most popular

Table 8.5 Suggestions of session-based models

Test cases	Methods	
	Session co-occur	Session LLR
Amazon	Facebook	eBay
	eBay	Walmart
	Google	Target
	Youtube	Best buy
	Yahoo	Barnes and nobel
Cell phone	Facebook	Cheap cell phones
	Verizon wireless	Phone
	Sprint	All cell phone companies
	Verizon	Verizon cell phones
	Google	Sprint

queries like "facebook" and "google" are always recommended. As a comparison, LLR addresses the bias systematically.

Table 8.6 presents several queries from high, medium, and low frequency categories with their suggestions. From suggestions generated by different methods, we have the following observations. (1) Session-based models often generate related queries in a broad range such as providing "verizon" as a suggestion to query "att." (2) For low-frequency queries, task-based and session-based methods generate nearly same suggestions. (3) Task-based methods often generate more specific queries for further narrowing down user information need, which are different from session-based approach. As a result, suggestions provided by task-based methods can be treated as complementary to results from session-based approaches.

8.2.4 Summary

In this section, we described co-occurrence based query suggestion methods. Simple co-occurrence based approaches have a frequency bias towards popular queries. We saw that methods like MI or LLR can help address the issue systematically. In general, the quality of query suggestions based on LLR tends to be better than other co-occurrence based approaches.

The essential point of co-occurrence based method is to define query similarity based on co-occurrence. Most existing works are session-based, where sessions are segmented based on the timestamp between consecutive queries. Due to the nature of multi-tasking searching behavior by search engine users, extracting tasks from session is useful to generate related queries from the same search task. As illustrated in Table 8.6, task-based methods tend to be complementary to session-based methods. Feild and Allan [14] also studied the task-aware query recommendation problem and show that queries from the same search task are useful as context for

Table 8.6 Example of query suggestions provided by different methods [30]. Superscripts h, m, l are notations for high, medium, and low frequency queries

Test case	Methods	
	Session LLR	Task LLR
Amazon^h	eBay	Amazon books
	Walmart	Amazon kindle
	Target	Amazon electronics
	Best buy	Amazon music
	Barnes and nobel	Amazon DVD movies
ATT^h	AT&T my account	AT&T my account
	Verizon	ATT wireless
	Sprint	AT&T email
	Tmobile	AT&T bill pay
	ATT wireless	AT&T customer service
Exchange^m	Military exchange	Military exchange
	Exchange rate	Exchange rates
	Easyfreexbox360	Navy exchange
	Tennis	Microsoft exchange
	Aafes	Base exchange
Harry Truman^m	Winston Churchill	Harry Truman quotes
	Robert Byrd	Bess Truman
	Nelson Mandela	Harry Truman facts
	Neil Armstrong	Harry S Truman
	Teddy Roosevelt	
"Popular Irish baby names"^{l}	Top Irish baby names	Unique Irish baby names
	Unique Irish baby names	Irish baby names
	Irish baby boy names	Irish baby boy names
	Irish baby names	Top Irish baby names
	"Traditional Irish baby names"	Top 100 baby names

query suggestion. There is also task extraction across multi-sessions [45], which can be used to generate cross session query suggestions.

The co-occurrence based approaches usually work well for high and medium frequency queries and perform poorly in low-frequency queries. To help generating good suggestion for low-frequency queries, graph-based approaches are preferred. The idea of graph-based methods is to construct a graph with nodes as queries and edges as similarities between queries and leverage the entire graph to help finding relevant queries. Sections 8.3 and 8.4 describe graph-based methods using query-URL bipartite graph and query transition graph, respectively.

8.3   Query-URL Bipartite Graph Methods

Although the click information on SERP URLs are often noisy, aggregating clicks
from a large number of users tends to reflect the relevance between queries and
URLs. Such rich query-URL relevance information can be used for generating high
quality query suggestions. As an example, the co-occurrence based method may
fail to generate suggestion for a tail (typo) query "faecboek." If we can leverage
the top clicked URLs on the SERP of the query, it is likely to generate relevant
suggestions. In practice, such approach can help address the issues on tail queries
that lack enough co-occurrence information.

Typically, query-URL bipartite graph-based methods use clicks from queries
on URLs as signals. They usually work as follows. First, a probabilistic matrix is
constructed using click counts. Next, a starting node (i.e., a test query) is chosen.
Third, a random walk (RW) is performed on the graph using the probabilistic matrix.
Forth, final suggestion is generated using RW results.

Let $\mathbf{B}$ denote the matrix derived from the query-URL click-through bipartite
graph, where

$$\mathbf{B}_{ij} = Cnt(q_i, u_j). \tag{8.16}$$

Here $Cnt(q_i, u_j)$ represents the click count of query q_i on URL u_j. An alternative method using inverse query frequency (IQF) to initialize $\mathbf{B}_{ij}$ was proposed by
Deng et al. [12]:

$$\mathbf{B}_{ij} = Cnt(q_i, u_j) \cdot IQF(u_j), \tag{8.17}$$

where $IQF(u_j) = \log \frac{|Q|}{n(u_j)}$ and $n(u_j)$ is the number of distinct queries clicking
on u_j. It is suggested in [12] to apply the IQF to re-weight click counts, which
decreases the weight of frequently clicked URLs and increases the weight of less
frequent but more relevant URLs.

By normalizing the rows of $\mathbf{B}$, we can get the transition probability from query
q_i into url u_j using $P(u_j|q_i) = \frac{\mathbf{B}_{ij}}{\sum_k \mathbf{B}_{ik}}$. Similarly, we can derive the transition
probability from url u_j to query q_i using $P(q_i|u_j) = \frac{\mathbf{B}_{ij}}{\sum_k \mathbf{B}_{kj}}$. Based on these
probabilities, we can derive the transition probability from query q_i to q_j as:

$$P^u(q_j|q_i) = \sum_u P(q_j|u) \cdot P(u|q_i). \tag{8.18}$$

8.3.1   Forward and Backward Random Walks

Let matrix $\mathbf{A}$ represent the transition matrix derived from the Query-URL click graph, where $\mathbf{A}_{ij} = P^u(q_j|q_i)$. The forward random walk with restart approach (RWR) is formulated as [30, 40]:

$$\mathbf{v}_i^{t+1} = (1 - \alpha) \cdot (\mathbf{v}^t)^T \cdot \mathbf{A} + \alpha \cdot \mathbf{v}_i^0, \tag{8.19}$$

where α is the restarting probability. $\mathbf{v}_i^0$ is the initialized one-hot vector for query at index-i. t is the number of iteration.

If we set p to be 0, the process of iteration can be viewed as a Markov chain through the probabilistic matrix $\mathbf{A}$. According the Markov chain theory [37], if a Markov chain is irreducible and aperiodic, there exists a unique stationary distribution π. Additionally, in this case $\mathbf{A}^k$ converges to a rank-one matrix in which each row is the stationary distribution π, that is:

$$\lim_{k \to \infty} \mathbf{A}^k = \mathbf{1} \cdot \pi, \tag{8.20}$$

which produces vector π, where π_i can be interpreted as the popularity of query q_i.

Compared to forward propagation defined in Eq. (8.19), Craswell et al. [10] proposed a back propagation method, which leverages a back propagation matrix $\mathbf{A}^b$ defined as:

$$\mathbf{A}_{ij}^b = \begin{cases} (1 - s) \cdot \mathbf{A}_{ij}, & \text{if } i \neq j, \\ s, & \text{if } i = j. \end{cases} \tag{8.21}$$

Here s is a self-transition probability to keep the propagation stay on the current query.

Based on the matrix $\mathbf{A}^b$, the backward RW is computed by multiplying $\mathbf{A}^b$ with $\mathbf{v}_i(t)$, which is formulated as:

$$\mathbf{v}_i^{t+1} = norm(\mathbf{A}^b \cdot \mathbf{v}_i^t). \tag{8.22}$$

Here $norm(\cdot)$ denotes the normalization to make $\sum_k \mathbf{v}_i[k] = 1$. The basic idea of backward propagation is that given a query q_i at time t, we aim at finding the probability of starting from q_j at step 0 by using $P_{0|t}(q_j|q_i) = [(\mathbf{A}^b)^t \cdot \mathbf{Z}^{-1}]_{ij}$. Here $\mathbf{Z}$ is a diagonal matrix and $\mathbf{Z}_{jj} = \sum_i [(\mathbf{A}^b)^t]_{ij}$ is used for a row normalization purpose. To set up the parameters of s and t, from the experiment results shown in [10], a self-transition $s=0.9$ with step $t=101$ can result in a good performance in the application of image retrieval.

Equations (8.19) and (8.22) look similar but are different in nature. For example, let $\mathbf{v}_2(0)=[0, 1]^T$ denote the starting vector and $\mathbf{A} = \mathbf{A}^b$ denote the transition matrix between q_1 and q_2,

$$A = A^b = \begin{bmatrix} 0.7 \ 0.3 \\ 0.6 \ 0.4 \end{bmatrix}. \tag{8.23}$$

Then one step backward propagation gets $A \cdot v_2(0) = [0.3, 0.4]^T$, and one step forward propagation gets $v_2(0)^T \cdot A = [0.6, 0.4]^T$.

8.3.2 Hitting Time Approach

Both forward and backward propagations need to tune the parameters (e.g., restart probability α or self-transition probability s). Mei et al. [36] proposed a parameter-free method using hitting time. The hitting time $h_i[q_j]$ is defined as the expectation of arriving at q_j while starting at q_i. To compute the hitting time, Mei et al. [36] proposed an iterative process:

$$h_i^{t+1} = \sum_{j \neq s} P^u(q_j | q_i) \cdot h_j^t + 1, \tag{8.24}$$

where s denotes the index of a test query and $h_i(0) = 0$. Here $P^u(q_j | q_i)$ is the same as in Eq. (8.18). After certain steps of iterations, the final h_i^{t+1} is used for the suggestion. Note that hitting time represents the expected arriving steps from a suggested query to the test query; therefore, a smaller value indicates a higher relevance. The iteration can stop with a given maximum number of step (e.g., 1000), or when the difference of $h_i^{t+1} - h_i^t$ becomes insignificant (e.g., less than 10^{-3}).

8.3.3 Combining Click and Skip Graphs

It has been shown that click graph can benefit popular queries which have enough user click feedbacks. However, using only click graph tends to ignore the relevant information presented on SERP which causes potential issues particularly for tail queries. For rare queries with very few clicks, click graph is unable to capture the underlying relationship among queries. Comparing with click graph, a skip graph which contains information of (query, skipped URL) pairs can enrich the information for tail queries with fewer clicks. Here a URL is skipped if it was viewed by the user without being clicked. For instance, if a user only clicked the 3rd-ranked URL after issuing the query, the 1st and 2nd ranked URLs are skipped.

Figure 8.1 presents an example which shows the motivation of the combination of click and skip graphs approach. The left figure (a) shows the click graph for three queries and five URLs that returned as top SERP results. Ideally, *audi parts*

Fig. 8.1 An illustrative example of query-URL click graph (**a**) and skip graph (**b**). Query *audi parts* and *audi bodywork* are not correlated if only performs random walk on the click graph, but will be highly correlation if random walk is performed on the skip graph. More details on the text

should be a good suggested query for *audi bodywork* (and vice versa). However, after performing a random walk on the click graph, only the query *audi* can be suggested to *audi parts* because there is no commonly clicked URLs between *audi parts* and *audi bodywork* so that their correlation is zero. However, if we leverage the top-skipped URLs for *audi parts* and *audi bodywork* as shown in Fig. 8.1b, it can be clearly observed that both queries skipped their top-returned two URLs: *NwaAudidealers.com* and *en.wikipedia.org/wiki/Audi*. As a result, a random walk on the skip graph assigns a high correlation score to these two queries.

To show that skip graph contains rich information for tail queries, Fig. 8.2 shows user session statistics from a dataset with 40 million unique queries. The figure compares the query frequency (x-axis) against the number of clicked and skipped URLs (y-axis). It can be observed that when the query frequency is low, more URLs are skipped than clicked during the same user session. However, with the increase of query popularity, the click patterns become more stable. Generally, users tend to click more often on top-returned results for popular queries. While for rare queries, click distribution is more random.

For the quality of skipped URLs for rare queries, Song et al. [40] selected 6000 queries which have been issued less than 20 times within a week. They asked human raters to judge the relevance of clicked and skipped URLs on a 1–5 scale (5 means the best). Figure 8.3 demonstrates the comparative ratings. Overall, skipped URLs indicate slightly less relevance than clicked URLs. On average, clicked URLs have a rating of 3.78, while skipped URLs have 3.65. This observation further supports our claim that skipped URLs should be leveraged for rare queries in the context of relevance measurement.

Following the same notation as used previously, we define the query-to-query click transition matrix $\mathbf{A}^+$ using Eq. (8.16) or (8.17). Similarly, we can also define a query-to-query skip transition matrix $\mathbf{A}^-$ by replacing the click count as the skip count. Hence, we can conduct the random walk on both click graph with $\mathbf{A}^+$ and skip graph with $\mathbf{A}^-$ using Eq. (8.19) and generate the final suggestion vectors $\mathbf{v}_i^+$ and $\mathbf{v}_i^-$ for each graph. After that, we can combine both vector for final suggestions as:

$$\tilde{\mathbf{v}}_i^* = \alpha' \cdot \mathbf{v}_i^+ + (1 - \alpha') \cdot \mathbf{v}_i^-. \tag{8.25}$$

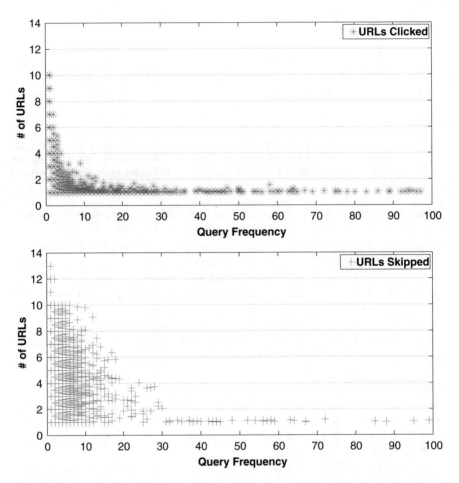

Fig. 8.2 Number of URLs clicked vs. number of URLs skipped in the same user sessions from 1 week search log. There are more URLs skipped than clicked for queries with lower frequencies

Together with restarting probability α, this approach has two parameters: α and α'. Cross validation can be used to tune the parameters to achieve the best results on held-out datasets.

We can construct a matrix $\mathbf{Q}^* = [\mathbf{v}_1^*, \ldots, \mathbf{v}_{|Q|}^*]$ as query similarity matrix where $|Q|$ is the total number of queries. A similar approach (e.g., compute URL transition probability $P(u_j|u_i) = \sum_q P(u_j|q) \cdot P(q|u_i)$ and conduct random walk on URL nodes) can be performed to get a URL similarity matrix $\mathbf{U}^* = [\mathbf{v}_1^*, \ldots, \mathbf{v}_{|U|}^*]$, where $|U|$ is the total number of URLs. Due to the difficulty of obtaining ground-truth for $\mathbf{Q}^*$ and $\mathbf{U}^*$, Song et al. [40] proposed to tune the parameters by minimizing the difference between URL correlation matrix $\mathbf{U}$ and $\mathbf{U}^*$ and apply same parameters for query suggestion.

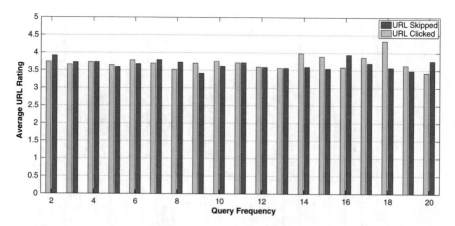

Fig. 8.3 Human judger ratings [40] in terms of relevance for clicked and skipped URLs in query logs. Break down accordingly to query frequency. Clicked URLs and skipped URLs have almost the same ratings for rare queries (queries with frequency less than 20)

8.3.4 Method Analysis and Comparison

To illustrate the differences among query-URL graph approaches, we show a few examples from [40]. The compared methods are defined as follows:

- **RW-F** The basic random walk on click graph using Eq. (8.19).
- **RW-B** The random walk approach with backward propagation using Eq. (8.22).
- **RW-P** Random walk based on pseudo relevance feedback where top-10 URLs of the testing queries are used to conduct random walk propagation on the click graph instead of the clicked URLs.
- **RW-C** This is to combine the random walk of click and skip graph using Eq. (8.25).

Table 8.7 illustrates the results with a few queries. From the table we can observe some interesting results: (1) RW-F and RW-B provide slightly different results. RW-F is more likely to suggest popular queries than RW-B since the propagation assigns larger probabilities to queries with more clicks. For example, for the query "nfl teams with 5 super bowl wins," RW-F recommends "super bowl champions" as the top suggestion and RW-B suggests "super bowl champs" on the 4th position. (2) RW-P has better suggestion quality than RW-F and RW-B, especially for tail and ambiguous queries. For example, for query "single ladies" the relevant query "single ladies by beyonce" is recommended as top candidate by RW-P. For tail queries with less clicks, non-clicked URLs on SERP becomes important for query suggestions. Therefore, RW-P performs better on tail queries than RW-F and RW-B. (3) RW-C works better than RW-P with more labeled relevant queries. The reason is that RW-P treats both clicked and skipped URLs equally, while RW-C utilizes the click and skip counts.

Table 8.7 Examples of query suggestions by different RW methods in [40]. Bold queries are judged as relevant

Query	RW-F	RW-B	RW-P	RW-C
Valentine one (shopping and car)	Valentines day	Valentine activities	Valentine gifts	**Best radar detector**
	Valentine activities	Valentine gifts	**Valentine one review**	**Escort radar**
	Valentine gifts	Valentines day	**Radar detector**	**Radar detector**
	Anniversary gifts	Free valentines crafts	Valentine one eBay	**Valentine one review**
	Free valentines crafts	Anniversary gifts	Valentine activities	Valentine one eBay
Single ladies (music)	Dating ladies	Single women	**Single ladies by beyonce**	**Beyonce single ladies**
	Beyonce single ladies	Dating single ladies	Single ladies mp3	**Single ladies by beyonce**
	Single women	Dating ladies	Dating single ladies	Single ladies lyrics
	Single women myspace	Dating ladies myspace	Single ladies myspace	Single ladies mp3
	Eharmony	Single moms	**Beyonce single ladies**	**Single ladies download**
NFL teams with 5 super bowl wins (sports and long)	**Super bowl champions**	Super bowl 2009	Super bowl history	**List super bowl winners**
	Super bowl	Super bowl 2008	**Super bowl winners**	**Super bowl winners**
	Super bowl 2009	**Super bowl champs**	**Past NFL super bowl winner**	Super bowl steelers
	Super bowl 2008	List of superbowl	Super bowl 2009	**Past NFL super bowl winner**
DC ups (ambiguous)	D-cups	DC power	**DC power supply**	DC power
	D cup	D-cups	DC ups power	**DC ups power**
	DC ups systems	**DC ups systems**	D-cups	**DC postal service**
	D-cup	**DC power system**	**DC ups systems**	**DC power supply**
	DC control	**Universal power supply**	DC USA	**DC ups systems**

8.3.5   Summary and Discussion

In this section we introduced several well-known query suggestion approaches using query-URL bipartite graph, namely forward random walk with restart, backward random walk, hitting time, and combining click and skip graphs. Existing study in [40] showed that random walk tends to get into data sparsity issue for tail queries with few clicks. Utilizing search result information (e.g., skipped URLs) can help improving both coverage and quality. Basically, the more relevant URLs we can obtain for a given query, the better suggestion results we are able to provide.

8.4   Query Transition Graph Methods

In this section, we introduce the query transition graph methods. Particularly, QFG and TTG approaches are described.

8.4.1   Query Flow Graph (QFG)

One typical approach to model the query refinement process is the QFG proposed by Boldi et al. [7]. The idea of QFG is to consider the whole search sequence as a flow of queries and model it in a probabilistic way.

Specifically, a transition probability between query q_i to q_j is defined as:

$$P^s(q_j|q_i) = \frac{Cnt(q_i \to q_j)}{Cnt(q_i)}, \tag{8.26}$$

which leverages the adjacent information between queries in the search sequence. Let matrix $\mathbf{A}$ denote the transition on the whole graph with $\mathbf{A}_{ij} = P^s(q_j|q_i)$. One can use either session or task described in Sect. 8.2 to organize the query sequence. The authors in [7] defined query chains to help identifying queries for the same information need, which is very similar to task defined in Sect. 8.2.2.

Second, similar to RWR in Eq. (8.19), an iteration process on QFG is defined as:

$$\mathbf{v}_i^{t+1} = \alpha \cdot (\mathbf{v}^t)^T \cdot \mathbf{A} + (1 - \alpha)\mathbf{v}_i^0. \tag{8.27}$$

Here α is restart probability of query node to itself.

The QFG approach was generalized as the query template flow graph (QTFG) in [43], where the phrases in a query were generalized by WordNet hierarchy. For example, "chocolate cookie recipe" can be generalized as "<food> cookie recipe."

For a test query q and a suggesting candidate q', suppose they can be generalized into templates x and x', respectively. A template-based similarity between q and q'

can be defined as:

$$f(q, q') = (1 - \tau) \cdot P(q'|q) + \tau \cdot \sum_{x,x'} P(q|x') \cdot P(x'|x) \cdot P(x|q), \qquad (8.28)$$

where τ is a parameter to combine query transition probability on QFG and the query transition probability on QTFG. One can define different types of template generalization for a query. In [43] the authors proposed to utilize the WordNet hierarchy to generalize each possible phrase in query as a template and compute all transition probabilities using the query co-occurrences in sessions. For example, following the definition in [43]: τ is set as 0.5, the term $P(q'|q)$ is the $\mathbf{v}_q^*[q']$ from Eq. (8.27) above, $P(q|x')$ is set as 1 if q can be generalized as x' and 0 otherwise, $P(x|q)$ is defined based on the WordNet hierarch distance of q to x. The term $P(x'|x)$ is defined as transition probability between all queries q to q' falling into template x and x', respectively.

8.4.2 Term Transition Graph (TTG)

Based on the observations that most of the time only the last term of the query is modified when users refine their queries for the same search tasks, Song et al. [42] proposed a TFG approach for query suggestion. Three types of actions, namely *Modification*, *Expansion*, and *Deletion* were proposed for a query refinement, where some examples are shown in Table 8.8.

Given a word vocabulary $W = \{\epsilon, w_1, \ldots w_n\}$ where ϵ is used to denote the empty string, three cases of user query refinements are formulated as [42]:

- *Modification*: user modifies the last term of the query, e.g., "single ladies song" → "single ladies lyrics." Denote as: $\{w_1, \ldots, w_m\} \rightarrow \{w_1, \ldots, w'_m\}$.
- *Expansion*: user adds one term to the end of the query, e.g., "sports illustrated" → "sports illustrated 2010." Denote as: $\{w_1, \ldots, w_m\} \rightarrow \{w_1, \ldots, w_m, w_{m+1}\}$.

Table 8.8 Three types of user refinement examples

Type	User activity	Pattern
Modification	1. q:{single ladies song}	song→lyrics
	2. q:{single ladies lyrics}	
	3. URL click	
Expansion	1. q:{sports illustrated}	$\epsilon \rightarrow 2010$
	2. q:{sports illustrated 2010}	
	3. URL click	
Deletion	1. q:{eBay auction}	auction $\rightarrow \epsilon$
	2. q:{eBay}	
	3. URL click	

- *Deletion*: user removes the last term of the query, e.g., "eBay auction" → "eBay." Denote as: $\{w_1, \ldots, w_{m-1}, w_m\} \rightarrow \{w_1, \ldots, w_{m-1}, \epsilon\}$.

Here the original query $q = \{w_1, \ldots, w_m\}$ and the refined query can be noted as q'.

A nature way to estimate the probability for *Modification* and *Deletion* can be formulated as:

$$P_{modify}(q'|q) = P(w_1, \ldots, w_{m-1}, w'_m | w_1, \ldots, w_m), \qquad (8.29)$$

where w'_m can be the empty string ϵ or other words in W.

Similarly, *Expansion* can be formulated as:

$$P_{expan}(q'|q) = P(w_1, \ldots, w_m, w_{m+1} | w_1, \ldots, w_m). \qquad (8.30)$$

However, this simple approach tends to fall back into the co-occurrence (or adjacency) based approach, where most frequent queries followed q are selected as suggestions. Hence it has issue to provide good quality suggestions for low-frequency queries. To address the issue, Song et al. [42] introduced a topic based method to generalize the words.

With topic T, the *Modification* and *Deletion* can be formulated as:

$$P_{modify}(q'|q) = \sum_T P(w_m \rightarrow w'_m | T) \cdot P(T | w_1, \ldots, w_m), \qquad (8.31)$$

while *Expansion* can be formulated as:

$$P_{expan}(q'|q) = \sum_T P(w_{m+1} | T) \cdot P(T | w_1, \ldots, w_m). \qquad (8.32)$$

Here $P(w_m \rightarrow w'_m | T) = P(w'_m | w_m, T)$ is the term transition probability under topic T, and $P(w_{m+1} | T)$ can be viewed as a popularity of w_{m+1} under topic T. The term $P(T | w_1, \ldots, w_m)$ is the probability of topic T for the given query. Note that Eq. (8.31) can be applied to any q' which has one word modified from q.

The topic T can be a predefined taxonomy (e.g., ODP as used in [42]), or an automatically learned topic distribution through approaches like LDA [6], pLSI [19], etc. Since the probability of $P(w_m \rightarrow w'_m | T)$ and $P(w_{m+1} | T)$ is not on the same magnitude, in [42] the authors proposed to multiply a $P(w_m)$ on $P_{modify}(q'|q)$ to make the final score comparable, based on the assumption that $P(w_{m+1} | T) \approx P(w_{m+1} | w_m, T) \cdot P(w_m)$.

Therefore, the final suggestion model can be formulated as:

$$P_{final}(q'|q) = \begin{cases} P_{modify}(q'|q) \cdot P(w_m), & \text{using Eq. (8.31)} \\ P_{expan}(q'|q), & \text{using Eq. (8.32)}. \end{cases} \qquad (8.33)$$

Table 8.9 Examples of query suggestions reported from [7, 42] (Q: test query, S: suggestion)

	Query flow graph		Term transition graph	
Q	Music	Evening dress	Battlefield bad company 2	Dante's inferno xbox 360
S	Music	Evening dress	Battlefield bad company 1	Dente's inferno xbox 260 wiki
	Yahoo music	Formal evening dress	Battlefield bad company 2 Ringtones	Dante's inferno ps3
	Music video	Red evening dress	Battlefield bad company 2 slots	Dante's inferno xbox 360 cheats
	Music download	Myevening dress	Battlefield bad company 2 realms	Dante's inferno xbox 360 walkthrough
	Free music	Prom 008 dress	Battlefield bad company 2 games	Dante's inferno

8.4.3 Analysis of Query Transition Methods

Table 8.9 shows query suggestions by QFG and TTG, respectively. From the table, we can observe that: (1) Suggestions from QFG for frequent queries are usually more specialized, which is in accordance to the query reformulation pattern statistics in Table 8.4. (2) TFG can provide relevant suggestions for long queries which are more likely tail queries. This is in accordance with the QTFG approach [43] which leverages term/phrase information in queries.

8.4.4 Summary

In this section, we introduced methods using query transition graph information. Both QFG and TTF approaches are introduced with a few examples to show their effectiveness. Query transition graph may have issue for low-frequency queries with less follow-up queries. To address the problem, we can either generalize the query into template or utilize the term transition information extracted from query refinements.

8.5 Short-Term Search Context Methods

In this section, we introduce the short-term search context methods. Short-term search context usually refers to queries and clicks issued shortly before the current one. One straightforward way of getting context-aware suggestions is to leverage the search history sequence $q_{1,...,i} = \{q_1, \ldots, q_i\}$ and predict the next query q_{i+1} based on the frequency of $(q_{1,...,i,i+1})$ in search logs. However, such approach suffers from the data sparsity problem due to the exponential growth of space of query sequences. Next, we introduce different types of methods to ease the data sparsity problem.

8.5.1 Decay Factor Based Approaches

Huang et al. [20] proposed a cosine based context-aware method, which is formulated as:

$$f(q_{1,...,i}, q') = \sum_{k=1}^{i} \beta^{i-k} \cdot Cosine(q_k, q'). \tag{8.34}$$

Here $\beta \in [0, 1]$ is a decay factor to control the quality of suggestion.

Following [7, 36], we can initialize vectors $\mathbf{v}_k(0) = \beta^{i-k}$ for $k = 1, \ldots, i$ and conduct random walks. To assign higher weights to more recent queries, β^{i-k} is used as a decay factor. Specifically, we can formulate the suggestion method as:

$$\mathbf{v}^*_{context} = \sum_{k=1}^{i} \mathbf{v}^*_k, \text{ and } \mathbf{v}^{t+1}_k = (1 - \alpha) \cdot (\mathbf{v}^t_k)^T \cdot \mathbf{A} + \alpha \cdot \mathbf{v}^0_k, \tag{8.35}$$

where $\mathbf{v}^*_k$ is the final result of $\mathbf{v}^{t+1}_k$ and $\mathbf{A}$ is the query transition probability matrix.

8.5.2 Sequence Mining Approaches

Next, we introduce sequence mining approaches: concept mining [8, 29], mixture variable Markov Model [18], and variable length Hidden Markov Model [8, 31].

Cao et al. [8, 29] proposed to mine the concept sequence instead of query sequence for suggestion. The idea is straightforward, i.e., instead of matching query sequence $q_1, q_2, \ldots, q_i$ with search history for query suggestions, we can first map each query into a concept (e.g., a cluster of queries) and utilize the concept sequence $c_1, c_2, \ldots, c_i$ for query suggestions. The suggestion method based on concept sequence proposed in [8, 29] can be formulated as:

$$f(q_{1,...,i}, q') = Cnt(Back\_Off(c_{1,...,i}), c'). \tag{8.36}$$

Here $c_{1,...,i}$ represents the concept sequence for $q_{1,...,i}$, and c' is the concept of q'. Back_Off($\cdot$) is a function to get the longest pattern $(c_{a,...,i}, c')$ $(1 < a <= i)$ which exists in the model. For example, if we have an input concept sequence (c_1, c_2, c_3) but our model mined from search logs can provide suggestion for (c_2), (c_3), and (c_2, c_3), the Back_Off function returns longest found sequence (c_2, c_3) and ignores (c_1, c_2, c_3) since it is not found in the model.

Similarly, He et al. [18] proposed a mixture Variable Markov Model (MVMM) to model the search sequence for query suggestions. Using MVMM, the query suggestion of a given query sequence $q_{1,...,i}$ can be formulated as:

$$f(q_{1,...,i}, q') = \sum_{k=1}^{i} w(q_{k,...i}, q') \cdot Cnt(q_{k,...,i}, q'), \tag{8.37}$$

where $w(q_{k,...,i}, q')$ is the weight for the sequence. The weight function is dynamically changing for different query sequences. If we set all $w(\cdot)$ to be 1, the model falls back as a combination of suggestions from different length matching of query sequences. In [18], the optimal weight parameters are learnt to maximize the generalization probability for next queries in the search logs. An alternative way of learning the weight is to build two separate datasets, where the first one is to estimate the frequency of search sequences, and the second one is used to optimize the weights of the sequences for better generalization ability.

A more generic extension of the search context modeling is proposed in [9, 31], namely the variable length Hidden Markov Model (vlHMM), where each hidden state in the model represents a hidden concept for each query. Using vlHMM, the query suggestion function can be formulated as:

$$f(q_{1,...,i}, q') = P(q'|z_{i+1}) \cdot P(z_{i+1}|q_{1,...,i}), \tag{8.38}$$

where z_{i+1} is the predicted hidden state at time $i + 1$, $P(q'|z_{i+1})$ is the probability of generating q' from state z_{i+1}, and $P(z_{i+1}|q_{1,...,i})$ is the probability of generating the next search state z_{i+1} given the sequence $q_{1,...,i}$. Similar to optimizing hidden Markov models, the parameters of $P(z_{i+1}|q_{1,...,i})$ and $P(q'|z_{i+1})$ are learned to maximize the probability of predicting the next query. By initializing the state of concept using clustering methods [8, 29], the EM (Expectation–Maximization) learning process can be greatly accelerated to converge within 10 iterations, which makes this approach scalable to large-scale datasets.

8.5.2.1 Concept Mining Using Clustering Algorithm

Concept mining has been shown to be useful for query suggestion, which is capable of alleviating the data sparsity problem by grouping queries into concepts. In this section, we introduce a fast clustering algorithm, namely Query Stream Clustering (QSC) for concept mining proposed in [8, 29].

Generally, the process of the QSC algorithm can be summarized into the following steps. First, each query q is represented as a feature vector using its clicked URLs. Second, q is compared to existing clusters to find a closest match, where the distance between q and a cluster is given by their URL feature vectors. Finally, if the diameter of a cluster after adding q is smaller than a predefined threshold, q is added into the cluster. Otherwise, a new cluster with only q is created.

Due to the fact that the average number of clicked URLs of a query is small, QSC algorithm can be very efficient in practice since it scans the dataset only once. For each query q, the number of clusters to be accessed is at most number of queries shared at least one clicked URL with q. Therefore, the computation cost for each query is near constant, which leads to the complexity of the whole algorithm to be $O(|Q|)$, where $|Q|$ is the number of queries in the dataset.

The QSC algorithm is memory-intensive since it needs to hold all data structure in the memory to conduct fast clustering. Therefore, once the data becomes large and cannot be stored on a single machine, the algorithm fails. To address such limitation, Liao et al. [29] proposed two extensions of QSC: (1) for datasets with small size, an efficient iterative clustering method is proposed and (2) for large datasets, a distributed master–slave framework is proposed for clustering. Interested readers can find more details in [29].

8.5.3 Method Analysis and Comparison

We presented experiment results from [29] to illustrate the difference of query suggestion methods, where the input is a query sequence $q_{1,\dots,i} = q_1, \dots, q_i$:

- **Adjacency**. It ranks queries by their frequencies immediately following the last query q_i in the training sessions and output top queries as suggestions.
- **N-Gram**. It ranks queries by their frequencies of immediately following the entire query sequence in training sessions and output top queries as suggestions.
- **Cosine**. It ranks queries by their cosine similarities with every query in the sequence $q_{1,\dots,i}$ as in Eq. (8.34).
- **CACB**. Short for context-aware concept-based method which uses the concept sequence to provide suggestions as formulated in Eq. (8.36).

Table 8.10 shows a few queries with suggestions from above methods. We can find that N-Gram method fails when the input query sequence is not frequently occurring in the search logs (e.g., providing no suggestion for query sequence"www. chevrolet.com $\Rightarrow$ www.gmc.com"). Similarly, the results from Adjacency indicates that the method ignores the context information (e.g., suggesting repeated query "www.chevrolet.com" for query sequence"www.chevrolet.com $\Rightarrow$ www.gmc. com"). Conversely, CACB provides better suggestions and avoids the duplications by other methods (e.g., "msnnews" provided by Cosine to query "msn news").

Table 8.11 shows a few ambiguous queries with or without context information, where the suggestions are provided by CACB. We can see that utilizing the context can help disambiguate the query intent and yield more relevant suggestions.

Table 8.10 Examples of query suggestions provided by different methods [29]

Test case	Methods			
	Adjacency	N-Gram	Cosine	CACB
www.at&t.com	AT&T	AT&T	ATT wireless	ATT wireless
	www.att.com	www.att.com	Cingular	Cingular
	Cingular	Cingular	ATT net	Bellsouth
	www.cingular.com	www.cingular.com	Bellsouth	Verizon
	ATT net	ATT net	AT&T	Tilt phone
msn news	CNN news	CNN news	CNN news	CNN news
	Fox news	Fox news	msnnews	Fox news
	CNN	CNN	MSNBC news	ABC news
	msn	msn	KSL news	CBS news
			Yahoo news	BBC news
www.chevrolet.com ⇒ www.gmc.com	www.chevy.com	<null>	www.chevy.com	Ford
	www.chevrolet.com		www.dodge.com	Toyota
	www.dodge.com		www.pontiac.com	Dodge
	www.pontiac.com			Pontiac
Circuit city ⇒ best buy	Circuit city	Walmart	Walmart	Radio shack
	Walmart	Target	Staples	Walmart
	Target	Sears	Office depot	Target
	Best buy stores	Office depot	Dell	Sears
	Sears		Amazon	Staples

8.5.4 Summary

In this section we introduced query suggestion methods based on short-term search context. We have shown that utilizing queries in the short-term search context can effectively improve query suggestion. Directly mining frequent query sequences from search logs suffered from the data sparsity problem, and decay factor and sequence mining based approach can alleviate this issue. A general way to address the data sparsity problem is to group queries into concepts using clustering approaches [8, 29], which can provide suggestions with both good precision and high coverage.

8.6 Other Query Suggestion Related Work

In this section, we briefly discuss other related work of query suggestion that are relevant but did not cover in this chapter.

Some early studies of query suggestion proposed to group queries into clusters and provide queries within same cluster as suggestions. Some examples are:

Table 8.11 Examples of query suggestions for ambiguous or multi-intent queries when context information is available and absent [29]

No context available	Context available	
Comcast	*eBay ⇒ Comcast*	*Cable ⇒ Comcast*
Myspace	Myspace	Verizon
eBay	AOL	AT&T
AOL	Comcast email login	Dish network
Comcast email login	Craiglist	Quest
Craigslit		T-mobile
MQ	*Games ⇒ MQ*	*Websphere ⇒ MQ*
Games	Dragonfable	MQ client
Dragonfable	Adventure quest	MQ document
Miniclip	Runescape	MQ training
Runescape	Miniclip	
Adventure quest	Tribal wars	
Webster	*Online dictionary ⇒ Webster*	*Citibank ⇒ Webster*
Dictionary	Encarta	Bank of America
Encarta	Thesaurus	American Express
Thesaurus	Free dictionary	Peoples Bank
Free dictionary	Oxford dictionary	Citizens
Bank of America	Spanish dictionary	Chase
CTC	*Tenax ⇒ CTC*	*Child tax ⇒ CTC*
Central Texas College Transcript	Central Texas College Transcript	Child tax benefit
Child tax benefit	GoArmyEd	Tax rebate
Tarleton State University	Tarleton State University	Working tax credit
GoArmyEd	University of Maryland	Tax credits
Tax rebate	Temple college	IRS

- **Agglomerative** Beeferman and Berfer [4] proposed an agglomerative clustering method to iteratively group queries and URLs into clusters.
- **DBScan** Wen et al. [46] used DBScan clustering algorithm to cluster queries based on both textual and click information.
- **K-means** Yates et al. [3] proposed to cluster queries using K-means algorithm and compute query similarity using the click-through information.

As pointed out by [8, 29], the aforementioned clustering algorithms have high time complexity (e.g., $O(N_q^2)$ for N_q queries). Therefore, the QSC algorithm [8, 29] was proposed as an alternative to efficiently generate the clusters in $O(N_q)$ time.

Different from traditional work which utilize query-URL click-through information to compute query similarities, some recent work [5, 15, 26] proposed to model query as bag-of-words or phrases and generate suggestions by considering the phrase similarity.

- **Phrase substitution method** Jones et al. [26] proposed to segment queries into phrases using pointwise mutual information and find related phrase substitution through Log Likelihood Ratio (LLR). To rank suggestion candidates, they further applied a machine learning framework to classify whether a suggestion is more generic, specific, or irrelevant based on textual and LLR features.

- **SERP-based method** Feuer et al. [15] proposed a generalization/specification approach for suggesting phrases from the top ranked search results. They proposed to generate query suggestions using proximal sub-phrases and unordered super phrase based on the phrase frequency in top search documents.

- **External corpus based method** Bhatia et al. [5] proposed to mine a phrase set from documents in external corpus (e.g., news article dataset used in TREC). Their approach splits an input query q into the completed phrase Q_c and typing phrase Q_t and finds a suggesting candidate p_i which can both optimize the probability of $P(Q_c|p_i)$ and $P(p_i|Q_t)$. Here $P(Q_c|p_i)$ is estimated by the probability of document containing phrase Q_c while p_i presents, and $P(p_i|Q_t)$ is computed using normalized frequency of p_i containing a complete word c starting with Q_t.

Besides improving the quality and coverage of suggestions, the diversity of the suggestion results was studied in [24, 34, 41].

- **Diversifying Suggestion** Ma et al. [34] proposed a hitting time based iterative algorithm to add diversified suggestion candidates one by one. To generate all suggestions, they conducted the following steps: (1) given a test query q, get a top-1 query suggestion q' and add it into a set HS; (2) perform a hitting time algorithm to get next query q', add q' to HS; (3) repeat step 2 until obtaining enough suggestion results. The essential idea in [34] is that in step (2), the hitting time approach computes the hitting time of q starting from q' without visiting any nodes in HS. Therefore, all nodes already in HS are skipped for a diversification purpose.

- **Diversifying Search Results** Song et al. [41] proposed a machine learning framework to systematically optimize the relevance and diversity for query suggestion. The proposed learning framework utilized result set features to compute the similarity between queries. Note that diversification in [41] is to provide different SERP comparing with testing query q, where diversity in [34] is to diversify the queries in the suggestion results.

- **Diversifying and Personalization** Jiang et al. [24] proposed to address the diversity and personalization problem together through combining multiple bipartite graphs (e.g., query-URL graph, query-session graph, query-term graph) for query representation and diversification and utilizing offline user profile for personalization. Their diversification algorithm is similar to method in [34] described above. After getting all suggestions, they personalized the results by computing a similarity between suggesting queries and user profiles.

Several studies are proposed to improve the user interface for better utility and experience [27, 48]:

- **Text + Images** Zha et al. [48] proposed a suggestion UI where a picture along with the suggesting query is presented to users in the scenario of image search.

Such UI design is integrated into the commercial search engine nowadays where some suggestions show both textual and image information.

- **Structured UI** Kato et al. [27] studied structured suggestion style with specialization and parallel movements where suggesting queries are grouped as clusters with text labels. Based on the success rate on predefined search tasks, the new UI with grouping and tags outperforms the traditional UI with a plain list of results.

Machine learning approaches were applied to query suggestion to better combine different features. Jain et al. [21] proposed to synthesize query suggestion based on a CRF model to drop less important terms and combine click-through and session information to get good suggestions within a learning framework. Similarly, Ozerterm et al. [38] proposed to learn the suggestion function through both lexicon and result set features using Gradient Boosting Decision Tree (GBDT) method. They validated the importance of aboutness feature which measures the similarity between SERP of a suggesting query and the test query, which is accordance with findings in [41].

To evaluate the suggestion quality, several metrics were proposed in [1, 8, 27]:

- **Human Label** This is the most common evaluation strategy [8, 29–31, 40–42]. Given a test query q with a suggesting q', the annotator is presented with both queries with some necessary information (e.g., the search context of the query, the search results of q and q') to label whether q' is relevant or not.
- **Task Accomplishment** Kato et al. [27] proposed to evaluate the effectiveness of different query suggestion UI by the success rate of predefined search tasks.
- **SERP Annotation** Ma et al. [35] proposed to annotate the relevance of the suggestion by considering the result set information of whether a suggestion q' provides a better results or not comparing with testing query q.
- **User Behavior Prediction** He et al. [18] utilized search logs for automatic evaluation of their query suggestion methods. Part of users' search sequences were given to query suggestion methods to predict the next submitted queries. Albakour et al. [1] used daily search logs to measure the suggestion results in a similar manner. They leveraged MRR (Mean Reciprocal Rank) as the evaluation metric.

It has been shown that query suggestion techniques are useful for other applications as well. For example, Jones et al. [26] applied query suggestion techniques (e.g., LLR) for sponsored search and illustrated improvement of sponsored suggestion. Hasan et al. [17] proposed to leverage query suggestion techniques for e-commerce websites (e.g., eBay) and evaluate the effectiveness (e.g., CTR) for product search.

8.7   Discussions and Future Directions

In this chapter, we summarized several types of query suggestion methods: (1) Co-occurrence; (2) Query-URL bipartite graph; (3) Query transition graph; and (4) Short-term search context.

Co-occurrence methods [16, 20, 26, 30] use co-occurrence of query pairs in sessions or tasks. This type of method is usually straight-forward to understand and compute. One problem of such approach is that it usually can provide good suggestions for high-frequency queries and may not be able to provide suggestion to tail queries with few or no co-occurred queries.

Query-URL bipartite graph methods [10, 36, 40] use clicked URLs of a query to find similar queries. This type of method usually conducts random walk on the click graph to propagate the similarities. For tail queries with less or no clicks, one can leverage the post-web information (e.g., skipped URLs on the SERP [40]) to enrich the pseudo relevant URLs of a query. If the search engine performs bad on a query, it is hard to provide good query suggestions by using the click or post-web information.

Query transition graph methods [7, 42, 43] use the query refinement information in search logs to find next possible queries in the search process. This type of method usually constructs a query transition graph and performs random walk on the graph starting from testing queries. For tail query with less or no refinement information, one can leverage the query string information to generate the query as template [43] or construct term-level transition graph [42]. At the meantime, one needs to carefully design the approach for generalizing queries as templates or constructing term-level transition graph to achieve a good relevance.

Short-term search context methods [8, 18, 20, 29, 31] use search sequence information (e.g., queries within current session) to improve the relevance of suggestions. Sequence mining approaches [8, 18, 29] are usually applied to predict next possible queries given current search sequence. To address the data sparsity problem of search sequence, clustering algorithms are proposed in [8, 29] to group similar queries as clusters and mine cluster level search sequences.

Moving forward, tail queries with few click information or irrelevant search results need to draw more attention for better suggestion algorithms. Although graph and SERP based approaches are able to help certain types of tail queries, the coverage remains as a critical issue for most of the existing works.

References

1. M-Dyaa Albakour, Udo Kruschwitz, Nikolaos Nanas, Yunhyong Kim, Dawei Song, Maria Fasli, and Anne N. De Roeck. AutoEval: An evaluation methodology for evaluating query suggestions using query logs. In *European Conference on Information Retrieval*, pages 605–610, 2011.

2. Aris Anagnostopoulos, Luca Becchetti, Carlos Castillo, and Aristides Gionis. An optimization framework for query recommendation. In *Proceedings of the Third International Conference on Web Search and Data Mining*, pages 161–170, 2010.
3. Ricardo A. Baeza-Yates, Carlos A. Hurtado, and Marcelo Mendoza. Query recommendation using query logs in search engines. In *International conference on extending database technology*, pages 588–596, 2004.
4. Doug Beeferman and Adam L. Berger. Agglomerative clustering of a search engine query log. In *Proceedings of the sixth ACM SIGKDD international conference on Knowledge discovery and data mining*, pages 407–416, 2000.
5. Sumit Bhatia, Debapriyo Majumdar, and Prasenjit Mitra. Query suggestions in the absence of query logs. In *Proceeding of the 34th International ACM SIGIR Conference on Research and Development in Information Retrieval*, pages 795–804, 2011.
6. David M Blei, Andrew Y Ng, and Michael I Jordan. Latent Dirichlet allocation. *Journal of machine Learning research*, 3 (Jan): 993–1022, 2003.
7. Paolo Boldi, Francesco Bonchi, Carlos Castillo, Debora Donato, Aristides Gionis, and Sebastiano Vigna. The query-flow graph: model and applications. In *Proceedings of the 17th ACM conference on Information and knowledge management*, pages 609–618, 2008.
8. Huanhuan Cao, Daxin Jiang, Jian Pei, Qi He, Zhen Liao, Enhong Chen, and Hang Li. Context-aware query suggestion by mining click-through and session data. In *Proceedings of the 14th ACM SIGKDD International Conference on Knowledge Discovery and Data Mining*, pages 875–883, 2008.
9. Huanhuan Cao, Daxin Jiang, Jian Pei, Enhong Chen, and Hang Li. Towards context-aware search by learning a very large variable length hidden Markov model from search logs. In *Proceedings of the 18th International Conference on World Wide Web*, pages 191–200, 2009.
10. Nick Craswell and Martin Szummer. Random walks on the click graph. In *Proceedings of the 30th Annual International ACM SIGIR Conference on Research and Development in Information Retrieval*, pages 239–246, 2007.
11. Hang Cui, Ji-Rong Wen, Jian-Yun Nie, and Wei-Ying Ma. Probabilistic query expansion using query logs. In *Proceedings of the Eleventh International World Wide Web Conference*, pages 325–332, 2002.
12. Hongbo Deng, Irwin King, and Michael R. Lyu. Entropy-biased models for query representation on the click graph. In *Proceedings of the 32nd Annual International ACM SIGIR Conference on Research and Development in Information Retrieval*, pages 339–346, 2009.
13. Ted Dunning. Accurate methods for the statistics of surprise and coincidence. *Computational linguistics*, 19 (1): 61–74, 1993.
14. Henry Allen Feild and James Allan. Task-aware query recommendation. In *Proceedings of the 36th international ACM SIGIR conference on Research and development in information retrieval*, pages 83–92, 2013.
15. Alan Feuer, Stefan Savev, and Javed A. Aslam. Evaluation of phrasal query suggestions. In *Proceedings of the Sixteenth ACM Conference on Information and Knowledge Management*, pages 841–848, 2007.
16. Bruno M. Fonseca, Paulo Braz Golgher, Bruno Pôssas, Berthier A. Ribeiro-Neto, and Nivio Ziviani. Concept-based interactive query expansion. In *Proceedings of the 14th ACM international conference on Information and knowledge management*, pages 696–703, 2005.
17. Mohammad Al Hasan, Nish Parikh, Gyanit Singh, and Neel Sundaresan. Query suggestion for e-commerce sites. In *Proceedings of the Forth International Conference on Web Search and Data Mining*, pages 765–774, 2011.
18. Qi He, Daxin Jiang, Zhen Liao, Steven C. H. Hoi, Kuiyu Chang, Ee-Peng Lim, and Hang Li. Web query recommendation via sequential query prediction. In *Proceedings of the 25th International Conference on Data Engineering*, pages 1443–1454, 2009.
19. Thomas Hofmann. Probabilistic latent semantic indexing. In *Proceedings of the 22nd Annual International ACM SIGIR Conference on Research and Development in Information Retrieval*, pages 50–57, 1999.

20. Chien-Kang Huang, Lee-Feng Chien, and Yen-Jen Oyang. Relevant term suggestion in interactive web search based on contextual information in query session logs. *J. Assoc. Inf. Sci. Technol.*, 54 (7): 638–649, 2003.
21. Alpa Jain, Umut Ozertem, and Emre Velipasaoglu. Synthesizing high utility suggestions for rare web search queries. In *Proceeding of the 34th International ACM SIGIR Conference on Research and Development in Information Retrieval*, pages 805–814, 2011.
22. Bernard J. Jansen, Amanda Spink, Judy Bateman, and Tefko Saracevic. Real life information retrieval: A study of user queries on the web. *SIGIR Forum*, 32 (1): 5–17, 1998.
23. Eric C. Jensen, Steven M. Beitzel, Abdur Chowdhury, and Ophir Frieder. Query phrase suggestion from topically tagged session logs. In *International Conference on Flexible Query Answering Systems*, pages 185–196, 2006.
24. Di Jiang, Kenneth Wai-Ting Leung, Lingxiao Yang, and Wilfred Ng. Query suggestion with diversification and personalization. *Knowledge-Based Systems*, 89: 553–568, 2015.
25. Rosie Jones and Kristina Lisa Klinkner. Beyond the session timeout: automatic hierarchical segmentation of search topics in query logs. In *Proceedings of the 17th ACM Conference on Information and Knowledge Management*, pages 699–708, 2008.
26. Rosie Jones, Benjamin Rey, Omid Madani, and Wiley Greiner. Generating query substitutions. In *Proceedings of the 15th international conference on World Wide Web*, pages 387–396, 2006.
27. Makoto P. Kato, Tetsuya Sakai, and Katsumi Tanaka. Structured query suggestion for specialization and parallel movement: effect on search behaviors. In *Proceedings of the 21st World Wide Web Conference*, pages 389–398, 2012.
28. Makoto P. Kato, Tetsuya Sakai, and Katsumi Tanaka. When do people use query suggestion? A query suggestion log analysis. *Information retrieval*, 16 (6): 725–746, 2013.
29. Zhen Liao, Daxin Jiang, Enhong Chen, Jian Pei, Huanhuan Cao, and Hang Li. Mining concept sequences from large-scale search logs for context-aware query suggestion. *ACM Transactions on Intelligent Systems and Technology*, 3 (1): 17:1–17:40, 2011.
30. Zhen Liao, Yang Song, Li-wei He, and Yalou Huang. Evaluating the effectiveness of search task trails. In *Proceedings of the 21st World Wide Web Conference*, pages 489–498, 2012.
31. Zhen Liao, Daxin Jiang, Jian Pei, Yalou Huang, Enhong Chen, Huanhuan Cao, and Hang Li. A vlHMM approach to context-aware search. *ACM Transactions on the Web*, 7 (4): 22:1–22:38, 2013.
32. Zhen Liao, Yang Song, Yalou Huang, Li-wei He, and Qi He. Task trail: An effective segmentation of user search behavior. *IEEE Transactions on Knowledge and Data Engineering*, 26 (12): 3090–3102, 2014.
33. Claudio Lucchese, Salvatore Orlando, Raffaele Perego, Fabrizio Silvestri, and Gabriele Tolomei. Identifying task-based sessions in search engine query logs. In *Proceedings of the Forth International Conference on Web Search and Data Mining*, pages 277–286, 2011.
34. Hao Ma, Michael R. Lyu, and Irwin King. Diversifying query suggestion results. In *Proceedings of the Twenty-Fourth AAAI Conference on Artificial Intelligence*, pages 1399–1404, 2010.
35. Zhongrui Ma, Yu Chen, Ruihua Song, Tetsuya Sakai, Jiaheng Lu, and Ji-Rong Wen. New assessment criteria for query suggestion. In *Proceedings of the 35th International ACM SIGIR conference on research and development in Information Retrieval*, pages 1109–1110, 2012.
36. Qiaozhu Mei, Dengyong Zhou, and Kenneth Ward Church. Query suggestion using hitting time. In *Proceedings of the 17th ACM Conference on Information and Knowledge Management*, pages 469–478, 2008.
37. James R Norris and James Robert Norris. *Markov chains*. Number 2. Cambridge university press, 1998.
38. Umut Ozertem, Olivier Chapelle, Pinar Donmez, and Emre Velipasaoglu. Learning to suggest: a machine learning framework for ranking query suggestions. In *Proceedings of the 35th international ACM SIGIR conference on Research and development in information retrieval*, pages 25–34, 2012.
39. Craig Silverstein, Monika Rauch Henzinger, Hannes Marais, and Michael Moricz. Analysis of a very large web search engine query log. *SIGIR Forum*, 33 (1): 6–12, 1999.

40. Yang Song and Li-wei He. Optimal rare query suggestion with implicit user feedback. In *Proceedings of the 19th International Conference on World Wide Web*, pages 901–910, 2010.
41. Yang Song, Dengyong Zhou, and Li-wei He. Post-ranking query suggestion by diversifying search results. In *Proceeding of the 34th International ACM SIGIR Conference on Research and Development in Information Retrieval*, pages 815–824, 2011.
42. Yang Song, Dengyong Zhou, and Li-wei He. Query suggestion by constructing term-transition graphs. In *Proceedings of the Fifth International Conference on Web Search and Data Mining*, pages 353–362, 2012.
43. Idan Szpektor, Aristides Gionis, and Yoelle Maarek. Improving recommendation for long-tail queries via templates. In *Proceedings of the 20th International Conference on World Wide Web*, pages 47–56, 2011.
44. Hanghang Tong, Christos Faloutsos, and Jia-Yu Pan. Random walk with restart: fast solutions and applications. *Knowledge and Information Systems*, 14 (3): 327–346, 2008.
45. Hongning Wang, Yang Song, Ming-Wei Chang, Xiaodong He, Ryen W. White, and Wei Chu. Learning to extract cross-session search tasks. In *Proceedings of the 22nd international conference on World Wide Web*, pages 1353–1364, 2013.
46. Ji-Rong Wen, Jian-Yun Nie, and HongJiang Zhang. Clustering user queries of a search engine. In *Proceedings of the Tenth International World Wide Web Conference*, pages 162–168, 2001.
47. Ryen W. White, Mikhail Bilenko, and Silviu Cucerzan. Studying the use of popular destinations to enhance web search interaction. In *Proceedings of the 30th Annual International ACM SIGIR Conference on Research and Development in Information Retrieval*, pages 159–166, 2007.
48. Zheng-Jun Zha, Linjun Yang, Tao Mei, Meng Wang, and Zengfu Wang. Visual query suggestion. In *Proceedings of the 17th ACM international conference on Multimedia*, pages 15–24, 2009.

Chapter 9
Future Directions of Query Understanding

David Carmel, Yi Chang, Hongbo Deng, and Jian-Yun Nie

Abstract Query understanding bridges the gap and establishes a communication channel between the searcher and the search engine. An important challenge in question understanding is the enhancement of user interaction with the search engine in a more natural way, including spoken language querying, multi-turn search sessions and conversational question answering. This demands additional information sources, such as knowledge graphs, and advances in research areas, such as cross-language IR. Moreover, there are many open questions and settings in query understanding that have not yet been fully explored. We will review some of these directions in this chapter, and we hope that researchers interested in query understanding will find them challenging and inspiring for future research directions.

9.1 Personalized Query Understanding

Query understanding is essentially limited if the user's personal perspective is not taken into consideration. Different people specify the same information need in different manners, and the relevance of an item to the query is varied according

D. Carmel
Amazon Research, Haifa, Israel
e-mail: dacarmel@amazon.com

Y. Chang (✉)
Jilin University, Jilin, China
e-mail: yichang@jlu.edu.cn

H. Deng
Alibaba Group, Zhejiang, China
e-mail: hbdeng@acm.org

J.-Y. Nie
University of Montreal, Montreal, QC, Canada
e-mail: nie@iro.umontreal.ca

© Springer Nature Switzerland AG 2020
Y. Chang, H. Deng (eds.), *Query Understanding for Search Engines*,
The Information Retrieval Series 46, https://doi.org/10.1007/978-3-030-58334-7_9

to the user's private interests, prior knowledge, and the current context of the search session.

Personalized query understanding (PQU) is the initial process of personalized search, which analyzes the user query according to the user's specific needs, personal knowledge, and the context he or she is currently involved with. Search personalization has been extensively studied by the IR community (e.g., [34, 62]) and was invoked, to some extent, by all commercial search engines.[1] In this section we briefly discuss our own anticipation how PQU is expected to emerge in the coming future.

Search personalization can be done at certain levels of granularity. The most basic one is session analysis, where the user's query is analyzed with respect to the previous queries submitted during the user's current search session, and the responses as reflected by the user feedback on the search results [18]. For example, a user searching for "parking" while his or her previous query was "Golden Bridge, SF," should only be exposed to parking lots in the Golden bridge area. Other parking lots are unlikely to be relevant in this specific session. Similarly, previous search results and the corresponding user feedback should also be taken into account while analyzing the current query, e.g., by downgrading results that have already been clicked (or ignored) previously during the current search session [71].

While current instrumentation tools for session analysis are mostly based on the user online feedback, as reflected through his or her clicks, mouse tracking, and his or her abandonment rate [15], much better instrumentation tools for measuring user engagement are expected to emerge, such as eye tracking, face expression analysis, sentiment analysis, and many more. Such tools would let us better analyze the user satisfaction (or dissatisfaction) with the search results, thus letting us tuning our search engine for better understanding and serving our users.

The long history of the user interaction with the search engine also provides important clues about the user general interests [6]. Analyzing the current query in the context of the user's search history, e.g., by topic modeling, can assist in understanding the user general topics of interests, thus assisting us in query disambiguation and classification [29]. Current search personalization approaches are mostly based on analyzing previous queries and previously visited Web pages. It is very likely that in the near future many other types of user feedback, on any digital device, could be tracked, aggregated, and be used for better modeling the user interests [79]. For example, the list of applications that we use on our smartphones on a daily basis is extremely effective in identifying our interests and goals [4]. Another example is the user activity on social media sites where the user posts, comments, and shares provide valuable data about his or her areas of interest. The user's own social network can be further analyzed for better understanding of the topics and issues that are relevant to the user in the context of his or her community [12]. Analyzing such rich types of data sources will enrich our understanding of the users' goals and preferences and will let us to better serve their information needs.

---

[1]For example, https://googleblog.blogspot.co.il/2009/12/personalized-search-for-everyone.html.

While PQU is going to emerge significantly in typical search scenario, it is also critical and essential for personal digital assistants like Siri,[2] Cortana,[3] and Alexa.[4] These agents are expected to answer our questions, make orders for us in online shopping sites, recommend relevant content, assist us in organizing our travels, etc. Such assistants require advanced personalization capabilities in order to keep track of our knowledge, preferences, and the context we are currently involved with, in order to serve us optimally. For example, when ordering coffee from our favorite coffee shop, my personal assistance is expected to be aware of that I drink my coffee with cream, no sugar, and very hot, while my wife drinks it black and weak. When asking for recommendations for a birthday present for Jenny, my assistant should know that Jenny is my five-year-old daughter. When asking our agent to order shampoo for our family, it should be aware of the types of shampoo favored by all family members, our favorite suppliers, as well as all other relevant details.

The main tool for capturing personalized data is a personalized knowledge graph (PKG), which will encapsulate all related entities of the user such as family members, friends, neighbors, contacts, as well as preferences, biases, and interests. The PKG will complement the general knowledge graph (KG) that is already being widely used by search engines for providing up-to-date information about popular entities such as politicians, celebrities, organizations, products, locations, etc. The PKG will be focused on entities strongly relevant to the user. Our personal social network, locations (home, work, frequently visited sites), medicines, dietary ingredients, and media preferred entities should all be represented in our PKG. The PKG will be used by the assistant agents to personalize the interaction with the user. Each query will be analyzed by considering the personal entities in this graph, in addition to the entities extracted from the general KG, and their relationships with the user.

To summarize, we can safely anticipate that query understanding will become much more personalized in the coming future for supporting deep personalized search experience, provided through general-purpose search engines as well as through personal digital assistants.

9.2 Natural Language Question Understanding

Another popular trend in the IR domain is moving from keyword queries to natural language questions. Current mobile devices enable users to input spoken language queries into their search applications, taking advantage of recent developments in speech recognition technology that exceeds human performance in spoken language understanding [65]. Spoken queries are typically much longer and are usually

---

[2]https://www.apple.com/ios/siri/.

[3]https://www.microsoft.com/en-us/windows/cortana.

[4]https://www.alexa.com/.

pronounced as natural language questions, rather the standard keyword queries that we are used to issue in the current Web search services [28].

In contrast to short keyword queries, long queries can benefit from Natural Language Processing (NLP) methods. While NLP analysis for short queries typically fails to bring significant improvement over shallow statistical-based methods, they were found useful for long queries where syntactic analysis such as part-of-speech tagging and dependency parsing complement standard statistical term weighting methods [14].

Serving natural language questions strongly corresponds with the traditional question answering task, which has been mostly focused on answering factoid questions [40]. The standard flow of question answering process begins with question analysis for identifying the lexical answer type, i.e., the category type of the answer expected for that question (e.g., country, capital city, date, distance). Then, passages are identified in a given knowledge base, which are likely to contain an answer to the question. Candidate answers are then extracted from the top retrieved passages and are judged and scored according to many criteria. The top scored candidate is then selected for the final answer. A typical judge, for example, will filter out candidates not belonging to the question's lexical category type identified during the question analysis phase. This paradigm was successfully demonstrated by IBM Watson, which was able to outperform human trivia experts in the game of Jeopardy [24]. However, even the extremely complicated Jeopardy questions are limited to factoid questions only. More complex needs such as why questions, opinion and advice seeking questions, puzzles, and many other types are still an open challenge and deserve further research for understanding the actual information need behind them.

Another emerging direction for question understanding is the identification of Web queries having a question intent, which constitute about 10% of the issued queries [80]. Such queries, even formulated as keyword queries, seek for a direct and detailed answer rather than a list of search results. Current Web search engines usually handle such queries by developing a specific tool for any specific question type. Weather-based queries are served by the Weather agent, while stock-based queries are handled by the Finance agent. The same approach is taken for handling named-entity queries where the entity's relevant information, extracted from the general-purpose knowledge graph, is directly displayed on the SERP enriching the standard Web search results.

Furthermore, a new trend emerges recently of handling factoid questions by existing question answering techniques. This approach is immature yet and in its infant stages, but we can expect significant progress in the future. Complementary, any question-intent queries can be served by searching over an archive of community question answering sites, looking for similar questions that have already been manually answered by humans. This approach was dominant among participants in the TREC's Live-QA track [1] where participants were challenged to answer real human questions in real time (in less than 1 min). Real human questions submitted on the Yahoo Answers site were submitted to participant systems during the contest and were answered automatically and immediately by the participant systems. Most participants searched for the answer over a given archive of question–answer pairs to provide the most appropriate human answer for similar questions. Many approaches were examined for measuring the relevance of question–answer pairs to the given question. One interesting technology presented in the track was a combination of automatic search with human judgment; a list of candidate answers was retrieved by the search component and then was judged in real time by crowd-sourcing humans [66]. One of the conclusions of the Live-QA challenge was that while previously answered questions can be useful to answer popular questions, advanced answer generation techniques should be considered in order to answer, with high quality, long-tailed questions.

To conclude, the trend of moving from keyword queries to natural language questions enables users to better express their needs and to easily provide their questions through much more diverse and highly accessible input devices. However, these complicated questions open many new challenges in question analysis and question understanding and require the development of advanced techniques that should be further explored.

9.3 Dialog Query Conversational Query Understanding

The current search engines mainly focus on one-shot search: the search results are basically determined by the current query the user has formulated. Few attempts have been made to engage a conversation with the user to better understand the search intent of the user. The burden is on the user who has to learn to adapt to the search systems: when a query was not successful, the user has to modify it based on an analysis of the previous search results. Such modifications can be repeated several times before the user can find the desired documents. Even though, it is not rare to see frustrated users who fail to retrieve desired documents and to understand why their queries have not been successful. The interface of search engines is not user friendly and does not provide much help to the user to formulate better queries

Looking back into the history, IR was imagined as an intermediary between the library system and the user—a role that was played typically by a librarian. To understand what the user was looking for, the librarian usually held a conversation (negotiation) with the user to understand the information need of the user and to generate a good search query to be submitted to a library system [78]. Even though we do not think about using a human intermediary for search nowadays or have the luxury to do it, the existence of a human intermediary provided at least several advantages compared to the current interface:

- She/he knows better the useful search terms to use than most users, being familiar with the data collections;
- She/he knows better databases to search (when there are multiple search systems);
- She/he understands the search intent of the user.

These advantages are precious for users who are not familiar with the search engine, the documents indexed, or the searched topics. A conversational intermediary can play a similar role as human librarian to help the user. Some typical cases where the conversational assistance can be helpful are as follows:

- The user's initial query is ambiguous: either ambiguous terms are used or the whole query may lead to very different types of documents. If ambiguity is detected, a clarification question can be asked to the user [2].
- The query is underspecified: The query may be too general or too vague, leading to too many search results. It may be useful to ask the user to provide more details about the searched topics. For example, some choices can be offered to the user based on the distribution of the corresponding topics [72].
- The formulated query does not contain the best search terms. When formulating a query, a user may not have the experience to choose the best search terms. In this case, the conversational assistance can suggest better terms or a better formulation of the query.
- A search topic may be strongly related to other topics, which could be of interest to the user. For example, it may be useful to the user to also learn about the background information when searching about an event or to learn about its next evolution [8]. The conversational assistance can take a proactive role to suggest related topics to users.

While conceptually the above assistance can be useful, it has to be implemented correctly. A bad assistance tool can easily become annoying. To implement effective conversational assistance to understand search intents, we are faced with the following technical challenges:

- How to detect if a conversational assistance is needed?
- How to determine the best action? Should the system ask a clarification question? Provide some results and see how the user interacts with them? or Suggest alternative queries/topics?
- How to generate a natural and relevant reply or question? This aspect is particularly challenging for the current conversation technology, which is able to generate replies in task-oriented conversation in limited domains with predefined knowledge structure but has difficulty to do it in open-domain conversation [2]. A key issue to investigate is whether it is possible to develop some general conversation patterns for general search tasks. For example, when a query ambiguity is detected, a clarification question such as "do you mean X or Y by [original query]?" can be generated. To suggest alternative queries, the system can suggest "try the query [suggested query] that has been successful for other users," or "your search topic is related to [suggested query]."
- How to judge the success of a conversational query understanding process? The goal of new interaction methods, including conversational query understanding, is to help the users to do more effective search. When the user is involved in the loop, the current evaluation methodology becomes insufficient. Some attempts have been made to evaluate the search process in which the user participates [37],

but there is still no general consensus on the appropriate methodology for conversational IR.

- Finally, we also have to think about the possible forms of a conversational assistance. Dialog in natural language (either in speech or in text) is the first form of conversation we can think about. Should we limit conversational assistance to this narrow form, or should we give conversation a wider meaning, to include other forms of interactions such as providing choices to the user, let the user click on some results? [49]

In summary, conversational query understanding and assistance will likely change the face of search engines in the future, but many underlying problems remain to be explored and solved to make it effective in practice.

9.4 Medical Query Understanding

Medical IR is an important application area. People often use search engine to locate relevant information in addition to consulting physicians. However, the current search engines are limited in providing appropriate search tools in this specific area. In most cases, users are left with a search engine constructed with the general technology, even though the documents in the database may be in the medical domain. A good understanding of medical queries is particularly important because most users are not familiar with the specialized concepts used in the medical documents. This situation also makes the understanding very challenging. Some of the main difficulties are as follows:

- Vocabulary mismatch: End users may not know the exact specialized term of a medical concept. Even though some lexical resources have been constructed, trying to bridge the vocabulary gap between specialized documents and non-specialized end users [91], they are far from enough to solve the problem. The problem of vocabulary mismatch is not limited to the level of words or terms, it can be at a more global level. For example, a user may use several sentences to explain a health condition, which could be described by a specialized term.
- Concept mapping: A strongly related problem is to recognize correctly the concepts described in a text (a document or a query). This is a key step for correct query understanding. Concept mapping in medical domain has attracted a large amount of research work. Most approaches leverage the existing lexical resources (e.g., UMLS Metathesaurus[5]) and make use of syntactic rules, variations on word forms, and statistics to determine which concepts a sequence of words can correspond to. MetaMap[6] [3] is considered to be one of the best tools in

---

[5]https://www.nlm.nih.gov/research/umls/knowledge_sources/metathesaurus/.
[6]https://metamap.nlm.nih.gov/.

this area. However, its accuracy on query analysis was estimated at only about 70% [21, 67], making it difficult to rely on for document matching.

- Exploring more resources to learn concept mapping: The existing research on concept mapping has been limited to lexical mapping an observed sequence of words to the possible expressions of a concept in a lexical resource. The recent development on deep learning offers us a great opportunity to match a piece of text with a concept in a latent representation space: Both concepts and words/sentences could be mapped into the same representation space, allowing them to be directly compared. While some preliminary studies in this direction have been done [47, 48] showing promising results, more investigations are required to fully explore the potential of this approach.

- In addition to search queries, users tend to ask more complex questions. In forums of discussions where users can ask questions to physicians or other peer users, it is common to see long questions with a description about the patient and the problem and asking for advice. While we do not see, in the current stage, that human replies can be completely replaced by automatic replies, it is useful to process such long and complex questions to help users locate the most useful documents or pieces of information. We are then faced with the problem of understanding complex medical questions, which is not limited to merely identifying the key concepts involved but also relate them so as to construct a complete picture (graph) about the question. For example, we should not only recognize that the user's question involves the concept "pneumonia" but also that "pneumonia" happened to the patient 1 month ago rather than now, and the patient is a 50-year-old adult. This fine-grained analysis is crucial in this area.

In addition to query understanding, documents should also be understood in a similar way. Finally, new matching processes are required to compare complex query and document representations. All these problems require more research work.

9.5 Cross-Language Query Understanding and Translation

In the majority of cases, users are interested in searching documents in the same language as the query. However, this situation does not mean that there is no need for searching documents in other languages. Cross-language and multilingual search is needed in several typical cases [25]. For example, the topic may not be well covered in the language of the query but is well covered in another language; or the search needs to be completed (recall-oriented search such as patent retrieval) in all languages. In these typical cases, a search query has to be translated into one or several other languages. Query translation is a challenging task.

A general machine translation can do a good job for translating most queries: when there is no ambiguity and when terms in a query have a clear translation in another language. However, we are often faced with the translation ambiguity problem, especially for short queries that provide limited contextual information. The existing approaches have explored the utilization of the following information to select good translation terms:

- Translation probability
- How common a term is used in the target language

In addition to the problem of translation, query translation also plays the role of selection of good search terms: When several translation alternatives exist, it may be better to select the one that is more discriminative or to combine all of them. The inclusion of multiple translation terms in query translation has naturally produced a desired effect of query expansion [25, 82].

Cross-language query understanding is not limited to translation only. The search behaviors in different language communities could be different. For example, while people in North America are more concerned with water and soil pollution, people in China can be more concerned with air pollution. So a search on "pollution" in different language communities may lead to different results. Cross-language query understanding could be extended to the understanding of search intents in different language communities, and when possible, making the required adaptation. This has been found very useful in some existing work [25].

The further development on cross-language query understanding will certainly benefit from the development of deep learning approaches. Indeed, if both the query and the document can be mapped into a common representation space, whatever their language is, then the translation problem does not exist anymore. Such interlingua representation has been investigated in recent MT studies [23], which assumes that different languages share a common representation space, in addition to a private space specific to each language. However, much more investigations are required to make the approach effective in practice.

9.6   Temporal Dynamics of Queries

The World Wide Web is highly dynamic and is constantly evolving: as a large number of new Web pages are created or updated every second, information on those old Web pages are outdated quickly. At the same time, Web search is strongly influenced by time: some queries occasionally spike in popularity, some queries periodically spike, and others remain relatively constant. In order to help search engine users to find the latest updated information, it is foremost to detect those time-sensitive queries and understand their temporal dynamics, which benefits not only search ranking [22] but also query autocompletion [11, 70].

Given a query, we count its frequency during a predefined time interval and generate a time series about this query. In order to model the temporal shapes, power Law distribution is proposed as the function to model burst time series [17], and recently Hawkes process is leveraged to model temporal bursts with multiple spikes [64]. Another useful approach is to model occurrence of spikes using infinite-state automation approach [39]. Yet, the method uses spike locations as input, and thus it is not possible to directly apply the infinite-state automation approach for raw time-series data.

In addition, temporal information helps us to group topics together. Once a sudden spike appears on the extracted time series, most likely, many of the users are searching the same topic or the same event, which indicates a strong relationship between content information and temporal information. Therefore, it is necessary for us to combine temporal information with content information into the same framework, yet it is a very challenging and difficult task, as temporal shapes and textual content are heterogeneous. To combine temporal modeling with content analysis is not brand new, and there are a few excellent works [35, 42]. However, these existing works either assume topical distribution changes smoothly or just model temporal information as a sequence of bursts, which could not explicitly model the temporal shapes with the sudden spikes.

Furthermore, temporal dynamics of queries can be leveraged for prediction. Since whether a query is triggered by an event can be successfully predicted [64], it is possible to improve query autocompletion by leveraging terms related to the triggered event or to enhance search result ranking via boosting documents related to the triggered event, which are promising research ideas. Yet, how to handle prediction with intent shifting or triggered by multiple events are still unsolved open challenges.

9.7   Deep Learning for Query Understanding

With the success of deep learning in many research areas, Information Retrieval (IR) community has started to explore deep learning-based techniques to various query understanding problems. The key features of deep learning are representation learning and end-to-end training. We begin by introducing different neural approaches to learn vector representations of queries. We then review some shallow and deep neural methods that employ pretrained word embeddings as well as learn the end-to-end query understanding tasks such as query expansion, spelling correction, query classification, and so on.

Vector representations are fundamental to both information retrieval and deep learning. Different vector representations exhibit different levels of generalization and could derive different levels of similarity. In traditional IR, query and document are represented as bag of words, and many approaches rely on exact term matching between the query and the document text. To be able to perform soft term matching between semantically similar words, a number of studies have focused in particular on the use of word embeddings generated using shallow or deep NNs. For example, the terms "hotel" and "motel" are two separate words that cannot match each other with bag of words, while ideally they could share a large similarity using word embeddings. Word embedding, also known as distributed representation of words, refers to a set of machine learning algorithms that learn high-dimensional real-valued dense vector representation $\mathbf{w} \in R^d$ for each vocabulary term w, where d denotes the embedding dimensionality. Word2vec [52] and GloVe [60] are two well-known word embedding algorithms that learn embedding vectors in an unsupervised learning. The underlying idea is that the words that often appear in surrounding contexts are similar to each other. Such word embeddings can be used to capture a certain type of topical similarity, such as "hotel" to be similar to "motel," and "wife" to be similar to "husband." It is worth noting that learning different word embeddings can capture different types of similarities, which may not be appropriate for a certain retrieval scenario.

A better alternative is to learn embeddings as a set of parameters in an end-to-end neural network model for a specific IR task [19, 85, 90]. The word embeddings can be aggregated in different ways for estimating query embedding vectors, and using the average word embeddings is quite popular [44, 56, 81]. In [88], a theoretical framework has been proposed with different implementations for estimating query embedding vectors based on individual word embeddings, which shows that average word embeddings is a special case. In addition, Dehghani et al. [19] proposed to represent query as a weighted sum of word embeddings by learning the global weight for each term in the vocabulary set. Training word embedding vectors based on additional data, like query logs and click-through data, was also studied in [26, 32, 73]. Recently, Grbovic et al. [27] used query embeddings to include session-based information for sponsor search. Estimating accurate query embedding vectors can improve the performance of many of the embedding-based methods that need to compute query vectors. It should be noted that in a realistic case, many tail and rare queries are not available during the training time of embedding vectors, which makes direct training of query embedding vectors problematic. How to learn the embeddings for tail and rare queries is still a very challenge task.

There are many existing works [5, 20, 43, 73, 89] that attempt to leverage word embeddings for query expansion. One straightforward method [5, 43, 89] is to employ the pretrained term embeddings to select terms that are similar to the query as a whole or its constituent terms, and then the selected terms are used to expand the query in a unigram language model framework. For example, Zamani and Croft [89] presented a set of embedding-based query language models using the query expansion and pseudo-relevance feedback techniques that benefit from the word embedding vectors. Diaz et al. [20] proposed to train word embeddings on topically constrained corpora, instead of large topically unconstrained corpora. These locally trained embedding vectors were shown to perform well for the query expansion task. Zheng and Callan [94] proposed a supervised embedding-based term reweighting technique applied to the language modeling and BM25 retrieval models.

Convolutional neural networks (CNNs) and recurrent neural networks (RNNs) are two most common architectures, where CNNs were originally developed for image classification [33, 41] and RNNs have been successfully used in natural language processing [31, 51]. Recently, a number of deep neural networks with deep architectures have been applied to some specific query understanding approaches.

For example, CNNs and RNNs have emerged as top performing architectures in query classification and query intent detection [30, 36, 38, 69, 92]. Park and Chiba [59] proposed a neural language model with recurrent layers for query autocompletion task. Another special type of neural network architecture is Siamese networks. A Siamese network consists of two identical neural networks, each taking one of the two inputs, such as the query and the document. The last layers of the two networks are then fed to a contrastive loss function, which calculates the similarity between the two inputs. The Deep Semantic Similarity Model (DSSM) [32] is one such architecture that trains on query and document title pairs and learns the similarity between them. Convolutional DSSM (CDSSM) [68] employs more sophisticated architectures involving convolutional layers. Mitra and Craswell [54] trained the same CDSSM architecture using query prefix–suffix pairs and leveraged the model to suggest query completions for rare query prefixes. Obviously, an appropriate network architecture makes big difference for end-to-end training, but it can be difficult to determine when to use which kind of network architectures. For a given query understanding task, predicting in advance which will work best is usually impossible, and how to design an appropriate network architecture remains an open question.

Some deep learning methods operate at the character-level or character n-gram [32, 55, 68]. For instance, the deep learning method for spelling correction is usually sequence-to-sequence models. A sequence-to-sequence model [76] consists of an encoder and decoder. The encoder converts a sequence of characters or tokens into a single vector, while the decoder begins with this vector, and it keeps generating characters or tokens until it generates a special stop symbol. Note that the lengths of the source and target sequences do not need to be the same. Both the encoding and decoding are done using RNNs. Xie et al. [84] presented an encoder–decoder RNN with an attention mechanism by operating at the character level. Sordoni et al. [74] formulated a hierarchical recurrent encoder–decoder architecture and used it to produce query suggestions, which takes account for sequences of previous queries of arbitrary lengths as context. Another advanced query reformulation system proposed by Nogueira and Cho [57] is to train neural network with reinforcement learning. The actions correspond to selecting terms to build a reformulated query, and the reward is the document recall.

9.8 Semantic Understanding and Matching for Search Queries

Semantic matching is one of the most difficult challenges especially for tail queries [45]: query document mismatch occurs when the queries and documents use different terms to describe the same concept. For instance, for the query "how much is tesla," relevant documents may contain the term "price" rather than "how much," so the widely used bag-of-words approach is insufficient to solve this challenge [87].

The basic idea of semantic matching is to project a query or a document directly or indirectly onto its semantic space separately and then match the query and the document on their semantic spaces. The traditional semantic matching approach can be grouped into the following categories:

Semantic Matching with Machine Translation Model Its basic idea is to leverage machine translation models to deal with query and document mismatching, which is a supervised learning method. In particular, queries are considered as the source language, while the clicked documents derived from click-through data are considered as the target language, then search can be formulated as a statistical machine translation problem [7], in which query q is translated into document d with the largest conditional probability $P(d|q)$.

Semantic Matching with Topic Model It is well known that queries and documents with the same topic are more likely to be considered as relevant, as their semantic are consistent at the topic level. The basic idea of this approach is to use topic models, such as LDA or PLSI, to obtain the topics of each query or each document and then leverage topic matching techniques to deal with query document mismatching, which could successfully improve search relevance [86]. Generally speaking, this approach belongs to unsupervised learning.

Semantic Matching with Latent Space Model In this approach, queries and documents are trained to map into the same latent space, and the semantic matching function is defined as the inner product between the projection of the query and the projection of the document in the latent space, while each dimension of the latent space does not necessarily have its corresponding semantic meaning [32]. Generally speaking, this approach is a supervised learning approach.

Semantic Matching with Deep Learning Model Recent work on semantic matching is mainly based on deep learning algorithms [58], which can automatically learn relations among words from vast amount of search log data and fully make use of information from phrase patterns and text hierarchical structures, and experimental results usually show a better performance.

In fact, these different approaches of semantic matching are complementary, and how to effectively combine them into one generic framework is an open question. In addition, how to handle the semantic matching when queries are too short is still a challenging problem, since deep learning-based text matching approach works well when the queries are relatively lengthy. Furthermore, how to handle multimodal semantic matching is another challenging problem, such as the semantic matching between a text query and an image, or between an image query and a text document, which is critical for image search and video search in commercial search engines.

9.9   Query Understanding with Knowledge Graph

Knowledge bases, better known as knowledge graphs, such as Wikipedia, DBpedia, Freebase [10], and Yago [75], have emerged in recent years. Most of them are encyclopedic knowledge bases, containing entities and facts such as Barack Obama's birthday and birthplace. The knowledge graphs have been utilized for enhancing query understanding in an entity-aware way for the rich facts organized around entities. For example, Google took the first step in understanding and answering queries with the knowledge graph in 2012, and they started by providing information on individual entities like "Barack Obama" or "Brad Pitt." Recently, search engines become a little bit smarter and could answer simple questions about those entities, such as "How old is Barack Obama?" or "Who are the authors of Harry Potter?". All of these works rely on query understanding with knowledge graph. There are a few challenges as listed below:

First, a widely accepted way to use knowledge graph is to annotate the entities in the query and link them to a knowledge base, also known as entity linking. TagME [61] is a very early work on entity linking in queries. It generates candidates by searching Wikipedia page titles, anchors, and redirects then exploits the structure of the Wikipedia graph for disambiguation. Entity linking in queries is also viewed as the problem of finding multiple query interpretations [13], usually with three phrases: fetching, candidate-entity generation, and pruning. One challenge is that the queries are usually very short and contain insufficient information, thus it becomes very important to leverage additional information, such as Wikipedia [16, 77], query log, and search results [9].

Second, quite a few nonentity words are barely included in knowledge graph, and knowledge about how words interact with each other in a language (instead of encyclopedia knowledge) plays an important role in query understanding. As we discussed above, the encyclopedia knowledge base contains entities and facts, while the other type of knowledge base is mainly about common sense or linguistic knowledge among terms, such as KnowItAll [50], NELL [53], and Probase [46]. For nonentity words, recently there appears a tendency to mine a variety of relations among terms and map them to related concepts [83] or intent topics [93] and then propagate the enriched features in a graph consisting of concepts or intent topics using an unsupervised algorithm. How to effectively extract knowledge of nonentity words and represent them in a unified knowledge graph remains a challenging task for query understanding.

Third, with the extensive knowledge graph, structured query understanding is a critical component to improve the relevance of search engines. For example, identifying attributes in a query for e-commerce platforms could significantly improve the performance in connecting users to relevant items. In many cases, the queries might have multiple attributes, and some of them will be in conflict with each other. Leveraging the e-commerce catalog [63] as an additional knowledge base to supplement the textual information can help to resolve conflicting query attributes. Similarly, additional domain-specific knowledge graph will be very valuable for structured query understanding in other domains, such as healthcare.

As discussed above, the knowledge graph makes it possible to break down a query to understand the semantics of each piece and get the intent behind the entire query. Moreover, that makes it reliable to traverse the knowledge graph to find the right facts and compose a useful answer for a given query.

References

1. Eugene Agichtein, David Carmel, Dan Pelleg, Yuval Pinter, and Donna Harman. Overview of the TREC 2015 LiveQA track. In *Proceedings of The Twenty-Fourth Text REtrieval Conference*, volume 500-319, 2015.
2. Mohammad Aliannejadi, Hamed Zamani, Fabio Crestani, and W. Bruce Croft. Asking clarifying questions in open-domain information-seeking conversations. In *Proceedings of the 42nd International ACM SIGIR Conference on Research and Development in Information Retrieval*, pages 475–484, 2019.
3. Alan R. Aronson. Effective mapping of biomedical text to the UMLS metathesaurus: the metamap program. In *Proceedings of the American Medical Informatics Association Annual Symposium*, pages 17–21, 2001.
4. Ricardo Baeza-Yates, Di Jiang, Fabrizio Silvestri, and Beverly Harrison. Predicting the next app that you are going to use. In *Proceedings of the Eighth ACM International Conference on Web Search and Data Mining*, pages 285–294, 2015.
5. Saeid Balaneshinkordan and Alexander Kotov. Embedding-based query expansion for weighted sequential dependence retrieval model. In *Proceedings of the 40th International ACM SIGIR Conference on Research and Development in Information Retrieval*, pages 1213–1216, 2017.
6. Paul N. Bennett, Ryen W. White, Wei Chu, Susan T. Dumais, Peter Bailey, Fedor Borisyuk, and Xiaoyuan Cui. Modeling the impact of short- and long-term behavior on search personalization. In *Proceedings of the 35th International ACM SIGIR Conference on Research and Development in Information Retrieval*, pages 185–194, 2012.
7. Adam L. Berger and John D. Lafferty. Information retrieval as statistical translation. In *Proceedings of the 22nd International ACM SIGIR Conference on Research and Development in Information Retrieval*, pages 222–229, 1999.
8. Sumit Bhatia, Debapriyo Majumdar, and Nitish Aggarwal. Proactive information retrieval: Anticipating users' information need. In *Advances in Information Retrieval - 38th European Conference on IR Research*, volume 9626, pages 874–877, 2016.
9. Roi Blanco, Giuseppe Ottaviano, and Edgar Meij. Fast and space-efficient entity linking for queries. In *Proceedings of the Eighth ACM International Conference on Web Search and Data Mining*, pages 179–188, 2015.
10. Kurt D. Bollacker, Colin Evans, Praveen Paritosh, Tim Sturge, and Jamie Taylor. Freebase: a collaboratively created graph database for structuring human knowledge. In *Proceedings of the ACM SIGMOD International Conference on Management of Data*, pages 1247–1250, 2008.
11. Fei Cai, Shangsong Liang, and Maarten de Rijke. Time-sensitive personalized query autocompletion. In *Proceedings of the 23rd ACM International Conference on Conference on Information and Knowledge Management*, pages 1599–1608, 2014.
12. David Carmel, Naama Zwerdling, Ido Guy, Shila Ofek-Koifman, Nadav Har'El, Inbal Ronen, Erel Uziel, Sivan Yogev, and Sergey Chernov. Personalized social search based on the user's social network. In *Proceedings of the 18th ACM Conference on Information and Knowledge Management*, pages 1227–1236, 2009.

13. David Carmel, Ming-Wei Chang, Evgeniy Gabrilovich, Bo-June Paul Hsu, and Kuansan Wang, editors. *ERD'14, Proceedings of the First ACM International Workshop on Entity Recognition & Disambiguation*, 2014a. ACM. ISBN 978-1-4503-3023-7.
14. David Carmel, Avihai Mejer, Yuval Pinter, and Idan Szpektor. Improving term weighting for community question answering search using syntactic analysis. In *Proceedings of the 23rd ACM International Conference on Conference on Information and Knowledge Management*, pages 351–360, 2014b.
15. Aleksandr Chuklin, Ilya Markov, and Maarten de Rijke. *Click Models for Web Search*. Synthesis Lectures on Information Concepts, Retrieval, and Services. 2015.
16. Marco Cornolti, Paolo Ferragina, Massimiliano Ciaramita, Hinrich Schütze, and Stefan Rüd. The SMAPH system for query entity recognition and disambiguation. In *Proceedings of the First ACM International Workshop on Entity Recognition and Disambiguation*, pages 25–30, 2014.
17. Riley Crane and Didier Sornette. Robust dynamic classes revealed by measuring the response function of a social system. *Proceedings of the National Academy of Sciences*, 105 (41): 15649–15653, 2008.
18. Mariam Daoud, Lynda Tamine-Lechani, and Mohand Boughanem. Towards a graph-based user profile modeling for a session-based personalized search. *Knowl. Inf. Syst.*, 21 (3): 365–398, 2009.
19. Mostafa Dehghani, Hamed Zamani, Aliaksei Severyn, Jaap Kamps, and W. Bruce Croft. Neural ranking models with weak supervision. In *Proceedings of the 40th International ACM SIGIR Conference on Research and Development in Information Retrieval*, pages 65–74, 2017.
20. Fernando Diaz, Bhaskar Mitra, and Nick Craswell. Query expansion with locally-trained word embeddings. In *Proceedings of the 54th Annual Meeting of the Association for Computational Linguistics*, pages 367–377, 2016.
21. Guy Divita, Tony Tse, and Laura Roth. Failure analysis of metamap transfer (MMTx). In *Proceedings of the 11th World Congress on Medical Informatics*, volume 107, pages 763–767, 2004.
22. Anlei Dong, Yi Chang, Zhaohui Zheng, Gilad Mishne, Jing Bai, Ruiqiang Zhang, Karolina Buchner, Ciya Liao, and Fernando Diaz. Towards recency ranking in web search. In *Proceedings of the Third International Conference on Web Search and Data Mining*, pages 11–20, 2010.
23. Carlos Escolano, Marta R. Costa-jussà, and José A. R. Fonollosa. Towards interlingua neural machine translation. *CoRR*, abs/1905.06831, 2019.
24. David A. Ferrucci, Eric W. Brown, Jennifer Chu-Carroll, James Fan, David Gondek, Aditya Kalyanpur, Adam Lally, J. William Murdock, Eric Nyberg, John M. Prager, Nico Schlaefer, and Christopher A. Welty. Building Watson: An overview of the DeepQA project. *AI Magazine*, 31 (3): 59–79, 2010.
25. Wei Gao, Cheng Niu, Jian-Yun Nie, Ming Zhou, Kam-Fai Wong, and Hsiao-Wuen Hon. Exploiting query logs for cross-lingual query suggestions. *ACM Trans. Inf. Syst.*, 28 (2): 6:1–6:33, 2010.
26. Mihajlo Grbovic, Nemanja Djuric, Vladan Radosavljevic, and Narayan Bhamidipati. Search retargeting using directed query embeddings. In *Proceedings of the 24th International Conference on World Wide Web*, pages 37–38, 2015a.
27. Mihajlo Grbovic, Nemanja Djuric, Vladan Radosavljevic, Fabrizio Silvestri, and Narayan Bhamidipati. Context- and content-aware embeddings for query rewriting in sponsored search. In *Proceedings of the 38th International ACM SIGIR Conference on Research and Development in Information Retrieval*, pages 383–392, 2015b.
28. Ido Guy. Searching by talking: Analysis of voice queries on mobile web search. In *Proceedings of the 39th International ACM SIGIR Conference on Research and Development in Information Retrieval*, pages 35–44, 2016.
29. Morgan Harvey, Fabio Crestani, and Mark James Carman. Building user profiles from topic models for personalised search. In *Proceedings of the 22nd ACM international conference on Conference on information and knowledge management*, pages 2309–2314, 2013.

30. Homa B. Hashemi, Amir Asiaee, and Reiner Kraft. Query intern detection using convolutional neural networks. *WSDM QRUMS 2016 Workshop*, 2016.
31. Sepp Hochreiter and Jürgen Schmidhuber. Long short-term memory. *Neural Computation*, 9 (8): 1735–1780, 1997.
32. Po-Sen Huang, Xiaodong He, Jianfeng Gao, Li Deng, Alex Acero, and Larry P. Heck. Learning deep structured semantic models for web search using clickthrough data. In *Proceedings of the 22nd ACM International Conference on Information and Knowledge Management*, pages 2333–2338, 2013.
33. Kevin Jarrett, Koray Kavukcuoglu, Marc'Aurelio Ranzato, and Yann LeCun. What is the best multi-stage architecture for object recognition? In *Proceedings of the 12th IEEE International Conference on Computer Vision*, pages 2146–2153, 2009.
34. Glen Jeh and Jennifer Widom. Scaling personalized web search. In *Proceedings of the 12th International Conference on World Wide Web*, pages 271–279, 2003.
35. Rosie Jones and Fernando Diaz. Temporal profiles of queries. *ACM Trans. Inf. Syst.*, 25 (3): 14, 2007.
36. Nal Kalchbrenner, Edward Grefenstette, and Phil Blunsom. A convolutional neural network for modelling sentences. In *Proceedings of the 52nd Annual Meeting of the Association for Computational Linguistics*, pages 655–665, 2014.
37. Diane Kelly. Methods for evaluating interactive information retrieval systems with users. *Foundations and Trends in Information Retrieval*, 3 (1–2): 1–224, 2009.
38. Yoon Kim. Convolutional neural networks for sentence classification. In *Proceedings of the 2014 Conference on Empirical Methods in Natural Language Processing*, pages 1746–1751, 2014.
39. Jon M. Kleinberg. Bursty and hierarchical structure in streams. *Data Min. Knowl. Discov.*, 7 (4): 373–397, 2003.
40. Oleksandr Kolomiyets and Marie-Francine Moens. A survey on question answering technology from an information retrieval perspective. *Information Sciences*, 181 (24): 5412–5434, 2011.
41. Alex Krizhevsky, Ilya Sutskever, and Geoffrey E. Hinton. Imagenet classification with deep convolutional neural networks. In *Proceedings of the 26th Annual Conference on Neural Information Processing Systems*, pages 1106–1114, 2012.
42. Anagha Kulkarni, Jaime Teevan, Krysta Marie Svore, and Susan T. Dumais. Understanding temporal query dynamics. In *Proceedings of the Forth International Conference on Web Search and Data Mining*, pages 167–176, 2011.
43. Saar Kuzi, Anna Shtok, and Oren Kurland. Query expansion using word embeddings. In *Proceedings of the 25th ACM International Conference on Information and Knowledge Management*, pages 1929–1932, 2016.
44. Quoc V. Le and Tomas Mikolov. Distributed representations of sentences and documents. In *Proceedings of the 31th International Conference on Machine Learning*, pages 1188–1196, 2014.
45. Hang Li and Jun Xu. Semantic matching in search. *Foundations and Trends in Information Retrieval*, 7 (5): 343–469, 2014.
46. Jiaqing Liang, Yanghua Xiao, Haixun Wang, Yi Zhang, and Wei Wang. Probase+: Inferring missing links in conceptual taxonomies. *IEEE Trans. Knowl. Data Eng.*, 29 (6): 1281–1295, 2017.
47. Nut Limsopatham and Nigel Collier. Normalising medical concepts in social media texts by learning semantic representation. In *Proceedings of the 54th Annual Meeting of the Association for Computational Linguistics*, pages 1014–1023, 2016.
48. Xiaojie Liu, Jian-Yun Nie, and Alessandro Sordoni. Constraining word embeddings by prior knowledge - application to medical information retrieval. In *Proceedings of the 12th Asia Information Retrieval Societies Conference*, volume 9994, pages 155–167, 2016.
49. Z. Liu, Z. Niu, J.-Y. Nie, H. Wu, and H. Wang. Conversation in IR: its role and utility. In *SIGIR Workshop on Conversational Approaches to IR*, 2017.

50. Mausam. Open information extraction systems and downstream applications. In *Proceedings of the Twenty-Fifth International Joint Conference on Artificial Intelligence*, pages 4074–4077, 2016.
51. Tomas Mikolov, Martin Karafiát, Lukás Burget, Jan Cernocký, and Sanjeev Khudanpur. Recurrent neural network based language model. In *Proceedings of the 11th Annual Conference of the International Speech Communication Association*, pages 1045–1048, 2010.
52. Tomas Mikolov, Ilya Sutskever, Kai Chen, Gregory S. Corrado, and Jeffrey Dean. Distributed representations of words and phrases and their compositionality. In *Proceedings of the 27th Annual Conference on Neural Information Processing Systems*, pages 3111–3119, 2013.
53. Tom M. Mitchell, William W. Cohen, Estevam R. Hruschka Jr., Partha Pratim Talukdar, Justin Betteridge, Andrew Carlson, Bhavana Dalvi Mishra, Matthew Gardner, Bryan Kisiel, Jayant Krishnamurthy, Ni Lao, Kathryn Mazaitis, Thahir Mohamed, Ndapandula Nakashole, Emmanouil A. Platanios, Alan Ritter, Mehdi Samadi, Burr Settles, Richard C. Wang, Derry Wijaya, Abhinav Gupta, Xinlei Chen, Abulhair Saparov, Malcolm Greaves, and Joel Welling. Never-ending learning. In *Proceedings of the Twenty-Ninth AAAI Conference on Artificial Intelligence*, pages 2302–2310, 2015.
54. Bhaskar Mitra and Nick Craswell. Query auto-completion for rare prefixes. In *Proceedings of the 24th ACM International Conference on Information and Knowledge Management*, pages 1755–1758, 2015.
55. Bhaskar Mitra, Fernando Diaz, and Nick Craswell. Learning to match using local and distributed representations of text for web search. In *Proceedings of the 26th International Conference on World Wide Web*, pages 1291–1299, 2017.
56. Eric T. Nalisnick, Bhaskar Mitra, Nick Craswell, and Rich Caruana. Improving document ranking with dual word embeddings. In *Proceedings of the 25th International Conference on World Wide Web*, pages 83–84, 2016.
57. Rodrigo Nogueira and Kyunghyun Cho. Task-oriented query reformulation with reinforcement learning. *CoRR*, abs/1704.04572, 2017.
58. Hamid Palangi, Li Deng, Yelong Shen, Jianfeng Gao, Xiaodong He, Jianshu Chen, Xinying Song, and Rabab K. Ward. Deep sentence embedding using long short-term memory networks: Analysis and application to information retrieval. *IEEE/ACM Trans. Audio, Speech and Language Processing*, 24 (4): 694–707, 2016.
59. Dae Hoon Park and Rikio Chiba. A neural language model for query auto-completion. In *Proceedings of the 40th International ACM SIGIR Conference on Research and Development in Information Retrieval*, pages 1189–1192, 2017.
60. Jeffrey Pennington, Richard Socher, and Christopher D. Manning. Glove: Global vectors for word representation. In *Proceedings of the 2014 Conference on Empirical Methods in Natural Language Processing*, pages 1532–1543, 2014.
61. Francesco Piccinno and Paolo Ferragina. From TagME to WAT: a new entity annotator. In *Proceedings of the First ACM International Workshop on Entity Recognition and Disambiguation*, pages 55–62, 2014.
62. James E. Pitkow, Hinrich Schütze, Todd A. Cass, Robert Cooley, Don Turnbull, Andy Edmonds, Eytan Adar, and Thomas M. Breuel. Personalized search. *Commun. ACM*, 45 (9): 50–55, 2002.
63. Suhas Ranganath. Leveraging catalog knowledge graphs for query attribute identification in e-commerce sites. *CoRR*, abs/1807.04923, 2018.
64. Shubhra Kanti Karmaker Santu, Liangda Li, Dae Hoon Park, Yi Chang, and ChengXiang Zhai. Modeling the influence of popular trending events on user search behavior. In *Proceedings of the 26th International Conference on World Wide Web*, pages 535–544, 2017.
65. Ruhi Sarikaya. The technology behind personal digital assistants: An overview of the system architecture and key components. *IEEE Signal Processing Magazine*, 34 (1): 67–81, 2017.
66. Denis Savenkov, Scott Weitzner, and Eugene Agichtein. Crowdsourcing for (almost) real-time question answering. In *Workshop on Human-Computer Question Answering, NAACL*, 2016.
67. Wei Shen and Jian-Yun Nie. Is concept mapping useful for biomedical information retrieval? In *Proceedings of the 6th International Conference of the CLEF Association*, volume 9283, pages 281–286, 2015.

68. Yelong Shen, Xiaodong He, Jianfeng Gao, Li Deng, and Grégoire Mesnil. A latent semantic model with convolutional-pooling structure for information retrieval. In *Proceedings of the 23rd ACM International Conference on Conference on Information and Knowledge Management*, pages 101–110, 2014.

69. Yangyang Shi, Kaisheng Yao, Le Tian, and Daxin Jiang. Deep LSTM based feature mapping for query classification. In *Proceedings of the 2016 Conference of the North American Chapter of the Association for Computational Linguistics: Human Language Technologies*, pages 1501–1511, 2016.

70. Milad Shokouhi and Kira Radinsky. Time-sensitive query auto-completion. In *The 35th International ACM SIGIR conference on research and development in Information Retrieval*, pages 601–610, 2012.

71. Milad Shokouhi, Ryen W. White, Paul N. Bennett, and Filip Radlinski. Fighting search engine amnesia: reranking repeated results. In *Proceedings of the 36th International ACM SIGIR Conference on Research and Development in Information Retrieval*, pages 273–282, 2013.

72. Yang Song, Dengyong Zhou, and Li-wei He. Query suggestion by constructing term-transition graphs. In *Proceedings of the Fifth International Conference on Web Search and Data Mining*, pages 353–362, 2012.

73. Alessandro Sordoni, Yoshua Bengio, and Jian-Yun Nie. Learning concept embeddings for query expansion by quantum entropy minimization. In *Proceedings of the Twenty-Eighth AAAI Conference on Artificial Intelligence*, pages 1586–1592, 2014.

74. Alessandro Sordoni, Yoshua Bengio, Hossein Vahabi, Christina Lioma, Jakob Grue Simonsen, and Jian-Yun Nie. A hierarchical recurrent encoder-decoder for generative context-aware query suggestion. In *Proceedings of the 24th ACM International on Conference on Information and Knowledge Management*, pages 553–562, 2015.

75. Fabian M. Suchanek, Gjergji Kasneci, and Gerhard Weikum. Yago: a core of semantic knowledge. In *Proceedings of the 16th International Conference on World Wide Web*, pages 697–706, 2007.

76. Ilya Sutskever, Oriol Vinyals, and Quoc V. Le. Sequence to sequence learning with neural networks. In *Proceedings of the 27th Annual Conference on Neural Information Processing Systems*, pages 3104–3112, 2014.

77. Chuanqi Tan, Furu Wei, Pengjie Ren, Weifeng Lv, and Ming Zhou. Entity linking for queries by searching Wikipedia sentences. In *Proceedings of the 2017 Conference on Empirical Methods in Natural Language Processing*, pages 68–77, 2017.

78. Robert S. Taylor. Question negotiation and information seeking in libraries. In *A. W. Elias (Ed.), (pp. 36–55) American Society for Information Science.*

79. Jaime Teevan, Susan T. Dumais, and Eric Horvitz. Personalizing search via automated analysis of interests and activities. In *Proceedings of the 28th Annual International ACM SIGIR Conference on Research and Development in Information Retrieval*, pages 449–456, 2005.

80. Gilad Tsur, Yuval Pinter, Idan Szpektor, and David Carmel. Identifying web queries with question intent. In *Proceedings of the 25th International Conference on World Wide Web*, pages 783–793, 2016.

81. Ivan Vulic and Marie-Francine Moens. Monolingual and cross-lingual information retrieval models based on (bilingual) word embeddings. In *Proceedings of the 38th International ACM SIGIR Conference on Research and Development in Information Retrieval*, pages 363–372, 2015.

82. Jianqiang Wang and Douglas W. Oard. Matching meaning for cross-language information retrieval. *Information Processing and Management*, 48 (4): 631–653, 2012.

83. Zhongyuan Wang, Kejun Zhao, Haixun Wang, Xiaofeng Meng, and Ji-Rong Wen. Query understanding through knowledge-based conceptualization. In *Proceedings of the Twenty-Fourth International Joint Conference on Artificial Intelligence*, pages 3264–3270, 2015.

84. Ziang Xie, Anand Avati, Naveen Arivazhagan, Dan Jurafsky, and Andrew Y. Ng. Neural language correction with character-based attention. *CoRR*, abs/1603.09727, 2016.

85. Chenyan Xiong, Zhuyun Dai, Jamie Callan, Zhiyuan Liu, and Russell Power. End-to-end neural ad-hoc ranking with kernel pooling. In *Proceedings of the 40th International ACM SIGIR Conference on Research and Development in Information Retrieval*, pages 55–64, 2017.

86. Xing Yi and James Allan. A comparative study of utilizing topic models for information retrieval. In *Proceedings of the 31th European Conference on IR Research*, pages 29–41, 2009.

87. Dawei Yin, Yuening Hu, Jiliang Tang, Tim Daly Jr., Mianwei Zhou, Hua Ouyang, Jianhui Chen, Changsung Kang, Hongbo Deng, Chikashi Nobata, Jean-Marc Langlois, and Yi Chang. Ranking relevance in yahoo search. In *Proceedings of the 22nd ACM SIGKDD International Conference on Knowledge Discovery and Data Mining*, pages 323–332, 2016.

88. Hamed Zamani and W. Bruce Croft. Estimating embedding vectors for queries. In *Proceedings of the 2016 ACM on International Conference on the Theory of Information Retrieval*, pages 123–132, 2016a.

89. Hamed Zamani and W. Bruce Croft. Embedding-based query language models. In *Proceedings of the 2016 ACM on International Conference on the Theory of Information Retrieval*, pages 147–156, 2016b.

90. Hamed Zamani and W. Bruce Croft. Relevance-based word embedding. In *Proceedings of the 40th International ACM SIGIR Conference on Research and Development in Information Retrieval*, pages 505–514, 2017.

91. Qing T. Zeng and Tony Tse. Exploring and developing consumer health vocabularies. *J. Am. Medical Informatics Assoc.*, 13 (1): 24–29, 2006.

92. Ye Zhang and Byron C. Wallace. A sensitivity analysis of (and practitioners' guide to) convolutional neural networks for sentence classification. *CoRR*, abs/1510.03820, 2015.

93. Shi Zhao and Yan Zhang. Tailor knowledge graph for query understanding: linking intent topics by propagation. In *Proceedings of the 2014 Conference on Empirical Methods in Natural Language Processing*, pages 1070–1080, 2014.

94. Guoqing Zheng and Jamie Callan. Learning to reweight terms with distributed representations. In *Proceedings of the 38th International ACM SIGIR Conference on Research and Development in Information Retrieval*, pages 575–584, 2015.

Printed in the United States
by Baker & Taylor Publisher Services